CW00515961

Katie Puckrik has hosted numerous TV shows including *The Word*, *The Sunday Show* and *Pyjama Party*. She writes and presents programmes and documentaries for BBC Radio, as well as contributing regularly to major magazines and newspapers including *Elle*, the *Guardian* and *New Woman*.

shooting
from the lip

Katie Puckrik

HEADLINE

Copyright © 1998 Katie Puckrik

The right of Katie Puckrik to be identified as the Author of
the Work has been asserted by her in accordance with the
Copyright, Designs and Patents Act 1988.

First published in 1998
by HEADLINE BOOK PUBLISHING

First published in paperback in 1999
by HEADLINE BOOK PUBLISHING

10 9 8 7 6 5 4 3 2 1

All rights reserved. No part of this publication may be
reproduced, stored in a retrieval system, or transmitted,
in any form or by any means without the prior written
permission of the publisher, nor be otherwise circulated
in any form of binding or cover other than that in which
it is published and without a similar condition being
imposed on the subsequent purchaser.

ISBN 0 7472 6016 8

Typeset by
Letterpart Limited, Reigate, Surrey

Printed and bound in Great Britain by
Mackays of Chatham PLC, Chatham, Kent

HEADLINE BOOK PUBLISHING
A division of Hodder Headline PLC
338 Euston Road
London NW1 3BH

To my mother and my father

All my love and thanks to Tony Horkins, Desirée
Lafont, Bibi Lynch, Steve Miller, Andy Puchrik, David
Puchrik, Ann Roe, Jo Scarpino and Lindsay Symons
for living this book.

nostalgia *n.* regretful or wistful memory of an earlier time. [modern Latin, from Greek *nostos* 'homecoming', and *algos* 'pain']

Shooting from the Lip

1

Have You Seen Your Mother, Baby, Standing In The Shadow?

When I was three, I wanted a penis. The kid next door had one, and it was a doozy. Revelling in my undisguised envy, he triumphantly displayed his baloney pony at regular intervals. The fact that he also was three greatly limited his chances of getting arrested.

The most impressive aspect of my neighbour's kiddy dick was its 'point and shoot' feature. So compelling was the attraction of projectile urination that I encouraged him to pee against the side of our house as often as his bladder would allow.

I wanted a penis, but I got a gun instead. My parents gave me the cap pistol as part of a rootin' tootin' cowgirl get-up including a red stetson hat and holster. It is doubtful that my folks sensed my schlong complex and sought to offset wieners with weapons. Nope – that gun was nothing but plain ol' playtime fun.

Soon enough, Flasher Jr. had to take his trouser business elsewhere. I loved my gun, finding it more versatile than the male member, which, in all but the most unfortunate cases, remains firmly attached to its owner. I was tooled up with serious metal, pardner, swaggering with toddler bravado and threatening absolutely no one on Susquehannock Drive.

Susquehannock Drive, where our sixties split-level-with-carport crouched alongside countless other freshly built houses, was named after the Susquehanna River. Confusingly, the river was in Pennsylvania, not northern Virginia, where we lived. The Indian tribe who'd originally named the waterway had long gone, and the lone echo of their paleface foes was me in my cowpoke costume.

But I wasn't the only ranch hand knocking back Kool-Aid at the Puckrik Corral. Two brothers and a sister, all older, shared my access to Mom, Dad and the wood-panelled rec room. That was where my teenage brothers played their Rolling Stones 45s and taught me dirty words.

Even more incongruous than a trucker-talking tyke was the long-term impact of *My First Bible*. The illustrated book of Bible stories was a gift from my father – one of his earliest attempts to help me 'get with the Lord', as he would say. The way he saw it, *My First Bible* was My First Leg-Up to Jesus.

The way I saw it, it was freaky dream fodder. All those pictures of angels with rainbow wings got me hankering after strap-on flappy-flaps of my own. I copied the moves in my sleep, flying high in the friendly skies in nap after nap. Cruising while snoozing, I was the heavenly host with the most, the cherub with extra cheese.

Dream-wise, I veered slightly off Old Testament turf by the time I was a teenager. At this point, my night flights began to take on a few extra routes with recurring slumber visions of whirling tornadoes and crashing airplanes. Curiously, these ostensible disasters were always erotically charged.

Whether my dream had me standing smack dab in the path

2

of a twister, or watching a doomed jet scream down to the wrong patch of earth, inside I'd be molten with gusset-bustin' excitement. Decades on, I told a Jungian dream analyst about these nocturnal transmissions, and his evaluation was that I needed a more stimulating sex life. Then he asked me out on a date.

I'm sure that if Dad could have predicted the eventual flight path triggered by his angel book gift, he wouldn't have bashed that baby Bible quite so hard.

My father was as handsome as he was Catholic, which was excessively. At forty-six, his wavy black hair had turned prematurely silver, but his blue eyes, square jaw and small but muscular build still boasted the vigour of the football quarterback he'd been at West Point. He referred to himself as 'the Old Tiger'.

While spy-piloting his way through the ranks of the air force, my dad had racked up some impressive hero-guy exploits. He'd been a participant in the Berlin Airlift, flying food and other supplies to the blockaded city and its Commie-trapped citizens.

In 1960, he'd accompanied Khrushchev's second in command across American airspace. This was a mission for which my father was uniquely qualified, based on the fact that he was the only person in the entire United States who had equal fluency in flying and Russian.

The achievement made the local paper in Topeka, Kansas, where my pre-Katie family were then living. The article had been duly clipped, saved and eventually xeroxed by the time it fell into my hands.

Under the headline 'He Brought Kozlov: TOPEKAN MAY FLY NIKI TO U.S.' was a photo of my dad, dapper in a bow tie and wearing a buzz cut and a Hollywood sneer. Under the photo was the caption: 'Maj. A.S. Puckrik ... speaks nine tongues'.

> *Maj. A.S. Puckrik, an aircraft commander with the 55th Strategic Reconnaissance Wing, for about 21 hours had the second-ranking member of the Kremlin under his wing.*
>
> *In late June the Pentagon ordered the 40-year-old West Point graduate to work for Aeroflot, an airline owned by the Soviet government.*
>
> *Maj. Puckrik was flight safety officer and aircraft commander aboard the Tupolev TU-114 which brought Soviet First Deputy Premier Frol Romanovich Kozlov to the US June 28.*
>
> *Puckrik was chosen by the Pentagon because of his command of the Russian language. In addition to Russian he speaks Spanish, Polish, German, French, Italian, Hungarian, some Japanese, and English.*
>
> *Puckrik, father of three, said, 'It's all part of the job. Flight of a new Russian aircraft is not an opportunity we all have.'*

When I asked my dad about it years later, he told me his job was to ensure that 'those sneaky no-goodnik Russkis' didn't fly anywhere off-limits. He also had to get a little sneaky himself, taking secret notes on the new technology when the Russkis weren't looking. He mentioned that second banana Frol had changed into a pair of pyjamas as soon as they were airborne.

Speaking 'nine tongues' came relatively easy to my father, who spoke Slovak at home with his Bohemian parents. He was the youngest of ten children whose family had emigrated from the Austro-Hungarian Empire at the beginning of the twentieth century. Along with their Old World language, his parents

4

brought their Old World religion to their New World digs in California.

The Puckriks were pious but piss-taking. A childhood enduring the rapid-fire ripostes of his older brothers and sisters guaranteed my dad's acrid wit and deadly put-downs. He also did a fine line in frisky.

Wizard of the wind-up, my father got a kick out of summoning salesgirls with 'Hey sweetlips!' bellowed across the shop floor. A hearty 'Hiya lover!' was reserved for the *Washington Post* paperboys, who were invariably twelve and traumatized by his bizarre badinage. In the supermarket, he made a point of reading the cashiers' names off their tags and alarming them with jovial overfamiliarity.

'Hey, LeWanda! Got any of that chintzy Miracle Whip left? You've only got the cruddy house brand out there!'

You could always see the bewildered look in their eyes as they frantically tried to figure out how they knew him.

Also in the grocery store, or other places of casual social intercourse, Dad could identify a person's nationality at ten paces. A quick 'How's it goin'?' in Swahili or Spanish always served up high-eyebrowed smiles from Africans or Latinos happy to hear their local lingo.

As a teenager, I'd sit in my dad's book-lined study and watch *Star Trek* with him. By the time Captain Kirk lurched into his inevitable love scene with the horny green alien lady, my father would shout out, 'Watch it, lover boy!', making loud kissy-face noises as William Shatner moved in for the mash. 'Ol' Cap'n's gettin' cosy,' he'd say to me, by way of explaining his outburst. 'Gettin' cosy' was something to be warned against, apparently.

In addition to 'gettin' cosy', my dad had about fifteen other catchphrases on heavy rotation. When he was feeling chummy, he called you 'Palzo'. 'So guuuuuuuuud!' was oozed out as an all-purpose affirmative. Several featured a mock-English accent: 'How nobby, how neat!'; 'Clever, these Irishmen!'; and the upper-crustiest of them all, 'Raaah-thah!'

The rest of Dad's trad patter wasn't quite so frolicsome. Kids playing outside after nine p.m. on a school night were indisputably 'hoodlums'. His daughters' boyfriends were all unbudgeably 'that bum'. His absolute trademark expression was 'Germs!' delivered in a deep disapproving moo at anyone, family or stranger, who dared to sneeze or cough in public.

Along with raisins and the colour red, my father loved music, and was given to belting out Al Jolson's 'Hallelujah I'm a BUM' in his rich baritone. He yodelled, too. A burst of 'yodel-ay-DEE-whoo!' might be used to sign off a conversation, flummoxing those unfamiliar with this quirk.

Dad played the accordion with clumsy enthusiasm, punctuated by much swearing when he couldn't find the right chord.

My mother loved music, too, but she wasn't so crazy about the swearing. The worst she ever came out with – and this was only under extreme provocation – was 'Crap!' She would apologize immediately for such lamb-strength oaths, looking shaken by her loss of control.

Along with her singing voice, low and honeyed, my dad adored her luminous brunette beauty. Revlon's 'Cherries in the Snow' lipstick intensified the lushness of her mouth, which contrasted intriguingly with her genteel demeanour.

The sexy librarian angle was further amplified when she wore her rhinestone-edged cat-eye glasses. These fashionable accessories were required when she drove, a skill she'd reluctantly learned as an adult but had never managed to enjoy. Her cautious driving technique mirrored her general approach to life. By and large, the world was a fearful place for my mother, and her only buffers against its unruly nature were etiquette and protocol.

And art. She specialized in Native Maternal Art – the largely yarn-based handicrafts indigenous to full-time motherhood. Prolifically creative, she needlepointed canvases, crocheted afghans, knitted sweaters – all of her own design. Colours crashed into textures, sequins and more colours on her flamboyantly beautiful pullovers. Some were destined for me, others she sold to local industrialists' wives. She ran up little cloth dolls, painting their faces and sewing their clothes. She made quilts.

Her mind was as fast as her fingers. When my mother graduated from William and Mary University in the mid-forties, the school lost one of the most devoted sorority gals ever pledged. The way she waxed so nostalgically about old Alpha Beta Whatever made me suspect that she considered her years after college to be less than golden.

She was proud of being a Daughter of the American Revolution, a genealogy group whose members could trace their maternal ancestors practically all the way back to the *Mayflower*. In America, being a DAR is as close as you can get to having blue blood.

Over the years, she'd dreamily recount tales of the biggest branches on her well-leafed family tree: early colonial statesmen; the founder of a Quaker college; a furniture-maker who'd built George Washington's coffin. I was impressed by the stories and liked the fact that they meant I was automatically a DAR, too. However, I was never sure what those little old DAR ladies actually *did*, apart from ride in parades, waving wrinkledly from the backs of open-topped Cadillacs. This quip of mine did not go down well with Mom.

Daughter of an army colonel as well as the American

Revolution, my mother had spent her 'army brat' years growing up down south and far east. Georgia and the Philippines were places packed with sci-fi insects and creepy crawlies. In the Philippines, she'd had to get used to sharing her bedroom with geckos – lizards which kept her awake with their eponymous bark of 'Gecko!' The geckos had adhesive feet and hobnobbed vertically on her walls as they munched their midnight bugs.

In Germany, where my mother moved with her family just after the war, there were no lizards with suction-cup toes. There was, however, my father.

When my mother married him, her father promptly disowned her.

My grandfather had been a devout atheist, and because her new husband was Catholic, my mother got the axe with permafreeze speed. The issue seemed more one of bigotry than papacy, but either way, the result was the same: my mother no longer had a family. She was devastated.

My father may have been West Point's star quarterback, but here on his first and last chance to make their marriage work, the Old Tiger fumbled the ball. All he'd needed to do was to open his arms when her father had shut the door. All he'd needed to do was to love his wife.

Instead, angry because her father didn't approve of him, mine expressed his displeasure by rejecting her as well. He alternated silent treatments with generalized scorn. He embarrassed her in front of company. Deep down, he knew he was wrong, but my father was a hothead and could be stubborn beyond sense.

Shot by both sides, my mother retaliated the only way she could. She was twenty-four when they got married, and by the time I was born fourteen years later, she still hadn't *quite* gotten around to converting to Catholicism, as per their prenuptial discussions. This infuriated my father, as she knew it would. It was her one big power play.

The wider berth my mother gave conversion, the worse he behaved towards her. My father was Catholic to a fault, but according to him, the fault was all hers.

I was born during a temporary truce in the religious war, a good eight years after my sister had made her appearance. But while Dad toiled at Ground Zero in his Pentagon job, Mom was left to wrangle the kids on her own. She'd get fed up, fuming, 'Your father's a bachelor with a wife and four children.'

But at the age of three, I still had years to go before I was troubled by my parents' imbroglios. Blissfully unaware, I lived the good life. After a light lunch of Spam, applesauce, maybe some ice cream, I'd retire to the backyard to take its various entertainments. I had a small inflatable pool, as well as a swingset. The pool was essential equipment in the sweltering Virginia summer, which regularly jerked the mercury up to the high nineties.

The swingset was the place to score hits of the kid drug of choice, known by its street name as 'spinning'. The desired altered state could be achieved by sitting on the swing and slowly twisting it in one direction before letting it rip in the other. Spinning highs could also be copped by rolling down a hill, or by staring up at the sky while twirling around and around into a giddy fit.

The goal was to turn on and trip out at that fine line between consciousness and seasickness. Hours of recreational swing use regularly left me dizzy but exhilarated. After one of my wooze-induced binges, I jumped off the swingset and galloped through the garden at dangerous speed, determined to prolong the mind-warp.

Call Timothy Leary – I was having a bad trip, and baby, the

crash was harsh. There was a rose bush, there was a thorn, there was gore. I don't remember the ouch – just the drama. The blood gushing from my torn eyebrow painted my family, who had crowded on to the tiny back porch, bright red. Framed in the screen door like a suburban Munch painting, my mother, sister and brothers must have been hollering, but my setting was on mute. What I saw were four mouths in silent undulating Os. What they saw was a bawling kid holding a hand over her bloody eye which was, for all they knew, stuck back on the rosebush like a new bloom.

This violent encounter with nature left me instantly and forever changed, both physically and emotionally. My right eyebrow was now bisected by a scar. And, more significantly, I had discovered that the joy of being the centre of attention could override almost any pain.

2

Young Girl

It was time for my first real flight. Unlike my Bible-book angels, it wasn't just a matter of sprouting wings and zooming through clouds getting bugs in my teeth. No dice. My first baby-shoed step into the jet set was facilitated by slightly less celestial means: the airplane.

My father had been assigned to Berlin and the family was temporarily holed up at an army base motel, girding our britches for the long haul to Germany. I had a special outfit for the occasion: a seersucker dress and a straw hat that looked like a coconut cake with a cherry on top. Wearing something that resembled food gave me extra confidence.

Feeling every one of my four fabulous years, I slipped out of our room to investigate the international travel glamour of the parking lot. There wasn't any.

I returned to the motel room to watch as my mother slipped lavender clothes-freshening tablets into the pockets of our red vinyl suitcases. All the luggage bore the 'Amelia Earhart' brand name. Mom explained that Miss Earhart had been a great lady aviator who had mysteriously disappeared in the South Pacific.

11

To me, this did not bode well for our bags. Nevertheless, ten hours later, both the Earharts and Puckriks arrived safely together on our patch of Free Europe outside the Berlin Wall.

We moved into a rambling three-storeyed house on Max Eythe Strasse, quite a few rungs up from our Virginia split-level-with-carport. I never learned what Max's claim to fame had been, but the house was remarkable for many reasons: the glass-enclosed front porch against which birds routinely broke their necks; the sitting room that my mother had had painted blood-red. Visiting Russians nodded 'Da', approvingly, at the perceived pinko tribute; visiting Germans just shuddered and muttered about the war.

I played for hours in the sprawling back garden, in thrall to its smorgasbord of nature: birch trees, apple trees, weeping willow trees; hyacinths and daffodils, robins and rabbits. But for me, the most outstanding feature of our new home was the mechanized glass wall that ran along almost the whole back of the house.

The wall was part of the glassed-in conservatory that contained a rock garden, streamlined Danish sofas and coffee tables, and a wall mosaic of flamingoes. There was a control panel next to the mosaic with three buttons: 'Up', 'Down' and 'Stop'. With one touch, you entered futurist bachelor-pad splendour as the entire glass wall sank into the floor.

In this enchanted house, my parents threw a profusion of parties for Berlin's diplomatic community – the martini-glass-chinking, *James Bond* side of my father's intelligence work. Of the snoopier, *Dirty Dozen* aspect of his job I knew little, other than he would disappear for weeks at a time. A few years later he showed me a photograph of him on some sort of stake-out, hiding up a tree. The pencil scribble on the back of the snap read *Tiger im baum* – 'Tiger in tree' in *Deutsch*-speak.

Sometimes I'd undertake a little spywork of my own and sneak out of one of my brothers' basement bedroom windows. My trusty tricycle would be revved up outside ready to patrol the cobblestoned streets. Patient policemen would bring the four-year-old Puckrik girl home as late as nine o'clock at night.

On the evenings I stayed in, my mother flicked my book-loving switch by reading to me from *The Wizard of Oz*. I was bewitched by the story of young Dorothy and her nemesis: the fearsome Wizard who turns out to be just a little man with big PR.

Dorothy's lifestyle was appealing, too: cool shoes, new friends, plenty of travel, no mention of bedtime. I hated bedtime. After haggling for extra awake-time, I'd be drawn by the siren call of the Supremes and the Beatles to my sister's bedroom. I was too young to be of any interest to my teenage sis, so I played with my battery-powered choo-choo in the darkened hallway outside her closed door. But as long as I could hear her music, I was content. Gary Puckett and the Union Gap would leak sonically over the threshold:

Young girl – get out of my mind!
My love for you is way outa line –
Better ru-u-u-un girl – you're much too you-u-u-ng, girl.

Occasionally, my sister would open the door and let me play with her kittens. Like a good girl, I put my toys away after I was finished, cramming the wriggling kittens into my sock drawer. After one too many episodes of angrily mewing furniture, the kittens did an Amelia Earhart of their own and mysteriously vanished. In their place appeared a dog, a black poodle too big for sock-drawer-shoving.

The poodle's main contribution was to introduce me to Milk

13

Bones. The canine cookies were an incentive for good behaviour – his and mine. My policy was one for him, two for me.

Milk Bones were just a phase, but doughnuts were forever. My lifelong doughnut habit began in kindergarten. Every single day at school, my lunch was the same: milk, a hot dog and two powdered doughnuts. For me, the milk and hot dog were a formality, a token stab at nutrition. The whole point of the repast was doughnuts. They were sweet, my preferred taste sensation, and they were round with a hole, which meant that they worked as edible jewelry.

As demonstrated by my doughnut baubles, I never missed an opportunity to accessorize. I was a clothes horse, engineering a Diana Ross costume change at least three times a day. I didn't shy away from colour, either. From my box of Crayola 64 crayons, I'd memorized such arch shades as Salmon and Periwinkle. Shopping for school clothes with my mother, I gravely informed the saleswoman that 'my colour' was Burnt Sienna. She rolled her eyes. My mother beamed.

Experimenting with unusual combos, I fearlessly mixed the stage outfits that my dad bought for me with more conventional schoolwear. My red satin clown top with white polka dots and puffed sleeves was a key wardrobe piece. I never was able to make the distinction between costumes and real clothes.

My rag-tag chic aroused the concern of a German family down the street, who bought me a dress. Their innocent assumption that I was a hard-up cruddy-dudded urchin was somewhat embarrassing for my mother, but I was just glad to have more clothes.

My quest for self-expression didn't stop with togs. I loved to dance, too. My thinking was: why keep all that talent, however ill-defined, to myself? With this in mind, I'd rummage through my dress-up finery for long skirts and sparkly scarves, then slip out my brother's window to position myself under the weeping willow at the end of the street.

Fetchingly situated, I would begin to dance. The moves were basic but heartfelt. The delight I took in performing was pure. God knows what the neighbours thought.

My mother, looking for a way to channel my energy and wanderlust, not to mention my knack for entertaining the locals, enrolled me in a ballet class. In this environment, my natural leadership qualities asserted themselves as I organized the blank-eyed little moppets into rows of prancing ponies or flying fairies.

My initiative led straight into show business, via a humble stage at the local community centre. My theatre debut was as a bumble-bee. The costume was *dyn-o-mite*: a yellow fun-fur bodice with a black and yellow tutu, and clear plastic wings at the back. On my head was a pair of glittery antennae. If my mother had allowed it, I would have worn the bee gear non-stop.

The choreography dictated that I and a fellow bee-lette would buzz gracefully through a stageful of tiny girls dressed as flowers. The spectacle was nothing short of the facts of life made flesh, pollination made entertainment.

Twenty years later, I ran into my former bee colleague back in America. Melanie challenged me with the initially cryptic, 'Were you a bee?' I don't know how she recognized me without the antennae. The girl had grown up into a racy-looking babe in purple harem trousers and silver disco stilettos. That's what learning the facts of life too young can do to you.

Usually I played by myself, and happily. I was the queen of my stuffed animals – my right-hand toy was a pony with a poodle-nibbled ear. For my fifth birthday party, my well-meaning mother wheeled in some kids I'd never seen before.

The plan boomeranged after the juvenile crims ransacked my toy stash. I never saw that pony again.

When I voluntarily played with other children, I relied on my limited supply of swear words, the pre-eminent one among them being 'pieface'. My father, who employed a copious amount of profanity in his daily doings, usually confined his epithets to Eastern European oaths. Accordingly, *'yat toya mat'* was heard frequently in our household. My present understanding of the phrase is that it suggests inappropriate carnal knowledge of one's own mother. My father was naturally displeased when my brothers enthusiastically adopted the expression for their childhood karate games.

Blithe hours were whiled away in the bomb shelter outside my friend Becky's house. Actually, it was less a bomb shelter than a midget medieval fortress: a concrete turret set squatly next to the driveway. We'd squeeze through the heavy cement door and peer at enemy German neighbour boys through what looked like rifle slots. The slots were insufficient for screaming 'pieface' through, so I'd poke my head out the slab door and open my mouth wide to deliver the hardcore scurrility. Unfortunately, one time the Germans got there first with a mudball right in the kisser. The hole-in-one was humiliating, but they weren't the *real* enemy.

The real enemy was an American teenager who lived around the corner. He was the sixteen-year-old son of some of my parents' army friends.

'You wanna go for a walk?'

He was leaning against the railings of Becky's gate, looking towards us at the bomb shelter. Before we could answer, Becky's mother called her in for her nap. He focused on me.

'Do *you* wanna go for a walk?'

I hesitated. It was strange that this older boy was even

16

bothering to talk to a five-year-old. Usually I was completely ignored by other people's big brothers.

'C'mon. It'll be fun.'

I wasn't so sure. It was a cold November day. But the wheedling tone of his voice convinced me that I'd be missing out if I didn't go.

'OK,' I said.

We walked to a big derelict house across from Becky's that had stood empty since I'd moved to Berlin. Becky and I used to pretend it was haunted.

We entered the overgrown yard and he guided me around the back of the building, to a hole in the wall that looked into the basement. He knelt down in front of me so that he was at my eye level. It made it easier for him to take off my clothes. I didn't question him, even though the wind was bitter and I was shivering. He seemed to know what he was doing.

Hat, coat, mittens, dress, tights and shoes went in a neat pile next to the gash in the wall. When I was completely naked, he helped me through the hole and into the murky cellar. I was freezing but trusting. He took my hand and began to lead me into the darkness.

Footsteps approached. My abductor yanked me back, shushing my silence. The trance-like figure of a tall, bald man appeared, passing no more than ten feet in front of us. When the man was nearly opposite, he turned and walked slowly up the stairs.

We remained framed against the daylight. There was no way the man could have missed us. Was he blind? What was he doing in the empty house? Was he a ghost?

Unnerved, the teenager pulled me outside and hurried me back into my clothes.

'Don't ever tell anybody what we just did. Understand? Don't tell anyone!'

We headed back towards my house, him dropping behind as I walked on through the safety of my front gates.

'Don't tell!' he hissed.

My sister was in the driveway, busy popping wheelies on her bicycle. She stopped and we looked at each other.

I didn't tell.

3

Indiana Wants Me

After three years, my father finished his mission in Berlin and accepted a teaching post at Notre Dame University, Indiana. I readied my now battered coconut-cake hat for another whirl on a big silver bird, but I had a surprise. This time, transatlantic travel was going to be conducted by ocean, not sky. The SS *United States*, sister ship to the *QEII*, was to fetch us in a leisurely fashion back to my old New World.

For a six-year-old, a week on a cruise liner boiled down to one tantalizing statistic: the ship had eighteen elevators. When I wasn't examining every available shaft on the westbound vessel, I'd open the sick-bay door a crack to view my nauseated sister as she battled her sea-roused gorge from the top of a bunk bed.

Soon enough, we traded the infinite expanse of flat Atlantic blue for the infinite expanse of even flatter Midwestern yellow. Everything in Indiana was yellow: the cornfields, the tornado-torn skies, the sandy lots staked with 'Coming Soon – Brand New Homes!' signs. From my bedroom window of our brand-new home, I counted the endless stream of cars coursing by on the yellow highway.

I played on nearby plains, finding Indian arrowheads where cowgirls before me had chased off the Native Americans. In a matter of months, the arrowheads would be buried forever under freshly built subdivisions.

Initially, the neighbourhood kids regarded me with misgiving. I was clearly suspect because I always wore dresses – never jeans like everybody else. I learned quickly that frequent costume changes were not tolerated in South Bend, Indiana.

Nonetheless, my playmates lightened up when I turned them on to the good shit, kid-drug-wise. I let them play with my latest spinning device – an orange plastic egg-shaped frame big enough to sit in. Once installed, foetus-like, in the giant orange egg, the spinner could then roll down a hill with more speed and danger than ever before dreamed. I named my recreational device Herbie, after the Disney movie *Herbie the Love Bug*.

It was a short spin from love-buggin' to full-blown spooky-malookin'. I discovered the occult. This entailed spending a lot of time reading all the supernatural books I could carry home from the library, while swathed in sheets and staring into candles. I tried hard for visions in the flames, but my Sensory Perception was less than Extra.

I asked my father for a Magic 8 Ball, a sort of soothsaying pool ball with a little window in which appeared various 'fortunes'. The idea was that you'd ask the Magic 8 Ball a question, shake it, then look at the window. The answers were usually enigmatic: IT IS DECIDEDLY SO; OUTLOOK NOT SO GOOD; SIGNS POINT TO YES. My dad refused to supply me with this necessary piece of mystic equipment on the grounds that it wasn't 'wholesome'.

According to Dad, horoscopes were also not wholesome, and Ouija boards were especially not wholesome. Anything that wasn't biblically sanctioned was Not Wholesome.

Fortunately for me, cartoons fell within wholesome guidelines. Three years in Berlin had meant three years in a cartoon vacuum. I had a lot of catching up to do. Leaving the La-Z-Boy recliner for Dad, I flopped on our searingly aqua vinyl sofa in front of the mahogany-panelled television set. Slack-jawed, I communed with the tube for hours.

In 1969, the Japanese invaded America. The invasion was in animation form only, but I was conquered regardless. The Japanese offensive was headed up by *Speed Racer* and *Kimba the White Lion*. Even though the cartoons had been dubbed in English, there was still a tinge of strangeness surrounding Speed and Kimba. They were almost heartbreakingly cute with their big blinky eyes and round baby heads. Speed's head looked even rounder and baby-er when he wore his white racing helmet. Although Speed was a teenage human and Kimba a teenage lion, they both made the same softly orgasmic noises when they were fighting small-skulled and squinty-eyed bad guys. I was riveted.

After my Oriental interlude, I would sit stonily through *The Banana Splits*, which never made me laugh, until *Scooby Doo* came on. It took me years to spot the marijuana munchie implications of the 'Scooby Snack', an obvious bong-time treat. I naively assumed that the presence of Shaggy, with his drug-raddled demeanour, was merely to offset the neatness of Scooby's well-groomed fur. Even though the plot of *Scooby Doo* was the same every week, the ghost-chase element never failed to get me a little tense.

Post-ghost relaxation was provided by *Wacky Races*. I applied my burgeoning ballet technique to approximate Penelope Pitstop's slo-mo leaping run. Now I was warmed up for *The Pink Panther Show*.

The Pink Panther was the coolest. I demonstrated my allegiance to His Pinkness by stuffing a thin strip of pink carpet down the back of my purple bell-bottoms. Thus rendered unmistakably leopard-like, I'd re-enact his laid-back panther shuffle around the house for hours.

One day, I was sitting in front of the television with the carpet strip down my pants, when *The Pink Panther Show* was abruptly interrupted by a static-y black and white transmission. I was outraged – what was this crap?

This crap was the first man on the moon. Apollo 11 had landed, Neil Armstrong was doing some pretty convincing Penelope Pitstop leaps across the craters, but I was not impressed. Where were the laughs? Moon, schmoon – it didn't compare with the great Pink Panther.

It took NASA's advances trickling down to the supermarket shelves for me to have some respect. Once the astronauts shared their lunch-box secrets, I couldn't get enough of technology. Just as long as it was edible.

This was the era of 'space food': Tang, the powdered orange drink that our boys were meant to have quaffed in orbit; Space Food Sticks, the chewy, chalky fudge cylinders flavoured in chocolate, peanut butter and 'original'. I presumed the original flavour stick was a motivational tool designed to make the crew hurry back to Earth for food that didn't taste like freeze-dried faeces. Speaking of which, 'freeze-dried' was new, too, and if it was good enough for outer space, then why shouldn't inner-space travellers enjoy the same plastic tastelessness?

Getting in on the act, the Little Debbie cake company invented a chocolate-covered puffed-rice affair called Star Crunch. I guess they were meant to look like moon rocks. They tasted like them, too, but that didn't stop me eating them.

One small step for man had sure brought home the space bacon, but the vittles that were turning up in our pantry were already pretty way-out as it was.

Every morning before school, I chugged a glass of a powdered milk drink called Instant Breakfast. Like Space Food Sticks, it came in a variety of flavours. The day I knocked back strawberry Instant Breakfast was the day I puked bright pink puddles all the way down the hall to the girls' lavatory.

Thereafter, I played it safe with breakfast cereals, though their combination of colours and chemicals was no less lurid. The monster trio of Count Chocula, FrankenBerry and BooBerry cereals turned the milk brown, pink and blue respectively. God knows what it did to my internal organs.

The commercial for Lucky Charms showed a deranged leprechaun whose frantic jonesin' for the cereal's marshmallow pink hearts, blue stars, green clovers and yellow moons had pushed him over the edge. It wasn't hard to see why: each bowlful contained about as much sugar as a wedding cake. Naturally, I loved it.

It was the dawning of the Age of Aquarius, and its slogans were Quick! New! Improved! The quickest, newest and most improved were the foods you could cook in your toaster. After the arrival of Pop Tarts, suddenly even the most horizontally inclined nosh – pizzas, Danish pastries – stood sideways in toaster slots. I didn't question the molecular structure that enabled such miracles. I accepted it as the ambrosia of the American Dream.

Our kitchen was an Aladdin's Cave of junk food. Along with Little Debbie Star Crunch, I ate my inexorable way through other zestfully named goodies: Suzy Qs and Twinkies, Ho Hos and Sno Balls, Devil Dogs and Ding Dongs – all gusto for my gutso.

What wasn't already in the house could be tracked down via my banana-seat Chopper bike. I'd straddle my purple sparkle saddle, admiring the streamers on the U-shaped handlebars and the day-glo spoke clickers on the wheels. Satisfied that I looked sufficiently bad-ass, I'd ride off through cornfields to get to the dusty roadside general store that sold arcane regional confectionery.

They had everything that could possibly be fashioned from corn syrup: Pixy Stix (sherbet in a straw), Good & Plenty (liquorice pebbles); Sugar Daddy, Sugar Mama (both caramel suckers); Sugar Babies ('Delicious Caramel Tid-Bits', said the wrapper); Goobers, Raisinettes (chocolate-covered peanuts and raisins); ultra-chewy Chuckles, Jujubes and Bit-O-Honey (all three induced instant lockjaw); Lemonheads (sweet 'n' sour lemon drops); Tootsie Roll (looked like dog dirt); Jolly Rancher Fire Sticks (blew your head off); Candy Corn (transmogrified into pumpkin shapes at Hallowe'en, and cupids and hearts around Valentine's Day); Chick-O-Sticks (the name was misleading, as was the picture of a chicken on the wrapper – the sweet tasted like peanut butter and there was no poultry involved); and Goo Goo Supreme (a chocolate-covered cowpat of pecan, caramel and marshmallow). Goo Goo Supreme's nearest competitor was simply – and stoically – named Bun.

After Hallowe'en, Easter was the big candy holiday. The arrival of spring was heralded as much by fondant-filled chocolate eggs the size of your head as by the newly blooming trees. My preference was for Peeps. They were the baby-chick-shaped marshmallows covered in bright yellow sugar, and tasted better when slightly stale. By the time we left for morning Mass to celebrate the resurrection of Christ, I'd have polished off almost the entire contents of my Easter basket. The only niblet unnibbled would be the orange foam kidney shapes optimistically called Circus Peanuts. Eating the pants-end of my Pink Panther carpet-strip tail would have tasted better.

I knew I had the space programme to thank for introducing

myriad new routes to indigestion. However, I never found out which high tech think-tank was responsible for the bubblegum bands designed to frogmarch little girls into womanhood. Whoever they were, my hormones are eternally in their debt.

I was eight, and regarded Donny Osmond as irretrievably namby-pamby. And I was *terrified* of the Bay City Rollers, whom I'd seen on *American Bandstand*. They were all scared hair, big nostrils and no lips.

So I settled on Bobby Sherman, who had had one hit with 'Julie Julie Julie (Do Ya Love Me)'. I diligently purchased magazines with names like *Tiger Beat* and *Fave!* to delve into his deepest dimples.

These magazines were filled with lots of 'pointing at the camera' poses from various Osmonds, Rollers and Jacksons, along with questionnaires determining which pin-up you were going to marry.

Plenty of 'now' lingo such as 'outasight', 'groovy' and 'wow' laced the writing. While thumbing through a treasured old copy of *Fave!* several years into adulthood, I happened upon 'Bobby's Love Schedule', which bore the penmarks of my youthful self.

> *1 Getting up in the morning is*
>   *a. a drag*
>   *b. a groovy way to start the day.*

I'd circled b, attracted no doubt by the key word *groovy*. I noted that my answer tallied with Bobby's. Outasight.

> *11 I like sitting by the fireplace because I think –*
>   *a. it's romantic*
>   *b. it's great for toasting marshmallows.*

My gluttonous will to grill won out here, sadly for my future with Bobby. According to Bobby's Love Schedule, he thought fireside lounging was strictly romantic and no place for snacking. Drag.

I think I regained some ground by question 19:

19 I feel a wife should –
  a. devote her entire life to her husband.
  b. devote her entire life to her children.
  c. have interests of her own, in addition to her role as a wife and mother.

I circled c, which, as it turned out, was just what Bobby had in mind. But I never found out just how groovy it could have been with him, because my girlfriends convinced me that Bobby was 'stuck-up', on account of his smug fat face and hair that looked like a shiny brown pudding. Thence and forevermore, I set my cap at David Cassidy.

David was achingly pretty, with a wind-tousled shag cut and mischief in his eyes. The full extent of his mischief was later spelled out in his autobiography *C'mon, Get Happy . . . Fear and Loathing on the Partridge Family Bus*. In it, he revealed that his only contact with 'real life' in the heady days of Davidmania was constant sex with groupies, who were brought to his hotel rooms ready-stripped and in quick succession.

At eight, I was blissfully unaware of such monkeyshines, and busied myself ordering David trinkets from ads in *Tiger Beat*.

One ad ran: 'David's Choker "Luv" Beads. Now! New Groovy Bead Designs. Make and wear choker beads like David does.' Sure, when Dave wasn't smearing peanut butter on his dong or letting roadies slurp up his sloppy seconds, I'll bet he ran a regular knitting circle on the tour bus.

Another article beseeched: 'David Asks: Can You Love Me Enough?'

Could you love me enough to spend most of your waking hours in an empty house, while I work at the studio all day? Can you love me enough to keep my house just the way I like it?

David's *Partridge Family* co-star Susan Dey, who played his sister 'Susan', tried to love his enough, but she just didn't have what it took. Wrote David in his memoir:

Susan lacked the slutty aspect of a female that I always found so attractive. She was never going to say, 'I want to take that big piece of meat of yours, baby.'

Miss Uldin, my third-grade teacher, was never going to say that either – at least not to me – but I still thought she was alluring. She was in her early twenties, with long side-parted hair and sweater-girl breasts. I was transfixed by the locket she wore on a chain around her neck, following its progress as it looped first over one bosom, then the other.

Miss Uldin wanted to tape-record the class singing the Hollies' 'He Ain't Heavy, He's My Brother' for her 'friend' in Vietnam. She ruthlessly weeded out the weak, off-key and generally sub-standard voices from the class until she was left with me. The flush of pleasure I received from being deemed the best singer was soon quelled by my vengeful classmates. They retaliated the next time I tried to organize a recess game of Partridge Family. I had considered it my inalienable right to be Susan, but vindictive group pressure forced me to play Tracy, the drearily simple 'little sister' character. I rebelled by forming a splinter Partridge

Family, in which I could always be Susan.

Partridge Family Two never really got off the ground, owing to the fact that the only other member I'd managed to recruit was a kid called Greg Legg. He was a scarily sombre child whose lips, gums and teeth were permanently stained indigo from constant pen-sucking. The blue would occasionally be varied by the red of the plaque-detecting tablets which schoolchildren were required to chew on Dental Awareness Days. Greg ate paste, too.

During my spirited renditions of 'I Think I Love You', Greg would shuffle around behind me, looking half asleep. His 'singing' consisted of a few mumbled words that would trickle out of his blue lips every so often.

When PF2 bombed, I drummed up a Bambi game. With Guess Who as star fawn, I again utilized my dance training, this time for stag leaps. I graciously allowed my school sidekick Terri to be Bambi's mother.

Sue Fountainblue was my *best* best friend. She wore glasses, had a freckle on the end of her nose, and lived across the street. Sue was two years older than I was and my link to the sophisticated ways of fifth-graders. For my part, I supplied enough zip and fizz to make having a 'baby' as a friend bearable.

When we weren't conducting week-long Monopoly-a-thons, Sue and I played What Shall I Be?, a femme-fraught board game in which players strove to attain one of the six officially designated OK-for-ladies occupations. These jobs were: nurse, stewardess, actress, model, teacher and ballerina. The game boiled women's options down to two: those who served and those who showed off. Being one of the latter, I always tried for the ballerina.

But what I *really* wanted to be was a spy.

The catalyst for my new career path wasn't the Old Tiger. It was a book by Louise Fitzhugh called *Harriet the Spy*. I was obsessed by Harriet, who spied relentlessly on all of her friends and neighbours and recorded her findings in a notebook. Inspired by *Harriet the Spy*, I began to keep a journal. In it, I wrote everything that happened to me, no matter how banal. My enthusiasm encouraged Sue to start one, too.

In my notebook, I disloyally trashed all my pals, including Sue, and she responded in kind. I knew this for a fact because we routinely snuck peeks at each other's diaries. There was a tacit understanding that we would use the other for bitch bait.

My first spy log was a spiral-bound notebook with yellow paper. The front cover was scrawled with warnings to keep out, with abundant use of the phrase 'big fink'. On the inside, I detailed the specifics of my threats: 'Note to anybody who gets this notebook: KEEP OUT, BUTTHOLE.' Then, obviously having second thoughts about the brutality of the language, I'd scratched out 'KEEP OUT, BUTTHOLE'. I then continued: 'YOU BIG ASS! KEEP OUT OF MY BUSINESS! Tell your mom and dad that they have a big fink and the fink is you.'

With security matters under control, I began the business of spying.

Like my guru, Harriet, I devised a spy route. I jotted the timetable in my notebook:

My route: 3:00 to 4:30 Saturdays and Sundays. 3:15 to 4:45 Tuesdays to Fridays. Mondays 5:00 to 6:30. Each place 15 minutes. Pirate Oak, The Rock, Tarzan Swings, Treehouse, behind Fink Mountain, around Tucker's house, in our evergreens (if necessary).

I followed my daily route with dedication, watching little neighbour kids doing profoundly uninteresting things. As I skulked in the shrubbery, the thought that local mothers might have considered the Puckrik child a sociopath didn't enter my mind. I was too busy engaging in high-level espionage.

George thinks he is the boss of Eight Ball Trail. He always has stuff coming out of his nose.

OK, so maybe it was medium-level. When George and his cronies let me down, I could rely on my sister to provide me with the real juice – especially when she had a boyfriend over. My technique, less than subtle, usually consisted of peering at them through the stair railings into the front room, where they'd be sitting. I'd continue to monitor them doing nothing more sensational than listening to Carol King's *Tapestry* album. As I remained in full view during the surveillance, it somewhat diminished the effectiveness of my intended stealth.

I was a small but intensely annoying albatross to my sister. To get rid of me, she utilized her superior cunning. Employing her knowledge of my Achilles heel – snacks – she would suggest unfeasible treats to get me out of her hair and into the kitchen. One of her more inspired ideas was that I fix myself a bowl of maple syrup with ice cubes. Leaping eagerly on to this fine recommendation, I completely missed the point that it was meant to taste disgusting and therefore provide my punishment for bothering her. As I lapped it up, I made a mental note to add 'Sap on the Rocks' to my regular menu. I was effectively too stupid to torture, which must have been discouraging for her.

Refreshed by my ice-cold bowl of syrup, I'd venture back outdoors to investigate any suspicious tots. My notebook accounts of the locals' movements were peppered with less-than-affectionate nicknames: 'Billy the Queer'; 'Patty the Mouse'; 'Ratfink'.

My lexicon didn't exactly dance off the page, but it was indicative of the jargon of the day. People were always described as 'weird' or 'such a queer'. Doing little more than simply existing could earn one the 'queer' tag. Stuff always 'cracked me up', which could either mean that it made me laugh or made me nuts. Fun stuff was 'a blast'. Cool stuff was 'tough'. 'Barf' was often employed as a brisk expression of approbation.

The wordplay in Sue's notebook was somewhat more vivid. I copied over her spicier segments because, as illustrated by George with the stuff coming out of his nose, I was sometimes low on quality spy material.

I have a note that Sandy gave to Sue. It says:
Ralph II,
I about died when Miller called on me! I haven't heard a fucking word he said. I was writing in my notebook! I made a jackass of myself. I hope Marcia gets her retarded butt kicked in if she has one. She's reading the blue box! Big shit! How about Rowley? He's cute and nice and dirty! Could you get him off my mind? Write back, Ralph III.
PS Why don't you ever curse in your notes?

'Retarded' was a good all-purpose put-down. When a *real* mentally handicapped kid moved in down the street, I noted the event in my notebook with fleeting compassion and abiding morbid curiosity.

I wonder what it feels like to be retarded? I wish that retarded kid would come outside more often. I would like to study him some more. One day I saw him run outside with his mother chasing him and he ran to his father and he yelled at him so he ran back to his mother. Then he went back into his house and ran upstairs. Then I heard more yelling. I think the retarded kid got in trouble.

Everyone was grist for my less-than-penetrating pen. It was satisfying to capture the world and pin it down to the page. Once I filled the first notebook, I started another. Then another. And another. With every year of my life, the spiral pile grew higher.

The journals became a paper time machine to my past. I could relive all experiences in fast-mo, with the bonus of knowing the consequences. It was like watching a high-speed film of a flower opening up in the sun. Or a corpse rotting, for that matter.

But for now, my childtime was filled with bouquets, not decay. I was energized by exploration, driven by discovery. I watched my family, my friends, myself, and wrote it all down.

Once in a while, I actually *played* with my friends instead of spying on them. As usual, the games were always of my own creation and on my own terms. A real after-school winner was an activity that took place in my neighbour Kerry's basement. Kerry's younger brother was still in diapers, which warranted the waiting plastic bucket filled with soiled loincloths. One putrid whiff was enough to bring the maple syrup and ice cubes right back to the starting gate.

My game was tag – with a twist. The person who was 'it' would chase all the others around the pool table and under the stairs. Whoever got caught would be forced to inhale the dirty diaper bucket as a penalty. Sometimes I sniffed, unbidden, just for the thrill of retching. Kerry's mother banned me from playing with her daughter for a week for devising these and other questionable pastimes.

The most questionable pastime was a game I called Born Free. Played in my basement at night, Born Free was a celebration of the female in her wild, natural state. For 'wild' and 'natural', read 'naked'. Preparing for Born Free was a ritual in itself. First of all, I'd light incense and put some atmospheric music on my portable record player, usually something psychedelic from my older brothers' collection. Floaty hippy-dip combo It's A Beautiful Day were favoured for this purpose. Then I'd place a flashlight in a strategic spot in the middle of the room, and turn off the other lights. Finally, Sue and I would remove all of our clothes.

As the music swelled to a crescendo of guitars, violins and drums, we would race around the basement, leaping nudely through the beam of the flashlight. We felt daring and exhilaratingly alive. And it sure beat doing homework.

Evenings over at Sue's were a tad more on the tame side. She had a board game called Mystery Date. The concept was to win your chance for a date with one of the five guy 'types' by rolling dice and picking up instruction cards. There was a prom king, a ski bum, a beatnik, a bookworm and a dud. They should have quintuple-dated with the gals from What Shall I Be?

The TV commercial for Mystery Date had the liltingly sung query, 'Are you ready for your mystery da-a-ate?' The girls in the ad demonstrated the proper reaction for winning the dud – a slacker guy in sandals and a Hawaiian shirt. The consequences of this tragic roll of the dice were met with a disappointed unison 'Ohhhhhhhh . . .' that trailed off at the end. Everybody sympathized with the loser who'd won the loser. Both the game and its marketing were designed to drill pre-pubescent girls into demanding the highest-status mates on the market. In this value system, the girl who won a date with the white-tuxedo-clad prom king was the winner.

But when it came to real life, there was no mystery date for me – because boys were plainly repulsive.

One fellow nine-year-old foolishly tried to confess his crush on me by phoning my home with a very formal 'May I speak to Kathleen?' He got as far as 'Kathl—' before I slammed the receiver down. Firm but certainly not fair, I recorded my assessment of the situation in my notebook.

What to do about Jim is kick him so that he has little dents all over him.

Even though I'd made it clear that any boy with the temerity to express his admiration deserved severe denting, a few wayward cravings of my own slipped past the thought police. Any documentation of my budding interest in suave ten-year-old Scott Whitehead, for instance, was hastily pre-empted by stern self-censorship:

Boy, I sure like Scott Whitehead. [scribbled out]

I AM BUGS ABOUT SCOTT WHITEHEAD. [scribbled out]

He's OK for a friend. Translation: FRIEND. [scribbled out]

I HATE HIM! [not scribbled out]

The first dawning of the old 'Can't live with them, can't live without them' maxim came with this remark about a boy who lived a couple of houses away:

Sometimes Joe Kolo is really weird. He always wants to find out stuff between Sue and Jeanie, Jeanie and me, Sue and me, or Sue, Jeanie and me. Otherwise Joe is really very nice. I mean, he can be a pain in the neck, but when his hair is long he looks really neat.

I never underestimated the power of hair to increase the neat-ability factor.

A furious scrawl nearly obliterated evidence of my feelings for my first actual boyfriend, who was a neighbour's nephew visiting for the summer:

I am beginning to like Ricky better and better.

This horrifyingly bold statement, having been duly pencilled over, was accompanied by the now-familiar disclaimer:

Not true. OK for a friend.

On the following page I had glued a passionate letter from Ricky, painstakingly written with multicoloured pens on groovy 'sun setting over the ocean' stationery. His prose was admirably unfettered for a ten-year-old boy:

Hi Katie,

I'm trying to write neat because this paper cost 30 cents a sheet but I don't care if it cost $100,000 a sheet, I'd still buy it just to write to you. If I get my allowance raised, I'll pay for every stamp you need to send a letter to me. Out of the ninety-eight million girlfriends I have, you're the only one I really LOVE.

LOVE ALWAYS, [drawn in puffy seventies letters with a purple felt tip]
Ricky

Along the bottom of the page, 'I love Katie' was written over and over. More puffy purple letters spelled out 'I LOVE YOU KATIE' on the back.

I was revolted. Typically, I had written next to the billet-doux: 'I DON'T LIKE MUSHY LETTERS!' But the truth was, it wasn't his tender tribute that had alarmed me. It was the fact that I apparently possessed some crazy mule-kick appeal, irresistible to icky boys, that even I couldn't control. Without me even wanting this oogie thing, Ricky was hooked.

I pondered the conundrum a few pages later:

I wonder why Ricky likes me? Strange. He's kinda nutty. I don't like him. He's OK. For a friend.

That said, I'd saved his letter, so I must have known a good thing when I saw it. The guy was flashing the pocket money and 'I love yous' around like no mystery date's business.

After establishing to my satisfaction how unredeemably *yecchh* boys were, I was appalled when Sue started to behave as if she actually *liked* them. This was reasonable enough, given that she was two whole hormone-packed years older than I was. She'd also started growing breasts and stopped wearing glasses. Nevertheless, I felt betrayed when she started hanging around Brad Norblad, a rich kid who lived a Chopper-bike ride away. It was even more chilling when she'd laughingly tell me all the mean things Brad had said about me.

Enraged, I turned to my notebook.

Sue likes Brad N. BARF! Brad said that he would ram a train up my ass and Sue started cracking up. She would because she is cracked. How she can think Brad is cute is beyond me. He is one of the most nastiest things on earth.

Sue thinks Brad is nice. Brad thinks Sue is nice. They should get married and call me names.

I rerouted my fury into mockery by concocting bogus love letters on behalf of my two newest enemies.

A letter from Sue to Brad.

'Dear Poopsie,

I am madly in love with you, Poopsie. I loved that joke about you ramming a train up Katie's ass. Why don't we get married and call her some more names?

And since you're so rich, why don't you buy a real train and ram it up Katie's butt. It's big enough!

Love and kisses,
Sue'

A letter from Brad to Sue.

'Dear Sue,

I am madly in love with you, too. I think we should get married, too.

I thought up another good joke about Katie, only it's too funny to write on this letter. Why not come over in my bed tonight and I'll tell you?

Love always [drawn in puffy letters as on Ricky's letter to me]

Poopsie'

Satisfied with the results of my bile-sharpened pencil, I sprayed the pages with cologne snitched from my sister's room to complete the mushy-letter vibe. If they were going to laugh at me, I was sure as heck going to get my own yuks in, too.

This position of strength through sarcasm was somewhat undermined by my entry two weeks later, disguised though it was in spy-style number code:

'2-18-1-4 9-19 7-5-20-20-9-14-7 19-5-24-9-5-18 5-22-5-18-25 4-1-25'

'Brad is getting sexier every day' was doubtless too obscene a sentiment to be safely expressed with ordinary letters. But it was grudging confirmation that as far as the opposite sex was concerned, maybe Sue wasn't as 'cracked' as I first thought.

4

Foxy Lady

If real relationships were too scary, I could always retreat into fantasy.

My bedroom was a hive of activity. I'd wunderkind away: cutting out construction paper stars, drawing with crayons, writing porn. Or at least writing what my callow nine-year-old mind considered to be unutterably depraved. I churned out piles of one-page stories incorporating much bowel-voiding and unauthorized uses of bras and underpants. Indication that my characters were a little harder-edged than, say, Dick and Jane, could be found in their names. With 'Barfy', 'Mushface' and 'Professor Bullshit' among the protagonists, readers knew that they were in for the rough stuff.

I'd staple on a title page and call it a book. Like real porn, quantity was more important than quality. I was keen to build up a body of work. Inside the 'front cover' of *Danny Dunce and Company*, for instance, I'd carefully pencilled:

Katie M. Puckrik, author of:
DANNY DUNCE STRIKES AGAIN!

DANNY DUNCE, NO. 1 QUEERO
MYSTERY OF THE MISSING SOCK
THE UNSTORY
DON'T WATCH TV!
A DOZEN RATS
DON'T WAKE ME UP

My mother never happened upon *Danny Dunce, No. 1 Queero*, or any of its scandalous sequels. However, she couldn't have missed the improvements I had made to an antique doll she'd saved from her childhood. I'd customized her treasured toy with tits 'n' twat drawn in red lipstick. Perhaps my mother recognized her 'Cherries in the Snow' put to imaginative new use. She tactfully never mentioned this incident to me.

My Barbie dolls also bore the brunt of my increasing sexual curiosity. I had four of them, and my favourite was the one who was the most stacked. I'd lock the bedroom door and dress her in her stewardess uniform. Minus the skirt. Making Barbie get kinky gave me a sharp surge of dirtiness. I didn't know *why* it was wrong for Barbie's plastic crack to remain uncovered, I just knew that it *was*. And I relished the wrongness. It made my pants itch.

Just like me, my Barbies were spies. They were always having to go undercover as prostitutes in order to tease information out of gangsters. I was effectively a Barbie pimp. My dolls of easy virtue had names like 'Velvet' or 'Blackie' or 'PJ', and I recorded their sexploits in individual doll diaries. One narrative detailed PJ's close call with a jewel thief who had a prosthetic face:

John Black was pretty sexy . . . told me to strip so we could fuck. I slapped his face. He said, 'Excuse me.' Then he left.

*When I slapped his face it was kind of mushy. It also had
wrinkles on it. When he came back, all the wrinkles were
gone. He told me if I got in his gang he'd tell me the plan to
rob the billion-dollar jewelled crown.*

On this occasion, the 'pretty sexy' John Black had misjudged
the fornication situation, but at least he had the class to
apologize. My dolls may have been trollops, but they were
ladies, too.

Of course, the real reason I had PJ slap the hoodlum was
simply because if she *had* spread her bendable rubber legs, I
didn't actually know what was supposed to happen next –
technically, that is. I was ignorant of the nuts and bolts of the
sex act, and not particularly interested, either. It wasn't what
the Barbies did with their nakedness that excited me. Just the
fact that they were naked was enough.

Another one of my behind-closed-doors activities was looking
at the cover of a sound effects album that belonged to my
parents. Among the pictured steam engines and brass bands
was a stripper with big sparkly blue pasties over her nipples. I
never bothered to find out what her associated 'sound' was –
the muffled chafing of her doughy inner thighs? Her screams at
the yanking-off of over-glued pasties? It didn't matter; the sight,
not the sound, was my stimulant.

And it didn't matter that I was a girl – naked ladies were
where it was *at*. In fact, compared to the buxotic babes that so
captivated me, I barely counted as one. I was as far away from
Pasty Lady's blue sparkled ripeness as a tadpole was from a
frog. I looked upon these cheesecake queens as inspirational,
but not necessarily aspirational. How could a shrimpy little kid
in a Tweety Bird t-shirt ever hope to look so foxy?

Ever resourceful in my smut search, I formed the Mad

Scientists Club. As President, and indeed, sole member of this organization, my aims were simple: to locate, steal and read my big brother's *Playboy* magazines. After a successful commando raid, I'd hide in my bedroom closet – which doubled as the Clubhouse – to peruse bosom flesh.

After many sweaty afternoons poring over *Playboy* with a flashlight, I hit on the bright idea of starting my own girly mag stockpile. After all, there was something undignified, even for me, about scrabbling around beneath my brother's bed. The only problem was, I didn't have the cash.

The solution to my lack of funds presented itself on the back page of a Spiderman comic. I didn't read the fine print for the 'Magic Money Making Machine', but the words 'money' and 'making' were enough for me to send away for it.

Sadly, I read those ads in backs of comics with the seriousness others reserve for the *Financial Times*. I beetled my brows in earnest consideration over teasers for trick black soap, whoopee cushions, onion gum. I fully believed that x-ray specs were functional, and that girl 'Sea Monkeys', the just-add-water pet, really did have bouffant flip dos with tiny tiaras perched on top.

Did I ever feel like a dupe when my 'Magic Money Making Machine' arrived. Sandwiched between two plastic rollers was a slip of printed green 'funny money', along with instructions for how to make your real loot dis- and reappear. Disgusted, I threw the thing away. What did I expect for a dollar, anyway?

Dreams of my own *Playboy* stash thus dashed, I resorted to cutting out pictures of every scantily clad female I could find and gluing them into a notebook. I called it *WOW! Magazine*. To drive the 'WOW!' factor home, I pasted pictures of dogs with their tongues hanging out next to the sexy ladies. Speech balloons saying 'WOW!' were drawn over the salivating pooches.

In *Time* magazine, I was delighted to find a paparazzi shot of *Playboy* supremo Hugh Hefner at his swingingest – all Paisley and crushed velvet with a hot-panted Playmate on each arm. I scissored it out and glued it to a page on its own. Hef was my mentor, but did I want to be him or the Bunny?

The answer came a few *WOW! Magazine* pages later. Under the heading 'A Page of Chicks', I'd plastered practically a whole farmyard of fillies, selected from 'Mark Eden Bust Developer' advertisements. The ads featured ample-racked women proudly flaunting the results of their 'development', which were barely restrained by teeny op-art bikinis. Mr Eden had applied his considerable scientific know-how to the mail-order creams and rubber plungers designed to make boobs big. It was a given that 'big' was a boob's only acceptable size.

The eight-week course worked a treat for former flatsies 'Yvonne' or 'Molly' or 'Rachel', who always managed to pump up the mammary volume by at least four cup sizes. The jubilance of their bazoombas was matched only by their smiles, which you could just about make out behind the twin peaks of their newly heaving cleavages.

I was getting my friends in on the nude-nik shtick, too. Sue had already been recruited for the Born Free scene, so I turned my attentions schoolward. My zest for breasts captured the imagination of best-friend-in-school Terri. At least it gave her a break from having to play Bambi's mother to my diva deer.

Terri, impressed with my home-made skin rags, began one of her own. There was panic the day she was rumbled by her mother.

Terri had nude pictures of girls in her notebook and her mom saw them. She thought that Terri collected them because they were like works of art and the human body is beautiful and that kind of stuff. Terri's mom said that she would get her more pictures like that! WOW! Terri got lucky. If my mom saw the stuff that's in my notebook, I'd be a dead mess. Man, she should see what I write, too.

As if my poor mother wouldn't have been traumatized enough by her anatomically corrected antique doll.

Months of studying smuggled *Playboys* led me to understand that upon reaching womanhood, I would automatically explode out to Playmate proportions. But my run-in with the bogus 'Magic Money Making Machine' had made me cynical, for the first time in my life. I stopped believing everything I read. But I never stopped ogling.

5

American Pie

It was starting to look like I was going to spend the whole summer in the closet. My mother had to do something drastic.

She sent me to camp.

Camp Tannadoonah – or 'Big T' as it was known to insiders – was a Girl Scout camp on Lost Lake, Michigan. I tagged along with Sue as an honorary 'Brownie'. Sue was the real deal – a fully fledged scout with a green felt sash dotted with merit badges. I couldn't be bothered with all that Girl Scout 'duty to God and my country' jive – I was there for the social whirl.

Sue and I were housed in a cute wooden cabin with three other girls and two 'counsellors'. The counsellors were about eighteen years old and cool because they had pierced ears, long, centre-parted hair, and could play 'Where Have All the Flowers Gone?' on their guitars. They taught us catchy sea shanties and nonsense folk songs. To this day, I recall every note, word and hand gesture of 'Are You A Camel?'.

Are you a camel, a flip-floppy camel,
And say, do you have a HUMP?

Do you sit at the table, as straight as you're able,
Or do you sit there and SLUMP SLUMP SLUMP SLUMP?
Are you a camel, a flip-floppy camel,
Without any starch in your SPINE?
If you are a camel, a flip-floppy camel,
Please go somewhere else to DI-I-INE!

To begin with, I revelled in the great outdoors.

Camp is neat. I love camp. I love the singing of the birds. I
love nature and anybody who tries to look in this notebook
may think this is queer. I don't blame them.

Then, things got ugly.

As opposed to the holiday spa spread I had anticipated, it turned out Tannadoonah was run like a Marine boot camp. The military manqué set-up included meals taken in the mess hall, and some tricksy trumpet-playing counsellor honking taps at lights out. Even though it was July, it was cold, and we were mushed forward daily on long 'character-building' hikes through poison ivy. By the end of the week, pink calamine lotion was crusting up on our skin like Pink Panther eczema.

Just about every activity had a brusque one-word name. Breakfast, lunch and dinner were 'Mess', which, given the calibre of the grub, made it easy to remember. Swimming lessons in Lost Lake were 'Swim'. Singing around the campfire was 'Sing'. The highlight of any day was 'Store', which was Big T's tuck shop, opened only during 'Rest'. I snacked away my battle fatigue with Sugar Daddy suckers and strips of purple-striped Laffy Taffy.

Relief from the basic training theme was provided by 'Crafts'. At last, the girls were allowed to be nancy boys instead

46

of soldier boys. We made jewelry boxes by gluing together forestfuls of Popsicle sticks. We wove 'god's eyes' with variegated yarn around twig crosses. The major project of the week was tie-dyeing our 'Big T' souvenir t-shirts. Mine was pink with faint and dainty rings, owing to the fact that I was too impatient to let it stew for the required length of time.

At twilight, I shivered happily in the still drying tee, waiting my turn to toast my twig-speared marshmallow in the bonfire. I was gearing up for the pièce de résistance of camp life: S'mores. Every veteran of summer camp knew how to make these survival training staples:

1 Toast marshmallow over open flame until charred and gooey.
2 Place now cindered wad of sucrose on graham cracker with one square of chocolate.
3 Place second graham cracker on top.
4 Smoosh gently together and eat.

I smooshed, ate and tripped my sugar-freak high. If S'mores were an indication of life in the rough, then mama call me Nature Girl. But this was not the shape of S'mores to come. It turned out that the cookies were just the counsellors' way of softening us up for the next day.

After 'Reveille' and 'Mess' on S'mores day plus one, the troops were summoned to a steep hillside in the woods. As the sun streamed through the ceiling of trees, forty little girls were ordered to clear the area of all underbrush. Unfortunately for us, 'all underbrush' consisted of one thing: stinging nettles.

Outranked and bare-handed, I huffed up the slope, pulling at the tough stalks. Before too long, the hills were alive with the sound of shrieking. I was getting stung like a schmuck.

Big T's little campers were nothing more than slave labour. By the end of the day, we'd cleared out the entire nettle-covered hillside. At evening 'Sing', we huddled around the campfire, exhausted, as the counsellors tried to cheer us up with another chorus of 'Are You A Camel?' It didn't work. We sat there in a collective 'SLUMP SLUMP SLUMP SLUMP'.

Sensing the distinct lack of starch in our spines, the counsellors told us they had a surprise. The day's toil wasn't just sadistic busy work, they reassured us. It was all in preparation for Big T's amphitheatre – an arboreal palace of culture to be completed by next summer. I could only hope that the next week's batch of campers would be brawnier than we were – the counsellors would probably be making them chop down trees and pour concrete.

The real surprise was that we never got to use the amphitheatre the next year.

This was because as soon as our week was up, Camp Tannadoonah was condemned.

After being 'Big T'd', I'd never been so glad to get back to school. At least at school, I never had to harvest nettles bare-handed. At school, I never had to sing 'Are You A Camel?'

At school, I never had to sing 'As Long As He Needs Me', either. The ballad was the big number for my role in the fourth-graders' production of *Oliver*. I played Nancy, the kindly wench who mothers Oliver and his adorable thug chums. It was decided that the song, with its pro-codependency message ('As long as he needs me/I know where I must be/I'll cling on selflessly', etc.), was too advanced for a nine-year-old. All that pointless sacrifice and devotion to a creep – jeez, I still had years to go before a girl was expected to do that for real. Even so, I had Nancy's fiery scenes with villainous lover Bill Sykes to negotiate. Tastefully, his actual murder of my character was set discreetly in the wings.

Bill was played by Bud Lipscomb, a boy whose name sounded worse than it looked. He was tall for his age with the roundest head I'd ever seen – even rounder than Speed Racer's with his helmet on. Bud had peachy-blond hair and several smatterings of freckles. The freckles somewhat diminished his menace in the role of psychopathic Bill.

Bud made up for any lack of theatrical credibility by being mean to me in real life. I always had the vague feeling he was overdoing it to disguise the fact that he really liked me. Maybe the dysfunctional pattern of our relationship had been set by Bill and Nancy's stormy love.

I hung tough about Bud in my notebook.

Bud Lipscomb has a too big mouth and is fat.

Yeah!

Bud Lipscomb is too tall for me.

So there!

Bud Lipscomb is a nut. He likes basketball. His head looks like a basketball. The only way he could like girls is if they were basketballs.

Preach, sister girl!

Bud and John are planning to take a firecracker and blow up somebody or something. Maybe I should stay a reasonable distance away from those guys.

49

In the circumstances, the use of the word 'reasonable' was, well, reasonable. There was always the chance that that firecracker had my name on it.

Worryingly, my favourite part of *Oliver* was always when 'Bill' yanked me off-stage to murder me. I never knew how much Bud was acting, and the frisson was disturbing. In a good way.

The theatrical visionary behind *Oliver* was the teacher whose name, unlike 'Lipscomb', looked *just* as bad as it sounded. 'Mrs Kumm' was a mouthful. I now wonder how long it took Mr Kumm to convince her to marry him. Then again, maybe it doesn't take any persuading to marry a man called Mr Kumm.

Regardless of how she felt about her orgasmic appellation, it was a cinch that as long as she didn't teach any children older than ten, she'd never have to read about it on the school toilet walls.

In my eyes, Mrs Kumm ruled as boho queen. She taught us that everything we created was good. If one of us crumpled up some artwork and threw it away, she would get angry and make the person retrieve it from the trash can. Mrs Kumm believed in making every child feel worthwhile and unique. She certainly was.

Mrs Kumm is short and fat. She has white hair and sometimes makes it blue or pink. She is old and is an art nut.

She resembled *Poseidon Adventure*-era Shelley Winters, but her look was pure Peppermint Lounge. Her pink-tinted bouffant was so way-out it was in. It vibrated insanely against her hamster-orange foundation. Pucci minidresses, black tights and patent-leather stacked-heel ankle boots completed the moonage daydream. She was on a collision course with her fifties, but she wasn't too past it to be with it. The fact that she was dumpy made her funky threads even more of a statement.

Mrs Kumm wasn't the only one cutting a dash at Swanson Elementary School. It was 1972, and with the help of Sears's Lemon Frog 'boutique-wear' section, even the under-ten set could approximate the streetwalker swank of Jane Fonda in *Klute*. The palette was mustard, rust, orange, white, brown and purple. I wore Peter Max cosmic print shirts with patch-pocket flares. 'Midi'-length was big. The fluffy puffy ring of acrylic fur trimming on the bottom of my suedette midi coat cleared swathes through school bus aisles. The coat looked totally *Klute* with my front-lacing, knee-high black patent leatherette boots.

Total *Klute*ness was also attempted by Jeanie Grossick, but with less success, I felt. Trying for Jane Fonda's wispy shag, she'd ended up with too much wisp and not enough shag. Her hairdo failure provided me with one more reason to make fun of her.

Jeanie was a year older than I was, and lived at the end of my street. She fulfilled the scapegoat role, all-important in any neighbourhood feeding chain. Her scapegoat duties were occasionally handed over to me, when it was Jeanie's turn to be Sue's best friend in the revolving door of friendship. Insecurity over the power balance ensured my mindless hostility towards Jeanie.

Jeanie Grossick is fat and has short hair. She's going to be a fat lady, an elephant, a rhinoceros and mammoth mixed in one when she grows up. Jeanie has a big mouth and says she is fat because she has big ribs.

Even to a nine-year-old, the 'big ribs' excuse didn't hold water. Her nickname was 'Fatsicle', an inspired blend of 'Grossick', 'fat' and 'Popsicle'. Jeanie was on the temperamental side, and her rages were legendary. Inspired by her hissy fits, I penned the 'Fatsicle Cheer':

Fatsicle Cheer

Clap your hands
Stomp your feet.
Throw a tantrum
Can't be beat.
You know why
I'm so fat?
It's because
I have big ribs.
You know why
They picked me
To throw a tantrum?
It's because
I fall through floors
Even the basement floor.
I end up
In China.

So it didn't exactly scan, but you got the idea. My notebook was filled with remarks about how fat everybody was. By general assent, this was the worst thing you could say about a person.

If Fatsicle tackled Joe Kolo, he'd probably be as flat as a pancake. Maybe even thinner. I bet she feels weird in her bathing suit when Joe sees her. I would if I were her.

My intolerance for fat people, bordering on mania, was peculiar in the light that I was no slenderella myself. The Little Debbie Star Crunch and maple syrup on ice were beginning to take their toll. One day at school, my increasing pudginess was confirmed in an unsolicited and most disagreeable manner.

With that morning's carefully coordinated outfit, I had gone overkill on the matchy matchy. I was wearing a blue and red polyester double-knit sleeveless dress pulled over a white blouse. On my feet were red, white and blue sneakers striped with stars. The thing that really pulled the whole ensemble together was a pair of tights that were red with *trompe l'oeil* blue knee socks with white stars. Basically, I looked like a chubby American flag. *I* thought I looked fantastic, until snottily blonde Trina Spinaldi turned around in the post-playground line-up, gave me the once-over and announced flatly, 'You're fat.' I was mortified.

Even before the echo of Trina's words had decayed into the air, I began to despise my body and obsess about my weight. It was the spontaneous birth, several years premature, of teenage-girl self-hatred. It was true that Mom had started steering me past the hip Lemon Frog stuff towards the 'husky' section of kids' clothes, but even still, I was no roly-poly.

My perceived corpulence was nothing more than a little puppy fat. Nevertheless, my notebook began filling up with self-directed invective. I scrawled in page-high letters:

Why do I weigh so much? WHY AM I SO FAT?

Next page.

I HATE BEING FAT!

Next page.

IT'S THE WORST THING

Next page.

IN THE

Next page.

WORLD!!!!

These screams in number two pencil were followed by the seeming *non sequitur*:

> *Hitler was sure a weird guy. He baked people in ovens??!!*

My hysterical holocaust had segued into the historical one.

In my notebook, I compulsively recorded what I weighed and ate.

July 28	*Morning*	*74 lbs*
	Night	*74 lbs*
July 29	*Morning*	*74 lbs*
	Night	*75 lbs*
July 30	*Morning*	*74 lbs*
	Night	*74 lbs*
July 31	*Morning*	*74 lbs*
	Night	*75 lbs*

Despite the fact that there was virtually no daily change in my weight, this went on and on for weeks. I also monitored my food intake:

Aug 2	*Morning:*	*Instant Breakfast*
	Lunch:	*Sandwich*
	Snack:	*Orange Juice Slush*
Aug 3	*Morning:*	*Instant Breakfast*

	Lunch:	Sandwich
	Snack:	Orange Juice Slush
Aug 4	Morning:	Instant Breakfast
	Lunch:	Sandwich
	Snack:	Orange Juice Slush

At this point I stopped keeping the food diary, sensing a certain repetitiveness to my routine. My diet was too predictable even for compulsive me to continue writing down.

While I was battling my blubbery demons, my parents announced that we would be leaving South Bend. My father had been promoted to the rank of colonel, and his latest assignment meant that we would be spending the next two years in Moscow, via a stopover in London. My brothers weren't going – they were now in their twenties and had their own convertible Mustang lives to drive. It was hard saying goodbye to them, and to Sue, but I was looking forward to hitting the road again. And maybe it was a chance to ditch the 'fat kid' stigma.

Shortly before I left Indiana forever, something unexpected lifted my turgid murk of plumpocentric misery. I discovered, written cramped and spiky on one of the back pages of my notebook, a secret message from Bud Lipscomb.

He'd spoofed Don McLean's current hit song:

> *Bye bye Miss American Pie.*
> *If you don't die,*
> *God will cry and so will I.*
> *Bye bye Miss Russian Queer.*

It was obvious. He loved me.

6

All The Young Dudes

Every time I hit a new city, I ask myself the same three questions:

1 What does the air smell like?
2 What's on the radio?
3 Are the doughnuts any good?

Odours, pop music and doughnuts are powerful potions – mood-altering substances with no risk of federal investigation. The chemicals released by sniffs, sounds and saliva medicate my way to a new up, a new down, a new career in a new town.

The new towns were beginning to pile up. My parents decided to turn the London stopover into a mini-holiday, a sort of appetizer for the main course of Moscow.

At nine, my knowledge of Britain, along with everything else, was sketchy. My main source of information on the country was the kids' TV show *H. R. Pufnstuf*, which I followed with an almost unbalanced zeal.

H. R. Pufnstuf – was it really underground code for marijuana? The rumour was that the initials stood for 'hand-rolled'. The programme *was* pretty trippy. 'Puf' was an incredibly camp Southern-accented dinosaurish thing in white go-go boots. His nemesis was 'Witchiepoo', a witch with a proto-punk band staffed by her animal minions.

The fact that *H. R. Pufnstuf* featured grown-ups cavorting moronically in unspecified critter costumes did not deter me in considering the show an authority on Anglo matters. This was because of its Cockney teenage star, Jack Wild.

Jack had a yellow shirt, brown bell-bottoms and an abnormal fixation on 'Freddy', a magic talking flute. This 'flute' looked disconcertingly phallus-like, especially while firmly gripped in Jack's hand. The dubious wind instrument had a castrato cry of 'Save me! Save me!' whenever Witchiepoo got her claws on it, which was every episode. The subtext was dicey, but hell, I was only a nugget, and besides, I had a big melting crush on Jack. I was enraptured by his English accent. I also dug his jaunty dance routines, which were an uncomfortable mix of Detroit soul brother and East End pearly king. I was oblivious to such nuances as I devotedly boogalooed in my living room along with Jack.

Jacked-up as I was, my parents' announcement that we were spending a week in London was great timing. I packed my yellow shirt and brown bell-bottoms, prepared to follow Jack to my future.

By 1972, the orange and yellow pavement on Carnaby Street was badly cracked and more of a health hazard than a tourist attraction. My family and I gamely stumbled over it and in and out of endless 'youthquake' establishments with names like 'Lord John' and 'Topper'. I successfully whined my way into a new pair of shoes that just screamed 'London' – orange suede loafers with cork platform soles.

Now standing three glam rock inches taller, I paused outside the shoe shop to soak up every molecule of London. On my new cork hoofs, I was a pony in a foreign field, nostrils flared, ears cocked. The city's DNA was borne on the wind in a code of odour and clamour.

I was electrified by the barrage of strange British whiffs: fishmongers, cheese shops, armpits. In deodorized America, where they zipped fish up and blanded glands out, such nasal tonics were rare.

I giggled at the funny way British police car sirens sounded like excited hot dogs: 'WIEner! WIEner! WIEner!' I tried to make out if English car horns really went 'Parp!' the way they did in my imported Noddy books, but all I heard were the standard beeps.

My dad, armed with a Super-8 camera, was warming up one of his nine tongues with some of the native patois.

'I say, old sport! How much are these bloody books, wot?'

'Puck, don't say that!' whispered my mother. ' "Bloody" is a bad word!'

My mom's disapproval was always his cue to step up the irritation factor.

'BLOODY nice day, wot? So about these BLOODY books – how's 'bout we make it two BLOODY quid for the whole BLOODY lot, OK palzo? Jolly good, you BLOODY bugger! Toodle-BLOODY-ooo! Yodel-ay-DEE-whoo!'

My mother set her mouth in a familiar tight line and didn't say anything.

As we strolled away from the market stall, my dad harrumphed, 'Yeah – those Limeys all sound like frooty-tooties.' 'Frooty-tooty' was another one of his catchphrases. He always rolled the *r* in 'frooty' for extra frooty-tootiness.

Our evenings were spent in a bewildering succession of theatrical diversions, most involving Agatha Christie in some capacity. I tried to steer the tribe back to youthquake territory with the suggestion that we see *Jesus Christ Superstar*. Many idyllic hours had been whiled away in my South Bend bedroom, acting out the rock Messiah romp to my sister's cast album. I did a mean Mary Magdalene. However, my mother vetoed it on the grounds of 'too much nudity'. She was getting it mixed up with *Hair*. I summed up the situation in a letter to Sue.

August 29, 1972
In London it was really fun. We went to a play every night. We saw a play called Company. *It was about married couples and it was kinda stupid but there was a lot of cussing in it like damn, hell, shithead, etc. And you know what the big put-down was? We didn't get to go see* Godspell *because they were all sold out and so was* Hair. *But I don't think* Jesus Christ Superstar *was. We could have gone to see that! Instead, we went to see some dumb old murder mystery. I even forgot what the name was.*

Regardless of maternal muddles, I was furious at being denied the full Jack Wildian experience of swinging London. I staged a sit-in on the tourist bus at the Tower of London in protest. My mother, eager for me not to spoil the entire vacation with a sulk, instigated a truce with the offer of lunch in Piccadilly Circus.

We went to a Wimpy Bar, and this was the pivotal episode of my week in London. This is where everything seemed *really* different, *truly* exotic, because it was in a context for which I actually had a reference point: food.

I thought I knew my way around a burger joint, but nothing

prepared me for the idiosyncratic affair that was the pre-US-clone Wimpy. Right off the bat, the very name was bemusing. What were they trying to do? Insult themselves before anybody else had a chance? And were they trying to pull a fast one with the so-called 'teacake'? I only ordered it because it was the closest thing on the menu to a doughnut. When I got it, I was surprised to see there was neither tea nor cake involved – just a sort of low-slung raisin bun.

I was also mystified at the presence of something called 'Salad Cream' lurking among the condiments. It seemed to be an unsuccessful compromise between dressing and pus. What purpose could it possibly serve on a menu of anaemic chocolate shakes and cakes masquerading as buns?

The waiter producing these culinary oddities excited my especial interest. He looked like an older Jack Wild, except with less zip and more zits. Smell-wise, my sudsed-up nose twitched to his distinctly lived-in tang. He was so louche, so London.

He was so *it*. *This* was what I had come to London to find. Suddenly Jack Wild seemed Junior League. The Wimpy worker obviously had better things to do than chase after talking penile flutes.

He certainly acted like he had better things to do than wait on us. By the time my dad had worked his seventeenth 'bloody' into our order of brown derbys, orange squashes and white coffees, my Limey loverboy's arrogance had curdled into curled-lip contempt.

My Happy Meal history was further scrambled by the pop music pumping out of someone's transistor radio. This was subversive stuff. You sure couldn't go to the A&W Root Beer Drive-In and get a blast of Mott The Hoople with your chilli dog. But in London, mod, fab, gear London, music that would annoy your parents was heard everywhere. And so, 'All The

Young Dudes' became my personal soundtrack for shyly eyeing my 'Jack' over a half eaten teacake.

Yep, it all comes down to chemicals. The complex compound of teacake, armpits and 'All The Young Dudes' had worked their magic on a young mind starved for sensation. Chemicals. They're all over the place – not just in laboratory test tubes handled by scientists in protective clothing. But maybe we *should* be more careful with them, because once they enter the system, chemicals can really rewire your life.

7

Black Dog

October 1973
I was wrong. You can't get much spying out of this place,
let alone the Russians. I can't understand a word they say,
but sometimes they do some sneaky stuff. A couple of
months ago I saw some Russians stealing windshield wip-
ers. They do it all the time here because parts are hard to
get.

I was crouched in the field behind the American embassy, where I lived with my family. My hideout was a copse of trees on the top of a hill. I closed my notebook. The tired light in the sky, not robust enough to qualify as sunshine, had begun to exhaust itself into gloom. It was only three-thirty, but the Moscow winter days were short. The snow-sharpened air was sulphurous with the fumes of cheap gasoline.

If it stayed this cold, soon I'd be able to go ice-skating in Gorky Park. Every winter, miles and miles of the pleasure ground's pathways were iced over for long-distance blading. I liked to go by myself, taking a Number 2 trolleybus from the embassy right up to the park's imposing gates. Stashing my snow boots in a locker, I would make for the ice. I'd glide for hours on splendid glacial avenues beside the Moscow River.

I was a good skater, fast and fearless. I'd shunt off the frozen esplanades into the enclosed rinks to practise a few tricky twirls and leaps kyped from ballet class. When I needed a break from figure-eighting, I headed straight for Gorky Park's main attraction.

I'm not talking about the giant Ferris wheel which towered over the onion domes of the nearby Kremlin. I'm talking about doughnuts. The Russians were smart enough to understand that hot doughnuts were the ideal accompaniment to a hard day's skating. And frankly, what *wasn't* compatible with that sugared ring of ecstasy?

Kvass wasn't. *Kvass* was a vile black fermented drink dispensed from a machine for five kopeks. It didn't fizz, bubble or tickle your tongue – it just turned your stomach. The *Kvass* machines were everywhere, on street corners, in parks, next to the doughnut kiosk where I was standing. While waiting in line, I made the mistake of taking an experimental taste. *Kvass* – arse, more like. It was putrid – sweet and bitter, all at the same time. I hastily put the communal glass back under the spigot.

This attracted the censure of a bunch of Russian schoolgirls ahead of me in line. They all had big white bows in their hair, like organza butterflies, and they were delighted at the opportunity to put a foreigner in her place. In no uncertain terms, the little martinets indicated that after each tipple, *Kvass* customers were meant to rinse the communal glass under the supplied faucet. The girls probably thought all Americans were slobs. I remembered what my mother kept repeating when we first moved to Moscow over a year ago, 'Remember, you're a little diplomat.' I felt like a little dip.

Shamefaced, I slunk up to the counter. Doughnuts would obliterate my faux pas, I thought. Twenty kopeks got me four hot balls of dough. I dropped the coin, grabbed my bag and skated away. Sliding, biting, zooming, chewing, I regained my equilibrium. This was the life. I loved Russia. Too bad about the Russians.

If temperatures weren't low enough to freeze up the park, I roller-skated. The whole burg was my beat. I roller-skated past czarist palaces and Stalinist hotels. I flashed my wheels of steel across Bolshevik bridges. I rolled on by bread sellers wearing bagels as bangles up the length of both arms like roaring twenties flappers. I brooked no obstacle in achieving my objective: TO GET TO THE TOY STORE.

I had pocket money, and dammit, I was going to spend it. Or try to, anyway. In Moscow in 1973, there wasn't very much to buy. Not unless I wanted to wait in line for hours to get fresh fruit or black market steak, which I didn't. And didn't have to – foreign diplomats were among the privileged who creamed off the goodies before the comrades got their chance.

What they lacked in strawberries or sirloin, the Soviets more than made up for in toys. Their cuddly toys were more esoteric in their sheer variety than any I had ever seen. Behind the Iron Curtain, virtually all flora and fauna, even squid, could be considered 'cuddly'. And from bears to bees, they all shared the same cry – a piteous bleat, courtesy of their sewn-in noise box. I steered clear of the bleating cuddly cabbage.

I selected a mewling elephant and stepped up to the cash register, which was an abacus, clacked at lightning speed by a thickset white-coated woman. The wooden-beaded counting machines were much more commonplace in Russia than the *ker-ching* variety. Suddenly, I became uncomfortably aware of the discrepancy between the other shoppers and me. To begin with, I was the only kid unaccompanied by an adult. The grown-ups were bundled in dark woollen overcoats and musk-rat fur hats, the accepted Russian get-up. I was in my hip Helsinki ski jacket and suede lace-up boots. In this arid environment of cheap sawdust-filled squids, I was impossibly western. Western, meaning 'wealthy', 'free'. Meaning 'spoiled'. I was the only child buying my own toys. Maybe it was incredibly tasteless. But I was eleven years old and I wanted toys, not taste.

Once I got my new elephant home, it wasn't long before it was filched by one of the workmen who serviced the embassy. I wasn't surprised – it had happened before. Just an elephant here, a squid there. I didn't really mind. I realized the Russkis must be hard up to steal a stuffed squid.

Back in the copse, my hands and face were beginning to feel frostbitten. I got up from my hilltop hidey-hole to go home. We'd be having dinner soon. I figured it'd be filet mignon or some kind of fondue – leftovers from my parents' party the night before. I hadn't seen macaroni and cheese or Spam since we'd left South Bend. I kind of missed Spam.

My father was the air force attaché to Moscow, which meant that as far as the Soviet Union was concerned, he represented the entire American air force. The USSR had eleven time zones, so it was a pretty big sphere of influence.

From what it looked like to me, his duties once again consisted of hosting numerous cocktail parties for swanky diplomat types. It was Berlin, but bigger: more men in tuxedos, more women in floor-length gowns, more ice cubes clinking into heavy crystal tumblers. Our maid, Mila, would keep the sterling-silver platters of hors d'oeuvres moving from cook to crowd, while Barbra Streisand's *People* shrilled out of the quad teak speakers.

My mother told me that she and my father were considered quite the cute couple at British embassy parties. This was on account of their nicknames, Dotty and Puck. 'The British just *love* to play games,' she trilled.

I nodded knowingly, but I wasn't really clear what she was talking about. What game were they playing – was it something to do with Shakespeare? Get a roomful of English people together, and Shakespeare was usually involved somewhere along the line.

In this instance, my sloppy cultural stereotyping was almost correct. It turned out that 'Puck' had slipped straight out of *A Midsummer Night's Dream* and into the Brit idiom to mean 'a mischievous sprite', which my father was. And those playful teabags couldn't get enough mileage out of 'She's dotty!' meaning 'silly', which my mother wasn't. During introductions, the pair of them probably sounded like a vaudeville act.

For the little I knew about my father's work, he might as well have been swallowing swords and juggling flowerpots. We couldn't talk about what Daddy did at the office, or indeed, where the office was. I knew it was somewhere in the embassy, parts of which were off-limits. For instance, the elevators couldn't go up past the seventh floor. Sometimes, men in military uniforms would call a number on the elevator phone and someone upstairs would unlock the block. When that happened, everyone else would have to get out of the lift and wait for it to come back down.

The constant hum of a generator droned from the uppermost reaches of the elevator shaft. Once when I asked my dad what was making all that noise, he put his finger to his lips and looked up at the ceiling. The gesture meant that because of the

KGB wire taps in the embassy walls, I wasn't to ask such questions. I decided for myself that the sound of machinery signalled classified stuff of the highest level.

When a fire gutted the embassy's top floors in 1977, nearly four years after we'd left Moscow, the *Washington Post* reported that the eighth, ninth and tenth floors contained 'sensitive documents and radio equipment' as well as 'top secret cryptographic and communications equipment'.

The Soviets gave as good as they got. It was Spy vs Spy. The KGB were everywhere, in the wires of our walls and the punchlines of our jokes. The standard gag as we walked in through the front door after a day away was to call out, 'Hi Boris – we're home!'

'Boris' and his KGB buddies were my *real* invisible friends. Alone in my bedroom, I chattered happily to them as I undertook one of my numerous artistic projects in the medium of Magic Marker. Any KGB boys tuned into my room were privy to classified information so hot even my dad didn't know about it. Mainly because it wasn't true. I was a fount of fake state secrets.

'The US are going to attack, you know,' I'd say to the empty room, colouring in my drawing of a bikini-wearing cat.

'Yep, you heard me, Boris. We've got bombs, missiles, everything – all pointed at the Kremlin. You'd better watch out.'

I was poisoning their minds with propaganda from inside their own country. I was Tokyo Rose – transposed.

Satisfied that I now had their undivided attention, I turned from disinformation to disc-information. I played DJ, spinning the latest sounds from the West as a way of rubbing their faces in what their inferior system of government had denied them. I taunted them with Led Zeppelin, The Rolling Stones, and, er, The Partridge Family.

'Yes, Boris. Capitalism has given us David Cassidy! Hah!'

Tell *that* to your Volga Boatman, Boris.

Rather than making me feel violated, I found the constant awareness that I was being listened to very much to my liking. For me, the KGB functioned as a captive audience. Perfect.

Sometimes, the moles came out from behind the walls and into full view. On a long journey in the Ukraine, our car was followed by two men in a beat-up Mercedes. They dogged us even when our driver got lost in the middle of a snowy nowhere. While maps were consulted, my parents and I got out of the car to stretch our legs. Fifty yards down the road, our shadows got out to stretch their legs, too. One of them lit a cigarette. It seemed silly not to just ask them for directions. But we all knew the rules. Spyers and spyees were to keep their Cold War distance at all times.

It made me feel important that we were considered suspicious enough to trail. Once back in the car, I spiced up the intrigue by sticking my tongue out at the 'spooks', as my dad called the other team's players. My mother pulled me away from the rear window, admonishing, 'They're only doing their job.'

The spooks were only doing their job – with some malicious little twists. Years later, the *Washington Post* revealed that a secret underground passageway had been discovered in Moscow, connecting the US embassy to the building across the street. In the building was special equipment designed to bombard the embassy with constant low-level microwaves. The idea was to trip up the capitalist pigs with stomach aches, diarrhoea, brain tumours. Shut down the spy machine.

While my dad was only doing *his* job, it was lonely for my mother. In the evenings, she skilfully performed her hostessing duties at my father's side. But in the day, she had no buddies.

Socializing with wives of lower-ranking officers was awkward – there was protocol to be observed. Whom would she 'favour' with her friendship? In the end, my mother favoured herself, sitting in her bedroom all day and needlepointing. She did the occasional ladies' ballet class.

I was still keeping up with my ballet classes, too. After the barre and centre practice, my teacher, a block-bodied yet graceful man, would demonstrate traditional folk dances. I was impatient with the proletariat pastiche – I wanted dying swans, not laughing cows. Where was the glamour in peasants?

On parents' day, I mazurka'd my socks off, trying to impress my dad. I already knew Mom was a solid fan. Clicking my heels like a jaunty serf, I checked to see that my father was clocking my talent. He wasn't. He was staring straight ahead at nothing, his face set in dried anger. Was he lost in some earlier confrontation – with work? With my mother? Why couldn't I cheer him up? Even if I hated heel-clicking, I was good at it. Wasn't he proud of me?

It was almost dark in the field, and my spy machine was about to shut down for the day. It was really 'nippy-toosa-pippy' – another classic Dad-ism. I hitched my long fleece mittens up to my elbows, liking how warm they kept my hands but not relishing the sweat that accompanied the heat. My fingers invariably smelled like wet puppies by the time I came in from the cold.

I didn't always need mittens in Moscow. On May Day, when processions of tanks rumbled past the American embassy and down the mile and a half to the Kremlin, it was sundress weather. That night, fireworks commemorating another victorious anniversary of the socialist worker would shower the capital. The great thing about Communism was that it staged spectacular pyrotechnics at the drop of a hammer and sickle. In the Motherland, there was always something to celebrate.

On these evenings, my friends and I would play 'war' in the wasteland behind the embassy, dodging the shells of the pretty rockets as they plummeted from the sky. The shells were hardboard bowls of varying sizes, and one could knock me out if it hit me, which it never did. I'd find a shell that was the right size for my head and wear it as a helmet.

I didn't see any helmets in the field now, as I picked my way down the steep hill. The next scheduled fireworks display wouldn't be until New Year's Day, a few months away. In the Soviet Union, Christmas was officially ignored.

Once I got to the wooden fence at the edge of the field, I turned left into the road. I was struck, as usual, by the blankness of the streets. No neon lights, no billboards. None of the commercial pizazz that put the pink in a city's cheeks. All the cars were off-white or sickly sputum-yellow.

A passing sputum car put me in mind of a man I'd seen earlier that day, blowing his nose, without a handkerchief, into the gutter. This was accepted mucus-moving practice in my latest new home. A person would pinch their nose with two fingers, lean away from their heavy winter coat and honk the contents of their shnozz right out on the street. Street-cleaning ladies with twig brooms would sweep up the freshly deposited snot. I thought the whole practice was kind of gross, but shucks, it was their country. If they wanted to blow their nose on it, it was their call.

I was now approaching Chaikovskovo Boulevard and the crumbling Yankee ghetto I called home. The central Moscow building had ten storeys and a roof bristling with antennae. It was surrounded by a high wall garnished with barbed wire. The two arched entrances were each guarded by a Soviet militia-man, supposedly for our protection, but really to keep the Russians out.

This was because the Russians kept trying to get in. Citizens sought asylum on a regular basis. It wasn't that they liked America so much – they just hated Russia.

Other citizens saw it as their socialist duty to drag the dissidents by their furry ear-flaps back into the bosom of Mother Russia. I was on the school bus the time our driver saw his chance to make a difference for Communism. As he pulled up to the embassy to drop us off, we all witnessed a Soviet family making a break for freedom past the grey-coated 'milimen'. Our driver leaped from the bus to help the guards tussle with their turncoat comrades. Unfortunately, he'd neglected to set the parking brake and our bus rolled off into traffic. An alert 'bus mother' jumped into the driver's seat and yanked the handbrake. The driver was sacked, and the family got in. They lived it up for a while in the embassy boiler room, before jetting off to somewhere with more than two car colours.

Over each milimanned entranceway were balconies that stacked straight up to the top of the embassy. We were forbidden to go out on them because they, like the rest of the building, were on the verge of collapse. I'd creep out on ours anyway, and peer through the plaster-clad railings to the top of the miliman's grey peaked hat six floors down.

I did my bit for mutual hostilities by dropping things on his head: usually popcorn seeds and black jelly beans, which were my least favourite kind. The next morning, as I strolled through the arches to the school bus, I'd see my missiles lined up neatly on the guard's podium, no doubt to be taken back to the lab for analysis.

I was on Chaikovskovo Boulevard now, but hadn't yet reached miliman-pelting distance when I was approached by a man. He was wearing a pea-coat and a flat cap, and he looked anxious.

'You American, yes?'

'Yes . . . ?'

'You from embassy, yes?' He jerked his head towards the dirty yellow building.

'Yes.' What did this guy want? I felt a little scared, but not as scared as he looked. He opened his pea-coat slightly and pulled out an envelope, holding it close to his body.

'Please. My family in America. In Philadelphia. You know Philadelphia? *Da*. I write letter for family. Please. No secrets. Just letter. Is nothing bad, but in Russia, they no mail. Please. You mail? At embassy, yes? For family. Please.'

He seemed desperate and sad. My initial reserve was sapped by sympathy. And zapped by excitement. I was to be the linchpin of a smuggling operation! Adopting what I felt was a discreet spy demeanour, I nodded my head curtly and answered, '*Da, tovarich*.' I tucked the letter into my nylon ski jacket.

The man melted back into the press of pedestrians. I moved forward towards the embassy, which in the dusk was now glowing a dull gold.

I kept my pace steady as I approached the miliman. I was about to breach eleven time zones' worth of security, so I had to stay calm. I was in luck. The guard seemed preoccupied by something in his hand. He moved it up to his nose, then into his mouth. He chewed. It was my jelly bean.

The jelly bean smokescreen had worked – in a way I had never even anticipated. I felt like I was born to spy. Triumphant, I marched up to our apartment and handed the letter to my dad. He looked quizzically at me, then turned businesslike as he scanned the envelope. As he placed it in his briefcase, he gave me the same curt 'spy nod' I'd used with the man outside.

'Thanks, palzo.'

I was elated. Now I was part of 'the firm'. Now, I had a connection to my father.

My best friend in Moscow was Jan Babbit, and she lived in the apartment directly beneath ours. She was twelve, a year older than I was, which meant that through her, I had access to the cool seventh-graders. Together, Jan and I cruised the pre-teen underworld of the embassy compound.

Our first stop would always be the snack bar, with its morale-boosting free world fare: pizza, French fries and Dr Pepper. Bellies now filled with all-American grease, we'd mosey past wisecracking Soviet chauffeurs hanging around in their black suits and ties outside the embassy garage.

Next to the garage was the playground, but Jan and I preferred to play in the adjacent garbage dump. The sweet, rank stink of rotting refuse was not a deterrent. The pit's attraction was the litters of kittens which sprang from its mephitic bowels. Most of the embassy kids managed to convince their parents to let them keep a couple of trash cats. I had three. Every bedtime, I was crowded by furry piles of purrs as they wedged themselves under my armpits for the night. I loved the discomfort of their affection.

Not all the cats were so lucky with their new homes, especially if they ended up with Tom Sawyer. Rumour had it that he'd killed his garbage-pit kitten by stuffing it into an acoustic guitar and smashing it over and over against a wall. Tom looked like a rock star in the Keith Richards mould with his pasty white skin, shaggy dark brown hair and permanent scowl. He was in my class at school, and his sunny *Huckleberry Finn* appellation belied his psychokid cruelty. He punched me whenever he saw me.

I took a shine to Michael Roof, another embassy boy who was also in the sixth grade. Like Tom, he had pasty skin and dark hair, but unlike Tom, with him the kittens and I were safe. Michael's brown eyes turned down at the outside corners, which gave him a sardonic air. He was a real wisenheimer. As per my m.o., I had difficulty facing up to my attraction to him.

Mike can really be funny sometimes, but I don't like his disposition. This may sound pretty prissy, but I don't think he's very nice.

In other words, I thought he was very nice. Otherwise, I wouldn't have sat next to him every day on the bus to school.

Our daily destination was the Anglo-American School, where the student body was comprised of the children of Moscow's international community. There were kids in my class from Malaysia, Australia, Canada, Iran, Italy, Greece and Holland, as well as Britain and America. You had to be able to speak English to attend.

The school was housed in neighbouring mini-mansions, two former homes of czarist princes. Frilly Corinthian columns cluttered the ornate one-storey buildings. Pediments perched with random grandeur. The school library, equally baroque, was a *bijou* ballroom with a blue and gilt cupid-covered ceiling.

Some mornings as we neared the school gates, we'd pass loitering Russian kids who'd yell, 'You! Americanski! Capitalist!' at us.

A wiry Young Pioneer once blustered at me, 'Money! You like money, don't you?' like it was a trick question.

For me, the answer was easy.

'Yeah, I like money. Don't you?'

Not expecting to have his rhetoric redirected, the YP faltered somewhat.

'You . . . you like money?'

This was getting tedious.

'Yes! And wouldn't *you* like a million roubles?'

Hey – that wasn't part of the script.

'Americanska – you like money,' he concluded, limply.

What was it to them, anyway? Didn't these Muscovite mites have something better to do? The notion of me standing outside Lenin Learning Institute No. 45 screaming, 'You! Collective farmers! You like tractors, don't you?' seemed preposterous. They'd obviously been getting too many sprinklings of propaganda on their bortsch.

All the Russian nippers spoke great English. Maybe their education was better, and maybe they worked harder. I put it down to the fact that our alphabet was manifestly easier to learn than the hieroglyphic mess they had to wrestle with. And certainly, the opportunity to harangue capitalist piglets through school railings was an incentive.

The multitudes of Russkis fluent in my language effectively crushed any motivation to learn theirs. Besides, I was too intimidated by my dad's command of languages to take more than a few tentative stabs at mastering Russian. In the end, it was easier to concentrate on just being good at English.

Our class had a day out at a Soviet school once, and even with its students graciously translating everything into English, their lessons were too hard. Even Lenin looked hard, in his portrait that hung at the front of every classroom.

In the cafeteria, I embarrassed myself by choking on a sausage. The whole day had put me on edge and my tubes weren't opening and closing in the right order. A menacing Russian boy cornered me with, 'Your father is a spy, yes?' I was stuck for an answer. Coughing back the gristle, I offered, lamely, 'No, we're all just capitalists.' I hoped my party-line line would squelch the interrogation.

I was glad to get back to the Anglo-American School. There, with its rainbow of nationalities, I got all the cultural exchange I could swallow.

Some of the school's 'Anglo' was provided by Louise, who was from London. She was *ever* so crispy-wispy, terribly, *terribly* lockjaw-proper. Louise had blonde hair and blue eyes, and her favourite word was 'stupid', which she pronounced 'styooo-pit'. Her preferred malediction usually came in twins and triplets, as in, 'Styoopit styoopit man!' or, 'Styoopit styoopit styoopit snow!'

One day, Louise brought in pudding for the whole class. Not knowing that 'pudding' was the all-purpose British term for 'dessert', I was perplexed not to see the cold creamy mousse that any Yank would expect. Instead, Louise's pudding was a tray of chewy bright pink sugar topped with a layer of chewy white coconut sugar. I was embarrassed for her as she tried to palm it off on the kids as a tasty snack. Talk about 'styoopit'. Was she brain-damaged or what? Why else would she have been at home the night before, thinking, 'I know, my friends will like congealed sugar covered in more congealed sugar'?

It wasn't until my next trip to London, a whole decade later, that I learned Louise's treat had been a variation on a legit Brit sweet called Coconut Ice. This tallied with the English penchant I'd by then discovered: matching a food's inside to its outside. They ate things like fried breaded bread on two pieces of bread, or something. I thought people were kidding around when they'd order a 'chip butty'.

'Oh that's a good one – a starch sandwich!' I'd chortled, until I realized I was the only one laughing.

Another Anglo-American student who avoided Louise's thoughtful offering was a beautiful Iranian boy called Sassan. He was tiny, with big dark eyes and sumptuous black curls. Sassan nixed coconut ice because of aesthetic sensibilities of a different sort: he didn't want to get any on his clothes. With his flashy *schmatte*, the kid was the Persian version of Prince – pre-dating the pop star by several years.

Sassan has really weird shoes for a boy. They're high heeled. Sometimes he wears a white shirt with white shorts. He wears rings on his short little fingers which makes him look corny.

I had to give him credit for trying. Throwing a look together in the Soviet Union was tough. Fashion was a Cold War casualty, and as soon as you moved behind the Iron Curtain, style was held hostage.

Everyone went native with a *shapka*, the big hairy hat that was like wearing a beaver on your head. At school, the ear-flapped *shapka* was the only acceptable item of indigenous kit, handy given how cold the winters were.

Whenever somebody new started at the Anglo-American, their latest western togs would be scrutinized by the rest of us with admiring interest. Parental trips to Paris or Germany or Finland ensured an intermittent trickle of new accessories. In one important seventies staple, we kids were fortunate in our proximity to Sweden: clogs. Resplendent in wooden shoes, we modishly clunked and scuffed our way though our Moscow days. I was especially enchanted with my pair, which were scarlet patent leather with a dappling of silver studs.

My friend Stephanie Stephanopolis had silver-studded clogs just like mine, except that hers were blue patent leather. Stephanie's father was the Greek ambassador and she lived in a pre-Revolutionary palace. She was real nice and had access to unlimited quantities of Toblerone chocolate. It would be shallow to suggest that food rationing in Moscow helped determine people's choice of friends, but the most popular parties *were* held at Stephanie's mansion.

Because of the rationing, food assumed even greater importance for me than usual. Families moving to Moscow were required to bring enough provisions to last for one half of their projected stay. We put our year's worth of food in the *sklod*, the larder in our back stairwell. The only stores that made any impact on me were the massed cans of violet pastilles and Chee-tos. Technically, these party nibbles were off-limits, but I was helpless to the call of the Chee-to. A Chee-tos-shaped scar carved down the back of a finger was the outcome of one of many ring-pull frenzies.

Rationing heightened the heinousness of the school lunch box thief. I suspected Anita Ndisi of the crime wave.

I am so mad! Yesterday something was taken out of my lunch box and today it happened with my cupcake. And for your information, I happen to know that those cupcakes are rationed at the commissary. Two a week, to be exact. Jan said that it was probably Anita Ndisi because she saw her take a whole gob of stuff from people's lunch boxes. Jan says that if I say something like 'How'd you like my cupcake?' Anita would kill me. Probably.

Anita's dad was an ambassador from an African country, so it wasn't like she was cupcake-deprived. She was just feisty. Too scared to sass her, I was jubilant when Anita got hers. It happened on a school outing to Lenin's tomb.

After waiting for over an hour in Red Square, we finally entered the reverent quiet of the tomb. The mummified body of Lenin lay waxily under glass in the centre of the room. We filed up, across and down the stairs surrounding the stiff in the dimly lit reliquary. It was the going down that tripped Anita up. Her six-inch platforms had given her the slip. The contents of her fringy suede bag clattered all over the marble floor: lipsticks, powder compacts, pens. I didn't see any cupcakes.

For several stretched seconds, a fog of appalled stillness enveloped guards and citizens, Anita and her fellow students. Her blunder was egregious *in extremis*; sacrilege in a holy socialist place. After an excruciating century of silence, the guards finally rushed forward and gathered her girly stuff up in a hurry. Anita had a big mouth, but she wasn't using it now.

After her gaffe, Anita lost all credibility as a bully. Admittedly, I still took the precaution of surrounding myself with Jan's older friends before ridiculing her. I had my future cupcakes to consider.

My teenage friends were a worldly bunch. They had cosmopolitan names: Saskia, Klaus, Uha, Jep. Australian Jep looked so tough with her long black ringleted hair, wire-rimmed glasses and white fluffy moon boots. Uha was a sexy Finnish boy who had Tartar cheekbones and shoulder-length brown hair. We were the in-crowd, and our in-est crowd scenes were at Stephanie's parties.

I never saw Steph's ambassador dad. It was hard to see much of anything in all that black light. Which was the way I liked it – the ultraviolet eclipse only intensified the grooviness of the music. Led Zeppelin's 'Black Dog' was *the* cool song that everyone loved even though it was impossible to dance to. This was because of its erratic tempo, which kept speeding up and slowing down. Nonetheless, when someone dropped the needle on 'Black Dog', I was flattered when Uha asked me to dance. He pawed the shag carpet like a heavy-metal bull, shouting out Robert Plant's caterwauled line as 'Eyes that shine, burnin' red – dreams of UHA through my head!' I laughed along with him. I stopped laughing when the song finished and he draped his arm around Jep.

Uha likes Jep now. He says, 'It's quite obvious that I like Jep and Jep likes me.' I must be jealous that Jep likes Uha and he likes her and nobody likes me. I will name all my faults on the next page.

Next page.

> *I am:*
> *fat*
> *loud-mouthed*
> *jealous*
> *vain*
> *too particular and practical*
> *bad-tempered*
> *contemptuous and bossy*
> *a show-off*
> *UNFORTUNATELY!*

I was being a little hard on myself. For one thing, 'contemptuous' was a pretty impressive word for an eleven-year-old, but I didn't write 'good vocabulary' on the plus side. That's because there wasn't a plus side.

But now it was time to pack up all my perceived faults, because my Americanska years were about to cross the finish line.

We're leaving January 27, 1974. I'm excited, but I'm also sad about leaving Moscow. I wonder how people will take me in the new school?

I like travelling. I'm glad I was born a diplomat's daughter. The only sad part is leaving your friends to go to a different country.

The only sad part was leaving Michael Roof, my school bus swain. Although we'd never formalized our glow with an Uha-style announcement, our attachment was undeniably real.

Without any prior discussion, we'd always managed to be partners for the square-dance lessons given by our batty Southern school principal. If Tom Sawyer was trying to punch me in the head again, Michael would help me to hide. And once, after setting fires together in the room-sized packing crates next to the garbage pit, Michael had given me his Bic lighter.

It took the imminence of my departure to crystallize our courtship. The day before I was due to leave, Michael and I found ourselves alone in the embassy playground. A poky 'warming shack', rickety and wooden, stood in one corner. Tree-strung coloured lights criss-crossed a makeshift skating rink. The effect was more forlorn than festive.

Quiescent, we stood next to the icicled jungle gym. I resisted a powerful urge to lick the frozen metal to see how many tastebuds I could rip out. After a spell, Michael and I moved intuitively from the outdoor chill to the indoor chill of the shack.

81

Sitting next to each other, with our backs against the black-painted walls, we watched our breath in the sub-zero air. It was my moment.

'You're cool.'

My confession floated towards him on tiny droplets of condensation. In the hush, it hovered.

Then Michael spoke.

'You're cool, too.'

Our mutual 'cools' met, meshed, then evaporated.

Together, we left the warming shack.

8

Dancing Machine

Spring 1974
I hate this place! Everyone in the States is so cruel and mean. I wish I was back in Moscow or South Bend. I am so miserable here.

The place I hated so much was Virginia, cradle of my birth. I must have grown out of it a smidge and now that I was back, the fit was mighty tight.

After Moscow, my dad had retired from the military. We'd resettled just a-ways beyond tobacco-spittin' distance of the Pentagon.

Though the Washington area is on the right side of the Mason–Dixon line – the southern side – its affluent mix of Kennedys and congressmen is too shallow to pass for the *Deep* South. But barely a few miles out of DC down Route 50, Virginia drops her candy pants and gets Deep real fast.

The state flares down and out from its northern apex like a plantation belle's hoop skirt, its ruffles tickling Tennessee, Kentucky and North Carolina. West Virginia snuggles on the side, a shy sister. Virginia is the heart of Dixie and the buttocks of the Confederacy. During the Civil War, the state capital Richmond had been the rebels' seat of power. But after the blue-coated Union men drove old Dixie down, rebels and slaves gave way to thoroughbred horse farms and the CIA headquarters.

And to the scene of the Puckriks' US comeback. For me, re-entry into American life was difficult. Even though I was in my own country, I'd never felt more alien.

Tad was calling me a Commie. He doesn't know what it means. I know I didn't, before I went to Moscow. I am definitely not Communist, but I surely don't like the way he calls Communists 'Commies'. He shouldn't make fun of what people believe. I never did anything to Tad. I gotta get him back, somehow. I don't like him.

Two years of having 'Capitalist' screamed at me by real Commies had left me unprepared to be lumped in with them. And this time, I *really* didn't like the boy in question. After making relentless cracks about my brown fur *shapka*, Tad stole it.

Tad was one of the kids at my new school in Falls Church, a seedy sprawl of strip malls and condos off Route 50. We were temporarily holed up in a rented apartment there while my parents looked for a house in a nicer suburb.

I didn't even bother trying to fit in. What was the point? I was only going to be there for a couple of months, and besides, these kids were riff-raff. This was an impression loosely based on the fact that some of them had divorced parents. I hadn't met any kids before who didn't have the complete set.

In a lacklustre fashion, I managed to acquire a couple of short-lease amigos. Our wariness was mutual.

Belva keeps giving me these weird looks if I do the least little different thing. Missy is a pretty good kid, but she also looks at me strangely if I do the least little thing. Obviously, these kids wouldn't last long in Moscow.

Like they gave a poopy-doop. Like it would have ever cropped up once in their collective lifetimes. The more relevant concern would seem to have been my own stateside durability, but I conveniently overlooked that angle. The only kid who was unreservedly nice to me was the class jerk, Rocky, but even misfits have pride, so I was horrible to him. Someone had to pay for my misery.

I perked up slightly the day all the eleven-year-old girls were sent down to the gym to watch *From Girl to Woman*. Our teacher joked that it was our first chance to see an X-rated movie. I pretended, along with the other sixth-graders, that the whole exercise was deeply corny, despite not having the slightest idea what puberty entailed. It was just important to take that world-weary stance. I brought my notebook along to document the event, and made a special notation regarding the teacher chaperoning the assembly:

Mrs Patch is really weird. She talks like a kid and she wears platform shoes, even though she is about thirty. She is always hanging around the male teachers.

I wasn't about to let the elderly Mrs Patch get away with such unseemly behaviour. To my mind, only Mrs Kumm had had the flair to carry off swingin' fashions.

The lights went down, and *From Girl to Woman* flickered on to the screen. The plot was a bit art-house. It seemed that a character called Judy finds a red flower in her underpants, after which she needs to wash vigorously under both arms. The narrator especially stressed the use of soap.

The approach was disappointingly cryptic. All that effort banning boys from the presentation, and even then we didn't get to see any gross-out stuff. We felt cheated.

Although I'd been exposed to *From Girl to Woman*, I was still emphatically a girl. A somewhat hostile girl. My parents had now found us a house, so I said my sour farewells to Falls Church. Then I said my sullen hellos to Venus.

When we moved to Venus, Virginia in 1974, it was pretty much the end of civilization before the world dropped off into a rural abyss of cow pastures and woodland. Our brand-new development of faux colonial family homes had been built on cow pastures. My dad set to work recreating the woodland by single-handedly planting hundreds of baby trees on our half-acre. He surrounded our house with maple, dogwood and weeping cherry trees. He ringed the entire property with a living barricade of evergreens.

The saplings were too small to keep out segments of the local 'party hearty' herd, a subculture I was as yet unfamiliar with.

At our new house, there were two seventeen-year-old boys walking up and down on our cellar door, so I snuck underneath to hear what they were saying. They were talking about hash, and how it feels so good going around in their heads. I was so scared. When I called for my mother and no answer came, I thought that they had caught her and that they were waiting for me. But they left.

The only thing these two were likely to catch was a bad case of the munchies. Kidnapping mothers was far too strenuous an activity, but I was innocent of the ways of the weed. The bucolic doobie-wielders had given me a fright. As long as the rustic drug scene was going down on our storm door, I was staying up in my bedroom. Preferably on my bean-bag chair, reading *Mad* magazines.

Before long, my various cats adopted the bean bag as a favoured place to relieve their kitty bladders, and their urine pooled up in polyurethane gullies. By the time they'd turned it into an inside-out waterbed, I faced up to the fact that it was time to get out of the house to meet my new neighbours.

Kelly, Petra and Carla were all my age, all lived nearby and all had horses. Since forever, Virginia had been horse country, and riding wasn't just a rich kids' hobby. It was a gen-U-ine down-home tradition.

Kelly, skinny and freckly, was my next-door neighbour and most trusted friend. Petra, pretty and sharp-tongued, provided an additional partner to pair off with when we all suffered our regular friendship snits.

Carla was exotically trashy. Her small house across the road from my big one had been there since our land had been cow food. When I first met her in the cafeteria line at school, I asked what her dad did for a living. Carla answered drily, 'He's a drunk.'

This was confirmed by the smell of stale beer and sweat in his beat-up Oldsmobile. I was scared of him. His normal speaking voice was an angry roar. Once, when her father conversationally screamed at me, 'DO YOU LIKE SOUR MILK?' I said 'Yes', because I didn't want any trouble. Maybe he was going to offer me some to drink, and if he had, I'd have done it.

Carla must have already found the red flower in her under-pants, because she had tits and hips before anyone else. She was impressively blasé about her womanly curves, and didn't mind when the older guys stared at her when we went swimming up at Timber Lake. We also went to the fairground together, soaking up the heady carnival sleaze.

When Carla and I were on the Scrambler, some cute guys came over and said, 'Chow, sweethearts.' I just about died. Carla goes, 'Chow,' and they go, 'Are you doing anything tonight?' and we go 'No,' and they just cracked up and drove away. Stuff like that happens to Carla all the time, and boy, do guys' eyes pop out when she says she's only twelve.

Friends of Carla's older brother would always stick around to talk to her. She'd laugh at my disapproval over her getting into strange men's vans and coming back with lovebites. She acted experienced, but I don't think she'd actually gone further than second base.

We'd hang out in Carla's messy bedroom and listen to Lynyrd Skynyrd's 'Free Bird'. She talked about earthy things that I was too prudish to discuss: hickeys, making out, getting drunk. I got her into Joni Mitchell, and she got me using tampons. Carla was the first person I knew who smoked pot.

Carla was also the first person I knew who employed the word 'redneck'. She used it proudly, to describe herself. The way she said it, redneck was an honourable thing to be. And sure as shootin' – Virginia was redneck turf.

The redneck ethos could be found in good ole boys drinking Pabst Blue Ribbon at the Elk Lodge, right down to kids my age chewing plugs of tobacco on the school bus. Boys – mostly – dipped snuff from the little tins of Skoal that wore rings into the back pockets of their Wranglers. They'd chew the tobacco and spit out wads of brown slimy gunk, leaving a Hansel and Gretel breadcrumb style trail behind them. The spitting was part of the pleasure, the aims being speed and distance.

If spitting wasn't enough and you wanted to actually swallow something, then redneck cuisine offered a fine line in cut-price comestibles.

The orange brick of Velveeta processed cheese is a cornerstone of Southern food. Pabst Blue Ribbon beer is another. Velveeta could be turned into sandwiches, casseroles or fudge. PBR enhanced chilli, fruit cobbler and cake. But Coca-Cola is the most versatile ingredient of them all, appearing in barbecue sauce, ham glaze, hot punch and baked beans. And drinking a bottle of Coke with a packet of salted peanuts poured into it was lunch-in-a-soda.

At our house, my mother's Georgia girlhood came out in the kitchen. We all inherited her predilection for peanut butter, mayonnaise and lettuce sandwiches. Sometimes, she made PBR beer bread. And for a special treat, she'd whack open a can of Pillsbury Poppin' Fresh Dough, wrap the perforated dough squares around 'fun-size' 3 Musketeers Bars and bake the whole mess in the oven. I loved biting through the warm bun into scalding chocolate lava.

For those with time enough for a sit-down meal, pulled pork on a bun at The Dixie Pig was recommended. The revolving neon sign outside the diner featured happy cartoon swine holding heaping plates of their barbecued pals while stabbing each other with forks. 'The Dixie Pig, where the pigs eat the pigs,' my friends and I used to sing out whenever we'd zoom by on the highway.

Roadside convenience shops offered a variety of regional bites for your 55 m.p.h. picnic. High's Dairy Store, which flourished before being swallowed up by 7–11, was my pitstop for banana Moon Pies and pecan Bama Pies. I'd wash down the hand-sized pies with Shasta soda pop, which came in a bewildering array of flavours. I usually stuck with cream soda, although tiki punch, black cherry or strawberry could give me a run for my allowance money. Chocolate Yoo-hoo, on the other hand, was just plain strange – I found the cocoa and carbonation combo too unsettling.

When I went up to the counter to pay for everything, I'd try not to look at the big jar of pig knuckles next to the cash register. The pink stumps in brown fluid were too much like something out of biology class.

Whether you were going to High's or horse shows, moms in Ford station wagons were a kid's usual mode of vehicular transport. I still had a few years to go before I could get my license and wang-dang down the backroads like the high-schoolers. The older guys squealed through Venus in their Trans Ams, Cameros or Firebirds, Allman Brothers on the radio and a Confederate flag on the antenna.

Those harbouring monster-truck rally ambitions might prop their Pinto chassis on a truck suspension with sixty-inch tyres off a manure spreader. No matter that on those giant wheels, the dinky car looked like a tick on a hound dog's back – the Godzilla'd Pinto was the ultimate redneck status symbol. The rebel yell could also be rendered automotive by driving a Ford or Chevy pick-up truck. It was a given that the trucks were Detroit-built – American-made was the American Way.

Frequently, American-made gas-guzzlers had to share the road with Virginia-bred hay-chompers. Folks on horseback ambled along the asphalt up to Difficult Run, the hilly park where they could really spank their steeds. One time, a bay gelding escaped from his field and galloped, riderless, all the way down Pamunkey Road. As cars swerved, a girl on a white nag barrelled down the equine expressway in hot-hoofed pursuit.

I knew how that horse felt   running alone the wrong way down the wrong road. In Venus, I was still having teething troubles. Especially at my new school. Especially with the popular girls.

Dee-Dee says I use too many big words. Hah. I just keep thinking of how she would be treated in Moscow for all her halter tops and eyeshadow. It would even be strange there for me to wear nail polish. The kids here (most of them) are so immature.

Immature? This Dee-Dee, 'for all her halter tops and eye-shadow', sounded like she'd heard the clarion call of teendom way the hell before I ever did. While she was dazzling the sixth-graders with her flashy ways, I was busy writing a poem to commemorate the obscure American holiday Arbor Day.

My poem, called 'The Tree', had the misfortune to win the Difficult Run Elementary poetry contest, which cemented my position as the school dork. 'The Tree' was an eco-centric elegy decrying Man's evil slaughter of green living things.

I read it in front of the whole school at a special outdoor assembly.

The Tree

There it stood,
The Tree.
Clothed in its leafy robe of green.
Majestic, Spectacular, Unmoving, Silent.
Its presence awed all that would
Pass by.

The tree's majesty thus established, my words went on to paint a vivid picture of anthropomorphic birds and vines vainly attempting to stop bad men with saws from killing it.

Movingly, I concluded:

> *There it laid,*
> *The Tree.*
> *Still majestic, but nevermore to live.*
> *It was dead and gone,*
> *But its spirit still lived.*
> *The Tree.*

Dee-Dee and her henchwomen were moved, too. Moved to kick my butt. In a pack, the girls would follow me across the playground, aiming the business end of their Earth Shoes at my tush. While roughing me up, they'd quote my poem back at me, spitefully:

'MaJEStic, QUEERbait.'

'SpecTACular, REtard.'

'Why'dja use so many big words, DIPstick?'

My bad fashion didn't help matters. Because of my two years in Moscow, my style clock had stopped at a critical point in the early seventies. By the time I'd been able to get my hands on some cool teen duds, they were, well, duds.

I never questioned why that sky-blue polyester pants suit with puffed sleeves and elephant flares was so inexpensive, even for K-Mart, but maybe I should have. As I made my sky-blue debut at Difficult Run, the wrongness of my clothes hit me like a fireball. To the sneers and jeers of my skinny-jeaned classmates, I was a pudgy vision of bell-bottomed hell.

In my final week at Difficult Run, my life changed. The last dance of the year was on the last Saturday of sixth grade.

Buddy-power was supplied by Kelly, Petra and Carla. Beauty-power was furnished by my mother. I felt pretty in an outfit she had sewn for me: a top and matching skirt in yellow and brown flowered cotton. The floor-length skirt was swirled in alternating stripes of yellow and brown fabric. With my centre-parted brown hair swinging down past my waist, I dared to think that for once, my appearance wouldn't make classmates blow chunks.

The only light in the school gym came through the doors of the fluorescent-lit hallways. The boys fidgeted in a clump under the basketball net. The girls lined up along the bleachers. Dee-Dee and her catty crowd whispered behind their hands and tried to look superior. Music boomed out of the speakers, but no one was really dancing.

Until 'Dancing Machine' came on. The Jackson Five song was my absolute favourite. Under my breath, I sang along with Michael:

She knows what she's doin' – she's super bad, now!
She's geared to really BLO-O-OW your mind!

Boppin' and finger-poppin', I swayed my way to the middle of the gym. I didn't care that I was on my own – it was the end of the school year and I didn't have anything left to lose. Besides, I wasn't going to waste the J5.

By the time the bruthas hit the second chorus, I was no longer alone. There was a hot papa for my mama, and he was none other than Ivan Bird, the coolest kid at Difficult Run.

Ivan was black, with a short 'fro and a jazzy shirt. Everybody knew he was the best dancer in school – and now he wanted to dance with *me*. Together, we busted loose on the floor.

She's a dance dance dance dance – dancin' machine!
Watch her get down, watch her get down,
As she do do do her thing – right on the scene!

I was ecstatic. And I was more than that. For the first time in Venus, I was – comfortable. Five days before school was over, I finally found my place. I was a dancing machine.

Revenge was sweeter than Velveeta fudge. While Dee-Dee stood on the sidelines, boy after boy came up to ask me to dance. Her face was awash with disbelief, then anger, then anxiety. Whatever it was awash with after that, I didn't care. I was too busy dancing.

9

Court And Spark

In junior high, I only had two years to get it right, as opposed to the six offered by grade school. The fresh kick-off at Louisa May Alcott Intermediate had a built-in bonus, which was that any bad reputations could be dismantled. The forfeit was that legends had to be rebuilt. Over the summer, my dance advances at Difficult Run had been forgotten, so I had to start from scratch. But then again, so did every other twelve-year-old. My advantage was, I was used to starting from scratch.

Socially, junior high is a dry run for senior high, in the way that puberty is a dry run for maturity. Except that the one thing puberty isn't, is dry.

And neither is the weather, in Virginia's hurricane season. Every autumn, Hurricane Arnold or Betty or Charles or Donna roars its alphabetical path of destruction up the Atlantic coast from Florida. A hurricane is nature's puberty: all that hot air, squally tantrums, rainy tears, then calm.

Most of the big 'look at me' damage is done by the time a gale hurls into Virginia: the flooding, the upside-down Winnebagos, the cows on people's roofs. But a Venus hurricane usually has a few good gusts left to turn garbage cans into UFOs – or to rip letters off the 'Crawdad's' sign down on Nutley Street.

Carla had the big red plastic 'C' in her bedroom. I don't know who got the 'F', but the agricultural supply store's sign now read 'rawdad's arm and Feed'. It suggested some vaguely cannibalistic command.

These upheavals to the lie of the land were mirrored by our changing bodies. The accoutrements of teenhood tumescence – jockstraps, training bras – were about battening down the hatches, making sure nothing flew off during the next storm. No boners here, miss. These buds are my biz, bucko. The straps and cups contained rampant bulging, both actual and potential.

Everything was to be kept smooth and under control. Lips were shiny; hair, sleek. The look you cooked was slick, slick, slick. Unguents and potions served adolescent enhancement as well as concealment.

Bonne Belle Lip Smackers were responsible for the petroleum scum on every girl's lips. Kelly liked the bubblegum flavour, but I preferred the prune-coloured stick of Dr Pepper. Funny smells in funnier places were the latest beauty trend. Improbably strawberry or lemon scents hummed from hair and labia, both upper and nether. I never went the douche route, preferring to leave the strawberry fields to the fields themselves. Perfume-wise, Love's Fresh Lemon was the main perpetrator of fruity funk. Wearing musk was only for the self-possessed, as it implied that you had your sights set on third base.

Hair was suddenly important. I knew girls who'd get up an extra hour early before school just to do their hair. 'Do' meant folding, spindling and mutilating it to within an inch of its follicular life. Hot combs and bulky blow-driers were deployed to get that Farrah Fawcett flick-back. The less ambitious could content themselves with 'wings', which were more Gregg Allman than Farrah. The feathered look was embraced by guys as well, whose big-handled combs reared from the back pockets of their tan needlecord jeans. Those with 'fro's had Afro picks with a little moulded plastic 'black power' clenched fist for a handle.

I didn't do anything fancy to my hair, other than use 'Gee, Your Hair Smells Terrific', the shampoo that came with its own built-in compliment. At this stage, I didn't mind paying for one.

I picked up on grooming tips, and more, in Home Ec class. In Home Ec, we learned about making white sauce, sifting flour and sewing. I could manage flour-sifting, but that was about it for my domestic skills. I regularly collapsed in frustrated tears over the sewing machine.

Home Ec was a glorified girls' club, although the class always had a boy in it – just one. The boy would either be what my dad deemed a 'frooty-tooty', or he'd be a sly swinger-in-the-making who'd figured out that the girl-to-boy ratio was exceedingly favourable for a young hustler like himself.

The Home Ec boy's flip side was the Shop girl. Shop was the place for guys to hone their gadget-loving instincts by woodworking and soldering. The Shop girl would be a tomboy in OshKoshB'Gosh overalls who had a great rapport with the guys and thought that other girls were boring. She usually soldered better than the boys.

I was a Shop girl, but not the soldering kind. The only Shop I cared about was The Mall. By the mid-seventies, malls were still recent developments in retail science. They were the newest novelty theme parks, the themes being touching, needing, wanting, eating, sighing, crying, buying. The whole spectrum of human emotion could be provoked by mere anticipation of a purchase. Malls were exciting even before you opened your wallet. And when you did, Galaxy Galleria was a Valhalla of merchandise. Kelly, Petra, Carla and I would pester our mothers to haul us up there for weekly merch worship.

Time stood still in Galaxy Galleria. As the strains of 'Scarborough Fair' muzaked through the static-y air, we'd float from kitsch cowboy burger bar to 'authentic' pioneer-gear boutique. Shoebox movie theatres nestled next to an ice-cream parlour that was a cross between *Happy Days* and *2001*. In the mall, America past and future was cartooned down and petrified in plastic.

We'd linger in The Wild Pair, marvelling at the slut shoes. I favoured Kork-Ease platforms, which I wore with stripy rainbow toe socks. The socks made my toes ache, but the shoes provided mall-trek comfort along with total bossness. All the girls had these suede platforms with the tan leather straps. If you got the length of your painter pants just right, Kork-Ease made you look an extra four inches taller.

Clomping on Kork-Ease out of The Wild Pair, we'd next peruse Foxmore for butterfly-wing-sleeved blouses. Foxmore also gave us a good vantage point for scoping guys choosing slacks and puka shell chokers in Chess King, the casual-wear store next door.

Spencer Gifts was the risqué way to finish our mall day. The cheesy gimmick emporium sold black light posters and day-glo foot-shaped rugs, gag sex toys and pet rocks. Ultraviolet light and the smell of incense gave the shop an air of the forbidden. With every visit, I made sure I checked out the poster depicting a man and woman pretzelled into twelve different sexual positions – one for each sign of the zodiac.

The position not featured on the sexual horoscope poster was the one involving Elton John, my favourite pop star.

Undaunted, I dreamed about it anyway. Or at least, the most sizzling scenario I could muster.

Spring 1975
I just woke up from the best dream! The Dream: I went over to Carla's house. I went to Carla's room and who should be there but Elton John!! He was just sitting around. I started talking to him and I became very clever and witty in my conversation. I could see Elton was becoming impressed and was beginning to like me. Then he stuck a basket in my face and said, 'Consider yourself lucky, you may be the first person to ever watch me dress!'

Since I had a basket stuck in my face, it wasn't too easy to watch, but I didn't bother to look anyway.

Then I told him I did ballet and he laughed right in my face, so I said, 'You shouldn't laugh because I'm pretty good at it.' Then I demonstrated how high I could lift my leg.

Then there were some girls outside that wanted his autograph. I said, 'Well, I better go out because I wouldn't want to take up space where another girl could be.' Elton said, 'Oh, you don't have to go, why don't you just stay here?' But I said no.

I tried to call up my house to tell them why I was late for dinner but the phone didn't work. I went outside and then Elton and the group of girls came out talking and laughing. Everybody got on their bikes and started riding off. I ran home to get my bike, and that's were the dream started to turn into a nightmare.

Started to turn into a nightmare? The whole *thing* sounds terrifying. Still, it was nice of me to dream an extra bike for

Elton, even if he didn't return the favour by waiting for me before he pedalled off.

In the only slightly more real world of Venus, I wanted to ride bikes with Kenny Butcher, the token neighbourhood love interest.

Far out. Ken is really nice. He was terrible in the sixth grade, and so-so last summer. I guess he's loosening up.

I craved Kenny. He was lean-limbed and golden-skinned, and a lot more local than Elton. Kelly, Petra, Carla and I slobbered over him like a litter of puppies with a bone. And Kenny showed about as much interest in our slobbering as said bone.

We were trying to figure out who Kenny liked and Kelly's brother said that he liked one of us. Andy said that it was either me or Carla. I think Carla really thinks that Ken likes her, because you can see it in the way she bounces over to him and starts touching him and seating herself so she can get maximum body connection. I think he likes it, but nothing romantic, just sexual. But anyway, today we got the final results. The winner is Kelly! Good for her. I hope that cures her of thinking she's such a weed. Now something's got to cure me.

Later.

Oh, the greatest thing that could happen has happened! Ken likes all of us as friends! Far out! No competition, no nuttin'.

Even later.

100

No nuttin' is right! No nobody liking me. Ken sticks up for Kelly. I never have a chance to get a boyfriend, and when I do, I blow it. I need help! I must quit acting like a loud-mouthed bitch, and start acting like a normal person!

Even later still.

Everything keeps changing. It really looked like Kenny liked Carla. Now I find out that he likes Carla just as much as the rest of us.

Even later still again.

I haven't seen Kenny in a couple of days. But, as they say: Absence makes the heart grow stronger. Or fonder? (And I also shouldn't bug him too much.)

Even later still yet again.

Seems like Kenny's been avoiding me. Maybe I'm just thinking that.

Later than I thought.

Petra made a good point today. If we bug Kenny like we have been, boy will he be turned off. We'll scare him off. If you want to keep a guy interested, you gotta make him feel big. Feed his ego. (Now I'm sounding like a woman doctor.) But I have to make him regret not playing STB last week.

STB stood for 'Spin the Bottle'. The game was major-scale sexy fun. So sexy, in fact, that it had to be abbreviated for secrecy.

STB was another kind of dry run – this time for gettin' cosy. It was my chance to do an up close and personal on the delicious Kenny while letting the bottle take the blame.

I can't wait until this weekend when the gang will play STB! Fun, fun, fun. I think if I get in a passion, I'll probably grab Ken and give him a hot one. Guess what happens if someone finds us?

Guess again, bozo. Kenny deftly dodged my grabbing, while quietly indicating his preference for another. Feeling fragile, I wrote in feeble green script:

I didn't know Kenny kissed Kelly while playing STB when they went in the closet.

My first year of junior high had finished. Realizing that I couldn't wait around for the bottle to snag me a boy, I decided on another strategy.

My plans this summer are to:
1 *Grow tall*
2 *Grow beautiful*
3 *Grow thin.*
In other words, Mission: Impossible.

At the end of the three-month summer vacation, I wrote:

I have to lose weight, get good clothes and good jewelry to get spiffed up for school.

Junior high was turning out to be a dry run for a dry run.

10

Bad Blood

Eighth grade automatically made every girl the potential queen of junior high. After serving my seventh-grade year as a lady-in-waiting, I was now ready to queen it up in my final year at Louisa May Alcott Intermediate. And since my final year of grade school had been disrupted by the move from Moscow to Virginia, this time I was determined to grab all the perks of being newly teened.

These perks included:

1 Being disparaging about the little seventh-graders and their pathetically stupid ways.
2 Getting to sit on the back seat of the school bus with the other cool eighth-graders.
3 Nabbing the cute boys.

Unfortunately, Perk 3 seemed to be temporarily unavailable to me. Gamely, I worked within the social structure of the school to rectify this.

The big event of the autumn season was the Sadie Hawkins

Dance. Named after a fictional hillbilly gal who plum turned the tables on backwoods ways by chasin' all the menfolk, the idea was that the girls invited the boys to be their dates. Everyone dressed up as country bumpkins, in gingham shirts with overalls or 'Hee-Haw Honeys' hot pants. Hick chic was heightened by chewing on a piece of straw or blacking out a couple of teeth.

Once in the scarecrow-decorated gym, the girls continued with the charade of this hog-crazy upside-down world by asking the boys to dance.

Naively, I assumed it was my chance to pick and choose at leisure from puka-shell-wearing, Puma-shoe-shod teenmeat. Wrong. Instead, it was my chance to experience first-hand the indignity of rejection, boy-style. The labyrinthine intricacies of this hayseed hop rivalled Jane Austen in their complexity.

November 1975
The Sadie Hawkins Dance was last night. First I had asked Kenny, of course, but then I figured that he and Shari were gonna go to the dance together since they liked each other. But then Shari stopped liking him. So recently Kelly asked him, and he said yes. Leanne LeRoy wanted to ask him, and she asked me what I thought. I said (in essence), 'Tough luck, cookie!' I asked Kenny what he would say if Leanne asked him and he said 'No!' I'm glad for Kelly.

Myself, I had asked Wendal Pender, but – sniff – he had a football game that night. Then I was thinking about asking Chip (wonder of wonders!) but Buck said that Jackie (the one with all the curves) had already asked him. So I ended up going stag.

At the dance, I got up my nerve and asked Duncan

McCloud to dance (like a fool!) but he said he was looking for someone. (He sure wasn't looking for me!)

Ah, the old 'looking for someone' routine. It seemed that while I was getting a crash course in humiliation, the boys were picking up a few pointers in girl-type bitchy evasion. Upon experiencing the Sadie Hawkins swap, I realized that the guys had gotten the better deal: feminine wiles were more fun than masculine responsibility.

Seeking to elevate my pariah status, I resorted to my time-tested technique – hitting the dance floor. A dance contest was announced, and as the first strains of KC And The Sunshine Band's 'That's The Way (I Like It)' pumped out of the speakers, I knew I was in there like swimwear. Even Jackie, with all the curves, didn't stand a chance against my funkified throw-downs.

By the time KC's final 'uh-huh, uh-huhs' faded into the stuffy gym air, I had my prize – a copy of the Neil Sedaka/Elton John single 'Bad Blood'. I was sweating and my hillbilly pigtails were coming loose from their polka-dot ribbons, but dagnabbit, I had won.

So I knew how to win a record, but I still couldn't crack how to win a guy. And as far as trophies went, 'Bad Blood' couldn't really compare to Kenny, Wendal, Duncan, Chip or Buck.

I just don't understand boys. And if I ever show this to a 13- or 14-year-old daughter of mine, I'm sure you're having the same trouble. Hey, I don't know if this notebook's gonna be in the trash by then or what, but wouldn't it be cool if I could shoot ahead in time or you could shoot back, and we could talk to each other, kid to kid? I wonder if you'll hate me or if there'll be a generation gap or something? I wonder if you'll have '70s Days' at school like I had '50s Days'? Far out, just

think, you'll be a child in the third century of this country.
When I think of the 'Gay 90s', I'll be thinking of the 1890s.
But you'll have the choice of thinking of my 1990s. Maybe
those'll be gay then, in the homosexual way.

Frankly, I've loved my life so far. Remind me to tell you
about it.

Love, Katie (or to put it simply, Mom!)

While I was fondly projecting a buddy-buddy relationship with
my future daughter, my relationship with my present family was
not quite so companionable.

As my thirteenth Christmas rolled around, I became
increasingly aware of flaring tensions between my parents.
They'd been sleeping in separate bedrooms for nine years,
since Berlin. And now that my dad had retired from the air
force, there were no longer the distractions of chi-chi parties
and other diplomatic duties to provide a diversion from my
parents' home-made Cold War.

Boy, are things ever goin' downhill around this house.
Mom and Dad are snivelling at each other (ie Dad throw-
ing tantrums and throwing out dirty names like an ill-
behaved little child, and Mom heaving big sighs and
having shit fits about any little thing). I s'pose I'm neutral
territory. They all talk to me about each other and I don't
really care to hear it. That's my job, I guess.

Like most kids caught in parental crossfire, I felt that it was my
responsibility to ease the discord.

My good ol' bro is moving here from Kentucky. Excellent.
I'd like to stay with him at his apartment on weekends to

get away from here. But now that I think of it, maybe I should stay at home to be a referee or warden for my dad and mom. Dad was mumbling about leaving Mom one of these days. Oh God, don't let that happen. I couldn't bear it. God, please help them, I can't. I'm miserable.

As bad as things might have been between my parents, to hear my father make that kind of threat was a complete shock to me. For such a hardcore Catholic to even remotely consider bailing out seemed like cruising for a papal bruising.

Every day, as my mother brushed and pinned my long hair up into a bun for ballet class, I stared at the newspaper clipping shoved into a corner of her vanity-table mirror:

Every person has three psychological needs:
1 Acceptance
2 Approval
3 Affection

Did this mean that she wasn't getting them? I wondered if it was a reproach to my father.

After one of their skirmishes, my dad would stomp off to play the accordion angrily, wheezing the bellows, forcing his frustrations on the squeezebox. The acid run-off from my parents' unhappiness poisoned everything.

April 1976
Lately, my father seems so far off, distant, cold and hard. He barks orders at me like he thinks I'm going to argue with him, which I never do when he talks like that – I wouldn't give him the pleasure. He's highly critical and he's beginning to make me paranoid about ballet

technique, washing dishes, anything. I wonder what's bothering him? Only sometimes he acts like he loves me.

I escaped from the strain by throwing myself wholeheartedly into dance classes. Ballet was one thing I could control – all I had to do was work hard and the hard work would be recognized. Simple equation. In school recitals, I began attracting as much notice for my stage presence as for my dancing. Praise came from my teachers and my mother, but when we'd get home from one of my shows, Dad would only say, 'Shari Sydenstricker kicked her leg higher.'

Even still, performing filled me with joy. Dancing, I shone. Nothing could take it away – I was, after all, a dancing machine. It was my identity, my buoy.

However, the buoy was floating me downriver from the anchor of my friends.

May
Sometimes I feel so left out of my natural world, the one with all my friends in the neighborhood. I am so wrapped up in my dancing that I am sort of losing touch with reality. I'm like a hermit because I never go outside.

I'm not like any other kid I know – everyone else goes to see friends, while I have ballet and jazz classes to take up my time. It scares me to realize that I don't have any deep feelings of friendship for Carla, mainly because she and I don't have anything in common. She's changed so much this year.

In seventh grade I was really dominating her and you could see my tastes in a lot of things she did and liked, especially music, but she's through that now. She's made new friends and discovered new things. She said in the sixth grade that she would never smoke pot and would never cuss like her father does, and wowie look at her go now! She swears so much she even offends me. One time, she told me I was behaving like an ass when I was dancing in the street, when before she would have laughed and maybe even have joined in. I used to make her get really crazy and fun to be with, but lately she has gotten boring with all her tales of rowdy drunk pothead boyfriends and weekends. She's one good friend when she tries to be, but she's drifting away into her own little world.

Petra has a lot of clique friends and she's clever, which makes her good at any gathering, but she's getting snottier. But Kelly has remained a good and faithful friend all through school.

Tonight I heard a whole bunch of kids talking and laughing under my window and it was Petra, Ken, Kelly and other voices. They were going somewhere and having fun, heading up to Lunar Lane. They were lighting up and talking about drinking and they were probably going to someone's house to live it up. I so desperately wanted to be with that group, but I knew that if I ran out there just then, I would be an outsider. I can't really define the sadness inside me, but I just feel alone, left out. What do I do?

11

Afternoon Delight

My official First Kiss, not one authorized by the aim of the spun bottle, was with Courtney Slusher. The First Kiss was hard won, the result of an unrelenting two-year campaign of devotion. It happened by the honeysuckle bushes at twilight and I experienced, as recorded in my notebook, 'a strange elation'. I was thirteen.

Courtney Slusher was also thirteen and had shiny blond hair, slanted blue eyes and very wet lips. He lived a school bus stop away. I would cycle over to my friend Daisy's house, who lived across the street from Courtney, just so I could be near him. As a consequence of an allergic reaction to make-up, Daisy had no eyelashes or eyebrows. She defiantly continued to wear bright blue eyeshadow and looked like a glam rock frog.

At the very beginning of my Courtney crusade, I consulted Kelly's Ouija board for information.

'Will Courtney marry me?' I asked it. Never mind the fact that he barely knew who I was. There were no half measures for the smitten.

When Ouija answered in the affirmative, I decided to share

the good news with my future husband.

Courtney was unflustered. He just smiled amiably and said, 'Could be.' This sounded like classic Magic 8 Ball material, blandly non-committal, but I chose to dwell on any dollop of positivity and rejoiced for months. I drew cartoons of him in my notebook as a fox, with me as a loveheart-surrounded hippo.

A year and a half later, I was still pining.

Spring 1976
Well, as usual, I like Courtney AGAIN. That guy turns me on and off every year. But he never quite likes me enough. Oh, love. Let's see:

First Courtney liked Lina, then Shari (but that was a farce) and now Casey. I don't see what's so special about her, but of course that's because I want him to like me. Maybe he just takes me for granted. If only Julie Plum would move. I mean, he always pays attention to her, but to Julie he's just another admirer, another fish she's caught. What goes on inside a boy's head?

I was beginning to ask the deep questions.

Courtney assisted my elementary gender studies by demonstrating a classic male manoeuvre:

Courtney doesn't really like Lina any more. He said she was a slut and she could get fucked in the cafeteria and would brag about it. Courtney's a real make-out man (by his own description). He always talks about how he did it (not a whole bunch of detail) but then he says that Lina is a braggart.

My first exposure to the double standard.

It was time for the big spring dance, the eighth grade prom, and in the argot of the day, 'I would just about die twice' if no boy asked me to go. I monitored Courtney's movements closely.

Courtney hasn't asked anyone to the prom yet. And he is currently unattached. Far out. But it's impossible that he would ask me.

Of course it was. Courtney asked Penny Bliss, a harmless girl who was hard to hate. Desperate not to be seen as a complete loser, I accepted the invitation of Chuck Jackson, a soft-eyed, frizzy-haired jock who excelled in football, baseball and wrestling. His muscular thighs were so big that he needed specially made slacks. Blue jeans were out of the question.

Chuck's dad took a polaroid of us before we left for the prom, and before he snapped, I strained away as far as I could from Big Thighs without actually moving my feet. I was a virtual Leaning Tower of Pisa in my efforts to appear as if I was not actually his date. To further emphasize how little he meant to me, I persisted in calling him 'Chuckles'.

Chuckles took me to the prom and was really gentlemanly and all that. I kept on doing stupid things like opening doors by myself, but it went all right. I don't know if he likes me for real or not. I just like him for a friend. He asked me to his baseball game, but I said no because of ballet class.

Whew – got out of that one.

On to the really good news. I only danced with Courtney about three times, but they were good. I danced one slow dance with him (oh heaven!). Chuck, Courtney, Penny and I all went to Pizza Hut afterward. Penny's nice (fantastically) and we all had a good time. Every time I talked to Courtney I expected Penny to show she was jealous, but she wasn't.

No duh, as we liked to say in junior high. Wilfully oblivious to the fact that it was Penny he'd asked to the prom, not me, I breathlessly recorded my analysis of the Courtney Slusher infatuation situation.

Things that lead me to believe Courtney might like me:

1 *Willing when asked to dance.*
2 *Absolutely charming personality.*
3 *When slow-dancing, at the end of the dance, he was still holding on when he pulled away, and he was still holding on when he said, 'Thank you, Katie.'*
4 *When Chuckles and I went to Pizza Hut and saved a seat for Penny and Courtney, they came and Courtney was very attentive to me.*
5 *Over all, he was very cute to me (little gestures and such).*
I am really crazy about Court. Shall I call him up? I wonder how he feels about me? I think he hasn't given another thought to me since that night.

I decided I needed to force myself into Dreamboy's consciousness, since I obviously hadn't made my interest clear enough. I devised a plan to distribute flyers on his street for an upcoming ballet school performance, figuring I would 'accidentally' run into him.

113

Guess what? Tremendous breakthrough! I went (casually, of course) over to Lunar Lane to put those sheets in the mailboxes, and fortunately Daisy was outside. I stopped to talk to her and I heard Courtney call out, 'Hey Puck!'

I yelled back, 'Hi!' and went on talking with Daisy. A few minutes later his little sister comes over and says, 'Courtney wants both of you to come up and see him,' sort of like His Royal Majesty ordering us around.

We got over there and were talking to Court. Daisy left and we went inside to watch TV. When I had to go home, Courtney rode bikes with me. We talked on my driveway for about a half-hour before I had to go in. And I noticed something – when I said I had to go, he didn't look real relieved like he was looking for an excuse to leave. Pretty good.

The main thing is that we talked. And I really mean talked. We spoke about people, life, what to do in the future, etc. etc. and I really found out what he was like.

Did you know . . .

. . . that Courtney likes soft rock and not hard?

. . . that Courtney shares my views about the clique people?

Anyway, the list goes on and on, and I find he's a very sensitive guy. You know? Also I believe that the preceding pages are the account of a serious infatuation, not actually loving him for his person. But now that I know him personally, I think I really like him. Whereas before there was a fiery feeling of longing in my body, there is now a sort of comfortable warm feeling. I know this whole thing makes me sound like an asshole.

Mmm.

114

The more obsessed I became with Courtney Slusher, the more contempt I felt for poor Chuckles.

Chuck Jackson is a person whose being sometimes repulses me. The way he's always picking and touching and wiping his nose and then flicking his fingers (shudder). The way he never has too much to say, as in: 'Who's your English teacher?' or, 'What did you get on your math test?'

Courtney likes me for sure. We talked on the phone last night for forty-five minutes. Whew. Tonight we're going ice-skating.

Triumph came on a late May evening right before school was out for the summer. Triumph was a sweaty-faced kiss in the honeysuckles on the side of the road where cars routinely creamed my cats. Triumph, if you asked me, was a fucking long time coming.

And a short time going.

I have been on an eating binge for about four days and I hate myself. I don't know where Courtney is, it's been raining all day, Mom wouldn't let me go to a movie and it's boring as hell. So I stuff my face. Now I'm getting pimples. My God, I thought girls were supposed to lose weight when they fell in love. I'm hairy, fat, tired and pimply. Why this self-torture?

I'll tell you why – it was that blasted kiss. What *was* in that smooch of Courtney's – the entire genetic code for puberty? It was like a scene from a horror movie – one minute I was an innocent maiden skipping across a sunny meadow, the next I was a monster in a thunderstorm.

Every time I hear 'Afternoon Delight' by Starland Vocal Band, I think of Court, because that was his favourite song at the time he liked me.

Wait a minute – *liked* me? As in the past tense? You betchum.

Courtney does not consider me a serious girlfriend. In fact, I was only his girlfriend for a couple of days. Then it petered out. I s'pose he just got bored with me.

So that was it. Two years of keeping the loin fires burning, and all I got from him were two measly days.

Understandably dissatisfied with this damp squib of a love affair, I resorted to fantasy.

I have a daydream that I take much pleasure in thinking about. It's me, tanned, thin and beautiful, just oozing with charm and wit, casually (oh so casually) riding my bike past Courtney's house.

'Gasp!' he will exclaim, and will come running out to stop me. 'Stop! Come here, Puck!'

With great hesitation I will change my direction and coast over to him. I will plant a big juicy wet kiss on his lips and say in a low husky voice, 'And where have you been, you naughty boy?'

Here's where the reverie dipped below the belt.

'Peter' will have problems in this great daydream, and Courtney will be embarrassed. I will pretend not to notice, and will make some incredibly smart comment about not seeing each other for so long.

> *Courtney, being such a gentleman, will not say anything
> about how beautiful (even more than I am presently) I've
> become. Instead he will say, 'We're going to a party tonight,
> and afterwards we can go swimming, and then . . .'*
> THE END

And then . . . 'Peter', presumably, would come into his own. At
the time, I felt the erection and its consequences were best left
to the area beyond the ellipses. Despite – or perhaps because of
– that sixth-grade screening of *From Girl to Woman*, I was hazy
on the specifics.

I now entered the official Period of Mourning.

> *Mom said that some guy called me up twice the last couple
> of days. My biggest wish is that it's Courtney, of course.
> But I know that it's not. My biggest horror would be that
> it's Chuck Jackson, that tepid kid who can't talk and picks
> his nose slowly and carefully.*

Even as I languished in my pain, I retained enough self-respect
to reject nose-pickers. Nobly alone, I wallowed.

> *I still long and ache for Courtney. If I ever get back to him,
> I think he will find that I'm a better kisser.*

Courtney was never to sample my upgraded kissing. I didn't see
him again after he and I moved on to different schools. Six
months of pointless yearning later, I phoned him.

> *New Year's Eve*
> *I'm really going to have to forget about Courtney. What is
> it about him that turns me into a babbling idiot every time*

I talk to him? What an ass I am.

I got tongue-tied and everything when I phoned him for a simple little 'wishing you a Happy New Year's Eve' call. There's never anything to talk about between us. Why do I keep thinking we're perfect for each other?

I'm a jerk, and he knows it. Hello cruel world.

12

Low Rider

The year America turned two hundred, I turned fourteen. We both had our birthdays in the same month. America's got a lot more attention than mine, but I didn't kick up a fuss. Anyway, how could I compete with the bicentennial?

The bicentennial year meant that there'd been independence fever for the whole six months leading up to Independence Day. Furniture store TV jingles were sung to the tune of Sousa marches. Car dealerships were swamped in cat's cradles of stars and stripes bunting. Gas stations gave away 'Old Glory' styrofoam beer chests with every ten gallons pumped. And when the Fourth of July finally did arrive, it stampeded Venus in a red, white and blue hullabaloo, with more Yankee Doodle hoopla than Uncle Sam's stag night.

I was lying on Timber Lake's sandy beach, writing in my notebook. Kelly, sitting next to me on her American flag towel, was slurping on an icy red, white and blue Bomb Pop. It was the day after the Fourth of July, and the Spirit of 1776 had given me a hangover. Last night's fireworks were repeating on me, hiccuping skyrocket afterglow to the back of my retinas.

119

The fact that the Founding Fathers' Declaration of Independence had changed entire centuries of history galvanized me into making a declaration of my own.

July 5, 1976
I made the absolute decision to become a professional ballerina on July 5, 1976. I get so much pleasure out of the pain and sweat of ballet class. It just fills me with ecstasy. Yup. I am positively going to be a ballet dancer when I grow up. I can dig it.

I felt open, expectant. It was fitting that the country's freedom was celebrated in midsummer, the season of teenage freedom. The season of STB, pyjama parties and all the Bacchanalian pleasures of pre-jaded youth. And the best thing about not being jaded was it whetted the anticipation of dissipation.

The first winds of dissipation were blown by *Fear of Flying*. Someone had left the Erica Jong paperback behind in the sand. The cover showed a woman's nude torso revealed by a peeled-down zipper. Grabbing the brick of a book, I flicked quickly, then slowly. Equal parts titillated and appalled; I ploughed through passages describing 'zipless fucks' and the pleasurable stench of urine on a man's testicles. It was cover-to-cover filth. What a find.

Fear of Flying was a breakthrough. Its heroine enjoyed her sexuality instead of getting punished for it. This concept was new to me. The lurid mags I was used to reading, like *True Confessions* and *True Detective Stories*, always made the girls pay for their wanton ways. The sudsy pulp for tired housewives in trailers was stuffed with stories about fallen women. 'Party Girl – Now I'm Paying!'; 'The Love Game I Played on My Bingo Nights Out'; 'Sex Gang on the School Bus'; 'My Bride is a

Man!' were some of the tantalizing titles.

The first I'd ever heard about masturbating with vibrators came from *True Confessions*. Slotted between columns of text about young girls seduced by their 'aunts', were ads for the 'Tingle Bullet'.

VIBRATOR TONING BULLET
For Satisfying Relaxation
Unique new bullet-shape cordless vibrator reaches difficult areas with its gentle, penetrating action. Try this stimulating new tool for toning throat muscles and other facial areas. Delicate, soothing action aids in relief from nervous fatigue. Excellent for waist, hips, thighs. 7″ hand-size Tingle Bullet in pink plastic operates on two C batteries not included.
6470 – Tingle Bullet.. $2.98

The copy would be accompanied by a picture of a woman holding the plastic pecker to her jaw, an expression of tranquillity on her face. Tipped off by the mention of hips and thighs, I was pretty sure that the 'difficult areas' in question were not throat muscles. Still, maybe they knew something I didn't.

I didn't have a Tingle Bullet to take care of my 'nervous fatigue'. But now I had *Fear of Flying*. When Kelly and I got back from the lake, we showed the book to Cherry. Cherry lived next door to Carla, and she had thyroid-bulged eyes and equally prominent lips, made even more so by her full set of braces.

We'd consulted Cherry because she was familiar with lewd material, owing to her with-it parents. To us, 'with-it' meant that they still had an active sex life. The tell-tale signs of nookie were a waterbed in the matrimonial chamber, and *Penthouse* tossed nonchalantly on the coffee table. I hadn't ever worked the naked lady fascination out of my system, though when looking at them in groups, I'd learned it was correct etiquette to say things like, 'Gross', or 'I'm *so* sure', just in case anybody thought you were a lesbian. Even still, my friends were plenty interested in looking at the magazines.

Cherry's parents also had a cache of dirty books, of which I was getting to be quite the aficionado. *The Harrad Experiment* was one: a steamy study of 'wife-swapping', which I assumed was merely an instruction manual that had come with the waterbed.

Inspired by Cherry's folks' home library, I trawled the strip malls for literature of my own. I hit pay dirt with *Let's Go Play at the Adams'*, a lurid text involving the sexual abuse, ritual torture and eventual murder of a babysitter by her young charges. It was disgusting but readable, and duly made the rounds of the neighbourhood book club until Kelly's father discovered it. He was understandably perturbed that I was playing librarian with such muck. But as far as I was concerned, it was just a little pulp – something I'd picked up at K-Mart.

Stupid Kelly's going to play dumb like she never read it (which she did), so I look like a dirty pornographic child who pushes these illicit trashy novels on clean kids. Sure. Kelly makes me sick. She can't even stand up to her own overprotecting pig-headed dad. He got all stuffy and said he was going to inform my father. Big deal. It isn't even anything bad and I didn't even like the dumb book in the first place. I'm just going to act like I've forgotten the book and like I have no interest in it whatsoever, which is the truth. Tough! Double tough!

There was more than a little pot-calling-the-kettle-black action with regard to playing dumb with dads. However, whether or not he'd shopped me to my father, my acting skills were never called upon.

After that, Kelly's father regarded me with distinct distaste.

I can feel this wave of dislike pummelling (whatever) me every time Kelly's dad glances my way.

One character who spared me his moral judgements was my cat, Sooky. He had short black fur with a white blaze on his face, a white bikini on his belly and white socks on his paws. The first thing I'd see when I woke up in the morning was Sooky sleeping under the covers next to me, his head on my pillow. I loved my kitty.

Kitty love was not shared by my father, who considered the cat a walking target for ridicule. In a rich, operatic voice, he'd sing, 'Dirty rotten Sooky, dirty rotten Sooky, I – hate – Sooky!' to my meatloaf of a pet.

Sooky worked off any pent-up aggressions by regularly culling the gerbil population in my basement. I had about four cages of the desert mice down there, eating and breeding. And bleeding, by the time Sooky pounced. I tried to keep the basement door closed, but every so often the cat managed to slink down and wreak gruesome scenes of rodent carnage. I'd go to feed them and find just the bottom half of a gerbil sitting quietly in its upended cage, with the survivors hiding under the refrigerator. The slaughter was curtailed by Sooky's snip.

Poor male cats! They have to suffer through all the kidding after they're neutered. Sooky's trying to take it easy after his operation and Dad keeps on making inane remarks like, 'Well, Sooky old boy, that was some operation!' etc. etc.

I commemorated his castration in alliterative verse:

Newly Neutered

Staring stonily into intervals of outer-space spots,
Tucking tearfully his hairy tired tail around a furry foot,
Sooky-Soo ponders poutfully:
'Where the hell are my balls?'

After Sooky recovered, he increasingly soothed his nervous fatigue with his own built-in Tingle Bullet. I noticed that he'd begun to take great care with his grooming sessions. By the time he'd reach the tail end of his bikini bottoms, his little lipstick penis would be waiting for him like the proverbial carrot at the end of the stick. Gently cupping a sheathed paw beneath the fuzzy undercarriage, Sooky would coax his corn cob towards the rasp of his tongue. Then tenderly, carefully, lovingly, he would lick.

His aplomb was something. He didn't care if people watched or not. In fact, I couldn't be sure if an audience wasn't part of the jerk-off appeal. In time, Sooky developed the ability to sit unsupported on the curved 'C' of his spine, his tail and back legs stretched out before him and the 'elbows' of his front legs resting on the downy pouch of his belly. He looked like a small man in a cat suit.

And acted like one, too. Guests would be charmed by Sooky's adorable sitting-like-a-person trick, until they noticed his erection.

I'd never encountered a flasher cat before, so I checked some of my feline reference books for guidance. Finding nothing, I turned to *Facts of Life and Love for Teenagers*, an old paperback I'd bought for five cents at a garage sale.

Published as it was in 1962, the book wasn't altogether convinced that masturbation – the human kind – was such a good idea. 'The handling of one's genitals is a very serious affair,' it read, though it did allow that there was no evidence that one could tell by 'looking into another's face whether or not he was an habitual masturbator. Circles under the eyes, pimples on the face, or a shifty look in the eye can mean a lot of things.'

Richard Cox had a shifty look in the eye. The soccer coach for the neighbourhood boys' pee-wee team was a skinny geek in his mid-twenties. In addition to the shifty look, Richard had the circles and the pimples, too. And he had something they didn't have back in 1962 – a van.

Vans were *the* primo vehicle of the seventies. Ordinary transit vans were converted to mobile sin bins with the help of trippy album art murals airbrushed on the outside. Galloping unicorns crashing through ocean surf were popular. Inside, the wall-to-wall, floor-to-ceiling shag carpeting was often dank with spilled bong water. Only guys had vans.

Richard had a fleet of them.

Richard was across the cul-de-sac in one of his vans. It was really cool 'cause the whole inside was carpeted, even the ceilings. The back was partitioned off. When I asked to see it, Richard goes, 'Well all right, but hurry up.' While I was looking around, he kept on telling me to hurry up, hurry up. I thought it was kind of rude but I didn't say anything and went out. Ken, Petra and I were kinda mad and we went around knocking on the sides and kicking the back door. I started climbing the ladder up the back and on to the roof where the starlight windows were open, and looked in.

First I saw the top of Richard's greasy hair and I was

about to make a wisecrack. But what I saw next sure shut me up!

One of the kids on the team, Chad, had a dirty magazine on his lap and Richard was carefully pulling down Chad's pants. I got down so fast I really surprised Petra and Ken. I told them in a whisper and I was so excited I was jumping up and down.

So the man (?) was really a pervert! There were rumours, but I was never really sure. After Chad got out, we asked him why he let the queer do it. Did he like it? Chad said no, Richard made him do it. What I want to know is why Chad didn't put up a big fuss and yell 'rape!' if it bugs him.

I had discounted the passive obedience so easily exploited in children, once so nearly exploited in myself.

The next time Itchy Dick showed up in his van, the whole neighbourhood was waiting for him.

Richard came over and all the kids were against him and his ways. Gayboy (his new name) was hostile from the beginning tonight, which brought out all the mob characteristics from us.

Richard was spreading rumours that I only fooled around with younger men 'cause I was afraid of getting pregnant and also I was a slut. According to old Gayboy here, while I was babysitting Chad, I took him down to the basement and fooled around with him. You don't know how raving mad this FREAK makes me. I am longing to tell my mother, just to have someone older to confide in, but of course she wouldn't understand.

Younger men? Chad was seven. I was outraged and sickened,

but too squeamish to tell my mother. It all seemed too rude to share with grown ups. Finally, I cracked.

I told the parents about Gayboy. They say that he can go to jail for all that perversion.

He didn't. Chad's parents backed down and Richard's pleasure dome rolled on to fresh cul-de-sacs.

If only he'd taken a page out of Sooky's book and stuck to self-abuse.

13

Young Hearts Run Free

September 1976
I love high school so much. I like all my friends there,
everyone's so nice. This year I'm getting whistled at by
guys and it's all so fun. I feel like such a happy person.
High school is really neat – a whole new beginning.

I was forever optimistic about fitting in at new schools. This
stout-heartedness was touching but tragic. At Venus High, it
wasn't long before I felt like my usual doofy self. The more
sophisticated girls on the scene deepened my feelings of awkwardness.

October
I'm getting disenchanted with people at school.
Everyone is part of their own little clique, and I feel like
SUCH an oddball. I feel so crude and not at ALL clever.
People like Mimi Van Upp and Sia Malatesta are so
self-assured-looking, while I flub around and say the
wrong thing.

Even though she was the same age as the rest of us – fourteen – Mimi Van Upp appeared so much more adult. She wore Gloria Vanderbilt jeans, Calvin Klein lip gloss, Candies mules, Halston perfume, and she slept with the teachers. In short, she was out of our league.

Her family had a swimming pool in their backyard and her pool parties were legendary. Her parents were never around and the liquor cabinet was a bottomless booze pit. The one time I was invited, I nervously grabbed a Tab and spent the entire afternoon floating on an inflatable duck, watching Mimi sparkle like a Park Avenue socialite. Mimi had even published a *Star Trek* trivia book with her older sister, which seemed ridiculously accomplished for a high-school girl.

Some years after we graduated, Mimi's dermatologist dad was busted for selling prescription drugs. He lost his licence, sold their house and left town with the family. Mimi always did have flair.

Sia Malatesta had a different flavour of flair. Her delicate blue-white complexion was curtained by dark brown hair as long and thick as a horse's tail. She wore her gauchos, the wide calf-length shorts, with square-toed Frye boots – part of the peasant couture craze. A dainty gold necklace dangled uselessly over the pink angora cliffs of her cowl-neck sweater.

Sia spoke in an itty-bitty whisper, and you had to lean in close to hear what she was saying. In art class, Sia breathed to me that she was convinced the man she'd lost her virginity to on her summer vacation was Roman Polanski. She'd seen pictures of the film director in the papers after he'd been accused of statutory rape of a minor.

'Why do you think he's the same guy?'

Sia's logic was flawless.

'His chest hair looks the same, and I'm a minor.'

Poise came in a joint, too. A certain *je ne sais quoi* could be copped by recreational drug use. The 'Why Do You Think They Call It DOPE?' campaign must have worked on me, because I was never tempted to try a toke of the Columbian Gold so beloved by young Virginians. Just the smell of it made me gag. But that didn't stop me from admiring the knowing languor of the stoner girls. At Venus High they were called 'freaks'.

Trish Tansy was a sexy freak with a pot-husked voice. The feathers on her roach-clip earrings brushed her cheek whenever she shrugged back her Indian maiden hair. Trish and I were two of three girls in a gym class with thirty guys.

One day in PE, I noticed that the third girl was missing. It turned out Jem Shellhammer had been killed in a car crash the night before. She and her friends were playing chicken with the trees in the centre strip on Nutley, and the trees won. Her dad's car was totalled.

I told Trish the news as we changed out of our rancid polyester gym suits.

'Did you hear Jem was in that crash last night?'

'Good way to get outta gym.'

'Trish, she's dead.'

'Bummer.'

Bummer? A masterful understatement. Why did freaks have the corner on wry one-liners?

In the freak vernacular, if the situation was satisfactory, it was 'copacetic'. 'Deece!' was short for 'decent', 'Ex!' for 'excellent', both used interchangeably. Reefer made you 'mellow'. And now I was to understand that death by a violent car crash was a 'bummer'. Ex!

In addition to freaks, Venus High society consisted of 'preps', 'jocks', 'brains' and 'drama fags'.

The larger than usual percentage of preps was due to Venus's relative proximity to DC. The Young Republicans' conservative nature was belied by their flipped out dress code. Haute preppie mode was Jerry Lewis circa '62: mad, plaid and White. Uptight toes slipped sockless into topsider yachting shoes in the summer, and waterproof rubber 'duck' shoes in the winter. Bass Weejun loafers, penny optional, were year-round footwear. Khaki slacks were standard, but the required Muffy/Buffy/Chip/Skip zing could be zapped with a pair of green and pink plaid Bermuda shorts. The ultimate prep hallmark was the Izod Lacoste alligator shirt. The Superprep wore two 'Izods' at once, in clashing shades, with the inside collar flipped up and the outside sleeves folded back so that both colours showed. The whole look was intensely asexual.

On big game days, jocks swaggered down the corridors in their leather-sleeved letter jackets. They all walked like giant babies with a diaperful of poo. Overtraining resulted in legs too bulky to move in any way other than a zombie waddle. Mammoth arms flanged out from their torsos, absurdly muscled, unable to hang straight down.

The biggest zombie-waddlers were Thor and Arn Gritsky, the wrestling brothers whose ears met their shoulders in batwings of hulk-pumped flesh. Years after high school, the brothers opened a wrestling-themed restaurant at Galaxy Galleria called The Hammerlock. It failed.

Cheerleaders were the jocks' geishas. They walked leaning back with tiny hobbled steps, textbooks clutched to their letter-sweater chests. The 'cheerleader wave' was a babyish sideways flutter of the hand. Extra coyness could be indicated by holding the palm stiff while wiggling the fingers together. Teasiest of all was the pinky wave, achieved by crooking only the pinky finger up and down.

The brains' badge of identification was a plastic pocket guard festooned with pens. The computer room and the after-school Chess Club was their natural habitat. Any respect gained by the brain's brains was nullified by their low social profile. In Venus, brains were invisible.

A drama fag was anyone tainted with the faintest whiff of the theatre department. The drama fag tag had the power to supersede all other classifications. If you were a freak, prep, jock or brain who'd appeared in a school play, forget it. You were a drama fag. I was a drama fag.

Initially, my clothes weren't the tip-off to drama fag-dom. In my ass-grabbing Levis worn with leg warmers and clogs, I was outwardly no different from a lot of girls. I liked to wear my shiny Spandex Danskin leotard with the jeans, which were alternated with long Mom-made peasant skirts. But in the space of the first semester, certain idiosyncratic components began to edge in: vintage dresses, stripy thigh-high socks, long hair braided into a snake-pit of plaits. I hadn't been in a play yet, but it didn't matter. Even minus the gig, I had the guise, so my DF deal was signed and sealed.

Tony Moroni wasn't a freak, prep, jock or brain. There wasn't even a place for him with the drama fags, haven for all oddballs. Membership of his niche numbered exactly one. This was because Tony had killed his little brother.

Accidentally, of course. Tony was no murderer – just unlucky. He was a skinny kid with a honkyfro and a face gobbled up by acne. He walked funny: half skittish, half defiant.

The mystery began when Tony's younger brother disappeared. For weeks, a search party scoured the town. Then they found the eight-year-old buried in his own backyard. The police report read that he'd died by a 'blow to the back of the head with a blunt object'. The story went that he'd been running away from Tony while playing when it happened. Some said a bookcase fell on top of the kid. Others heard he'd tripped and hit his head on the fireplace. In any event, Tony panicked and shovelled some flowerbed dirt over his brother's body.

Tony kept quiet. We kept our distance. Everyone was creeped by him. People weren't sure whether to feel sorry for Tony or fear for their lives. In sociology class, I especially watched him when our lessons turned to 'abnormal psychology'. Tony never moved his eyes from his hands, which were tightly clasped on top of his closed textbook.

I didn't bother inviting Tony to my first big bash. He'd already had his, and look where that got him. Besides, who wanted to be upstaged by a kid who knew his way around a blunt object?

One of the essential high-school skills was being able to throw a real bras-hanging-from-the-chandelier soirée. Clenching my teeth and my sphincter, I waded into the fray.

November
I had my first party last night, and I think I learned a lot. It was so weird. Beaux and Bobby came drunk and they brought the beer. Kelly drank three beers and was acting mighty queer. She kept falling asleep, then she was running around acting crazy. I found her standing in the middle of Pamunkey Road screaming to an oncoming car, 'Come and get me,' and it scared me to death. As she stumbled back to the basement, she complained to Theresa that I wouldn't let her kill herself. I didn't know what to do.

Petra and Leslie were really bad off. Petra was outside running around with Bobby screaming things like, 'I'm gonna get you, little boy!' Leslie was laughing and sleeping, but after a while, she started crying. She was sitting on the stairs, and every time she tried to get up, she saw Troy

and Pam slow-dancing and she got back down and contin-
ued crying. It wasn't because of them, though.

After a while, Petra was crying a whole lot and Kelly
was tapping on her face to try to get her out of it. Petra
started screaming and crying harder because she said it
hurt.

Then she started kissing everyone. She even kissed
Kelly's little brother on the mouth. Duh. Her language was
slurred and she was so sorry for getting drunk. She yelled
that no one was listening to her, so I said I would. She said
she loved me and that she would never do it again. It was
so heartbreaking. It's amazing how childish beer makes
one act. I'm still very confused.

I shouldn't have been. I was so busy being the bungling
ringmaster that I didn't realise everyone else was having a great
time.

And what else?

I was so busy being bugged out by Tony Moroni that I
ignored his torment.

And?

And I was so busy being down on myself that I couldn't see
how good I had it. I thought my problem was party-throwing,
or popularity, or my hallucinatory portliness. I didn't know what
my real problem was.

I found out after I broke my finger playing basketball in gym
class. The bone had splintered into the joint and after it was
surgically reset, the doctors told me what my real problem was.

March 1977
My spine is crooked. I have scoliosis. If I let it go, I'll be
humpbacked in two places when I grow up. Dr North says

it's lucky they caught it this early, because I still have soft bones. He says that I'll have to get a spinal fusion, meaning that they're going to fuse something in my spine to straighten it. You know what? That means one or two extra inches on my height! But the bad thing is that I'll lose some flexibility in my back. I'll be in the hospital for a few months, and it will take six months to a year to heal. The thing I'm worried about most is ballet, of course. Then school.

The chest X-ray showed that my spine looked like a bony 'S'. The curvature was severe: a hairpin of fifty-nine degrees bowed between shoulder blades, whiplashing back to forty in my lower spine. I had a slalom track for a back. I was the 'flip-floppy camel' from the Camp Tannadoonah song, the one with the hump. The one without any starch in the spine. Or too much starch, but ironed all twisty.

I was fourteen and female, the typical profile of a scoliosis sufferer. My scoliosis was 'idiopathic', meaning that the doctors had no idea why it was there. Its appearance was spontaneous and irrational, like a lot of bad ideas.

Before it squeezed the life out of my heart and lungs, the doctors wanted to operate. This meant welding my spine to a metal rod. The fact that I'd have to wear a plaster body cast for up to a year was one reason why I was desperate to avoid surgery at all costs. The likelihood of never being able to dance again was another.

The alternative to fusion was the Milwaukee Brace, a bulky metal contraption that shoved the spine into shape during the twenty-three hours a day it was worn. No way was I going to wear that and turn into the school spaz.

I just wanted the whole mess to go away.

They're catching up with me now. A doc from the hospital called today to try and get me in for an operation in August! Yelp! Mom said that I didn't want it, and the doc got stern and said that if I didn't, my breathing would be impaired and I'd die young.

Even with my mother running interference, the men in white coats were bearing down on me. The willy-nilly way operation dates were being scheduled made me feel like I was about to be conscripted. The gravity of my situation was starting to sink in. I began to refer to the surgery as 'being killed'. My tears smudged the ink as I wrote:

Kelly and Petra have their horses, many people I know have their music and singing. But something or someone or some plan is taking my dancing away, and I resent it bitterly. They want me to go crazy. They want me to be paranoid and miserable. I'm without direction. Most everyone has their talent to take them away, to save them from too much living with anxiety. Something that will always take the place of a more temporary thing that has fallen by the wayside. I had my body, my glorious, wonderful body and talent that I love and appreciate so much, and now that is temporary, THAT has fallen by the wayside.

In the kink of a spine, I had learned the worth of a body. Suddenly, mine was glorious and wonderful, not the curse I'd considered it. All those years ulcered by judging it too fat, too short, too wrong – when all those years it was nothing less than just right.

Twelve months later, I was granted a stay of execution. The

doctors told me that as long as my spine didn't get any worse, I was off the operation hook.

But in the meantime, I was scared.

I busied up my days to crowd out the worry. Deciding to cash in on my drama fag status, I auditioned for the big spring musical.

The state bird of Virginia is the cardinal. The state tree is the dogwood. There's even a state slogan: 'Virginia is for Lovers'. Doing the school play gave me the chance to discover this state for myself.

We met working on a 'greatest hits' review of American musical theatre. Chris was seventeen and a senior, three years older and three grades higher than my lowly freshman level. He was small and wiry, with blue eyes that crinkled at the corners when I made him laugh. Chris was the best piano player in the school, and I was the best dancer. It was perfect.

May
The play was about the best thing I've ever worked on, and I'm also in love! I love Chris Azalea. Let me list what I love about him (not necessarily in order):
His wit
His talent
His personality
His cool
His honesty
His directness
His eyes
His size
The way he pretends to walk bow-legged

Aren't I crazy?

No, baby. Just in love.

It feels neat to be older and wiser. This is the first time I've been in love. I feel terrific!

It doesn't get any neater than that.

The first time I asked Chris over to my house was an interesting experience that has helped me change, and I've even changed a little from that night only a week ago. When Chris and I were walking around my neighbourhood, I couldn't totally relax with him, but I was happy. When we sat down on the curb for a rest, he turned my face towards his and kissed me. Now that was a totally new experience for me because I've never had someone want to kiss me like that, and then do it. He kissed me another time that night when I didn't expect it and I wasn't used to it and I didn't know what to think. He kissed me really hard and I didn't know how to feel. The next day I awoke at 6.30 in the morning with a queasy feeling in my stomach, all because of that kiss! It was really weird.

All day my stomach was tight, and I felt light-headed, sick and maybe guilty. I really couldn't pinpoint the feeling. I HAD to talk to Kelly about my mixed emotions, and she calmed me down quite a bit. She suggested I tell him I didn't like the way he kissed, but I told her I didn't think that was it. I figured out then that I just didn't have enough experience, and I'd get used to it, then I'd enjoy it.

Feeling bad never felt so good. This was all new territory for me, because unlike the last few years' dead-end Courtney Slusher-worship, Chris actually liked me *back*. What a concept.

138

Our first real date was the junior/senior prom. This was a heapum big deal, for four reasons:

1 For *anyone's* first date to be the prom was an awesome planetary alignment – it was the Oscars, Superbowl and Studio 54 rolled into one.
2 For a mere freshman to attend the junior/senior prom was to fully achieve Mimi Van Upp-ness in the Beautiful People department.
3 For a mere freshman to attend the junior/senior prom on the arm of a *senior* was *so* Sia Malatesta on the going-out-with-an-older-man tip.
4 I'd never been on a date before – not counting the eighth grade prom with Chuckles, because that was really a date with Courtney, except that neither of them knew it.

With Chris's quease-inducing kiss, I had leapfrogged over age, rank and year. I was ready for the prom.

For this gala occasion, my mother made me a beautiful long dress based on old-fashioned Wild West undergarments. The lacy camisole top billowed into frothing petticoat skirts, all in virginal white broderie anglaise. On my feet were white ballet slippers tied at the ankles with white satin ribbon. I was pleased that I looked like Brooke Shields in *Pretty Baby*, a movie I hadn't actually seen because I was too young. All I knew was that Brooke played a twelve-year-old prostitute, and I figured if her wench-kitten style put a tiger in the big boys' tank, then I was all for it.

Chris turned up wearing a rented powder-blue tuxedo with big Las Vegas lapels. I *knew* he was cool. He pinned an orchid corsage to my ruffled shoulder strap.

The average prom has five distinct components: the hiring of the limo; the dance at some anonymous corporate hotel; the bearded covers band; the more adventurous students stealing up to pre-booked rooms for extra-curricular hanky-panky; then the traditional dawn breakfast at someone's house.

But for me, this prom could never be merely average. Its theme was 'Precious and Few', and as the band lurched into the schmaltzy old song, I felt the truth of it to my core. Chris kicked off his shoes and we slow-danced – Pretty Baby and Vegas Boy.

As the sun rose, I had metamorphosed from a gauche little girl into a savvy, self-possessed, debonair little girl. My vault from out to in elicited a satisfying amount of thinly veiled jealousy from my fellow fourteen-year-olds.

My freshman friends kept on asking me if I 'didn't feel out of place at the prom' because of all the juniors and seniors. I think they wished I had. But of COURSE not! I was familiar with everyone there – PLUS I was with Chris the whole evening.

All of my previous worries eased away.

I feel differently about certain things since I've met Chris. I feel more independent and like I've gained freedom. Clique-y girls at school no longer make me paranoid and self-conscious because I have something they may or may not have – someone to love.

One by one, the neighbourhood girls were getting relief.

Ah, the simplicity and complicatedness of young love. Kelly and Petra have found it. Kelly's been especially hard hit, from the way it looks on the outside. She's been out with lots of guys in such a short time span   it was funny to see her smile happily, fling her arms out and say, 'Well, what do you know? I'm normal!'

A teenage girl could never have enough proof.

My new-found euphoria was irritating to those I'd left behind in my fairy dust, particularly Kenny Butcher. Kenny had gotten used to his role as the love superintendent of Pamunkey Road, and now quite enjoyed it.

But after two years of being passed around for kissing practice between Kelly, Petra, Carla and me, he was gradually getting phased out as we grew up and moved on.

Smarting from his demotion, Kenny began to get testy.

August
Ken Butcher drives me up the wall. He criticizes every-thing about me: my ballet, my father, the colour of my front door – sheesh.

When Chris came over, Ken looked at his car and said in his all-knowing voice, 'That car's a piece of junk.'

At a quarter to six last night I came out of the house and said to the group sitting in Kelly's driveway, 'I just ate dinner.'

Ken contorted his face into a look of distaste and asked, incredulous, 'You had DINNER so EARLY?' making me feel like some sort of freak.

Today he gave me a disgusted look and stated, 'Every-body hates your cat.'

Poor Kenny. Not only was he losing the battle – he was running out of ammunition.

14

Jesus Children Of America

Dad never really did put the 'fun' in fundamentalism.

Now that he was retired from the military, my father gave up trying to straddle the line between the Almighty and all-RIGHTee and came down hard on the side of God. While my mother continued knitting a fortress around herself complete with needlepoint turrets, his religiousness revved up to warp speed.

With all that extra space to fill in his days and in his heart, my father joined every Catholic-compatible organization short of the Spanish Inquisition: charismatics, born-again Christians – even Jews for Jesus – along with still attending daily Mass. He was recreationally religious, but this was no hobby. It was a full-time job.

He began answering the phone with 'Ave Maria', spoken in the blandly affable tone others might use for 'Jones residence'. Anyone who wasn't named Maria would get confused and hang up. Sometimes he'd swap 'Ave Maria' for 'Praise the Lord'. Schoolfriends started asking if my father was 'foreign'.

Dad had banned Ouija boards as Hell's hotline, and was not

happy about rock 'n' roll, either. He gave me a fantastical comic book that highlighted the dangers of 'the devil's music'. The plot involved long-haired Beatles-esque musicians prowling back into the studio at midnight after everyone thought the album was finished. Slipping purple-hooded robes over their mop tops, they'd chant satanic incantations on backwards tracks. It didn't say where you could buy the record.

I found it increasingly hard to have a non-God conversation with my dad. He worked religion into every topic, no matter how seemingly unrelated. A discussion of dance as a career, for instance, always ended up with a thundering denouncement of the numerous 'godless ingrates and inverts' sliming up the profession. I could appreciate that he had fatherly concerns for me, but for once, just once, I wanted him to climb down from the pulpit. I wanted him to talk with me, not at me.

My father frequently expressed great remorse that his children were 'godless ingrates' and not 'with the Lord'. It was clear that he thought he had failed in this, and that we in turn were failures. I tried to reason with him.

'But Dad, we're all happy and healthy, we're not drug addicts, we're not crazy. Aren't you glad about that?'

He wasn't. He felt that as long as we weren't interested in the Church – in literally, precisely, *exactly* the same way he was – we were write-offs.

'You kids have been given a gift!' he railed, angry and dismayed. 'You've been offered the love of Our Lord Jesus – and you've rejected it!'

The only thing I rejected was my father's moral bullying. I wanted the judgement left to God, not to Dad.

As always when we had these kind of exchanges, I had a hard time trying not to cry. I couldn't trust my voice not to quaver as

I defended my worth to him, so in the end I'd just clam up.

One night after a family dinner, he leaned back from the table, sighed, then said wistfully, 'Yeah . . . I wish I'd been a priest.'

In his black turtleneck and trousers, he looked pretty priestly, all right. It was only the presence of his wife and children that ruined the fantasy.

There was a stunned silence. Knives and forks froze in mid-scrape. I couldn't believe he had said it. He'd heard a calling, but the voices in his head weren't ours.

Dating Chris Azalea increased tensions with my father. His apprehensions were unnecessary, because I'd stumbled upon the only senior at Venus High who could give the Osmonds a run for their clean-cut buck. Chris was Catholic, and he went to church every Sunday. *And* his father led a Catholic youth group, which I attended.

It wasn't good enough.

When Chris would come over to visit, as my bedroom was obviously off-limits, we'd hang out in the basement. Every time we passed my dad in the front hallway, he'd say, accusingly, 'Are you going down to that HOLE again?' The way he emphasized 'HOLE' always made me flinch. It sounded so lascivious, so . . . dirty. Any innocent kissing that actually took place down there could never live up to the debauched promise of my father's HOLE.

Once when I broke my ten o'clock curfew while out with Chris, I attempted to deflect my father's wrath away from my boyfriend.

'Don't blame Chris, Dad! It's all my fault we were late.'

His response was chilled and deliberate.

'I know it's your fault, Kate, because Eve tempted Adam.'

He meant it.

The next day he phoned Chris's father to take up the curfew issue with him.

'I don't want my daughter to be ruined!'

Ruined? What was this, the Middle Ages? 'Sorry Mimi, I can't come to your pool party – my chastity belt will rust.' And ruined for what? For the delectation of a future husband who only wanted one thing in a woman: a hymen? In that case, I'd send him the membrane and get on with real life.

The only reason why Mary, Mother of Grace was getting 'hailed' all over the place was that she'd managed to produce Jesu Bambino without breaking any eggs. There wasn't much hope for the rest of us girls. Next to her, we were fallen by default. And that was exactly my father's point.

Dad fulminated against free love and free rides. If you were enjoying life, you were definitely going to get it in the neck later. And if you were having a rough time, then you were to blame for not praying enough. That horsehair shirt was sure scratchy.

And some of it began to rub off on me. Since I had been diagnosed with scoliosis six months earlier, I had become more and more distressed about the prognosis of my crooked back. The latest consultation with the doctors came to the same conclusion as all the others: 'You're too far gone for a brace – you'll have to have the surgery.' This was my father's signal to chime in with Plan B.

'What about Our Lord?'

The surgeon was caught off guard.

'Our . . . Lord – sir?'

I cringed.

My father was slightly impatient.

'Yes – Our Holy Father! What about faith healing?'

'Faith healing. Yes.' The surgeon regained his footing.

'Well, we'll just do what we can here, sir, and leave the rest to Him.'

Dad was lobbying hard for a miracle.

October 1977
Jesus came into my room last night, and His presence was so overwhelming and loving. I had been all keyed up, wondering and worrying about the operation. Then, all of a sudden, it dawned on me – why do I have to worry? What if I didn't have to worry? What would I feel like then? That's when I felt Him fill me. All anxieties oozed out of me, and a supernatural peace and calm filled me. I started crying and crying with happiness. It was marvellous! I want to be straight.

Jesus came into my room? He must have been looking for Dad and taken a wrong turn. But they didn't call Him the Prince of Peace for nothing. The encounter – whatever it was – left me with a serenity that eased my constant dread. I opted not to go the Joan of Arc route and advertise my vision. I kept it to myself. Then I forgot about it.

March
What am I supposed to do? My father is pressing me to join his stupid prayer groups.

On a car ride to Giant Supermarket, my dad told me about our latest chance for beatification. The charismatic movement was a neo-pentecostal crusade sweeping the Church. The aim was to get so fired up by the Spirit that you'd collapse in a Lord-lovin' swoon, twitching and speaking in tongues. The charismatics were a peculiar mix: by-the-Book Holy Joes who worshipped with bell-ringin', yell-singin' exuberance. They were buttoned up show offs.

My father admired the charismatics' loss of control when shaken by Christly vibrations. He hungered for the absolute surrender that led to salvation.

He wanted to be redeemed, renewed, reborn. He wanted to crash backwards into the arms of believers with the Holy Ghost burning up his tongue. And he wanted to drag me along, kicking and screaming. I was happy that he liked churchy stuff. Why couldn't he be happy to leave me out of it? But it doesn't work like that. It's dogma's job to hound the customers who don't buy in.

Dad rallied his Christian soldiers to pray for my zigzag spine. He invited a charismatic group to set up shop at our house.

When I walked into his den, squeezed in with the familiar recliner, television, desk and books, were five strangers. After some stilted small talk, a woman grabbed both of my legs, yanked harder on one, and excitedly announced, 'They're uneven!' My hip cricked into temporary dislocation. As the group mumbled a few quick prayers, she moved her grip on my feet and trumpeted, 'They're even!' Then she did the same thing to my arms. It was so phoney. I was embarrassed for them, and for myself.

Now came the main attraction – the laying-on of hands. Standing, I was directed to bend at the hips to get all hands on deck. The shame of feeling fifty strange fingers on my body was excruciating. I knew my dad was only trying to help me, but here, bent over with my eyes to the floor, I felt grotesquely vulnerable.

Hands on my humps, the charismatics hosanna'd and hallelujah'ed. The leg-yanking lady crooned, 'You are the apple of Jesus' eye,' before disintegrating into glossolalia with the others. They were really breaking it down, getting their kumbaya-yas out. The oppressive air leadened further. I held my breath and pictured the Son of Man, with me as a big red pippin stuck in His eye.

He's fanatical he's charismatic he's a hypocrite oh the hate the hate we're confused and he takes it out on us oh Dad. 'Ah, in the old days I was a money-grabbing bastard – I'm trying to get with the Lord.' He is insulting the Lord not honouring Him . . . if this is what religion is, I'm leaving. St Dad with the big house and the family conveniently hidden away. Downstairs learning from St Dad or so they think, upstairs we are crying and confused we are in ruin he discards us when we depend on him he forgets us divorces us from his mind and adopts a family of charismatics – 'What a lucky family you are to have such a God-glowing father provider husband' . . . au contraire hate hate curses abuse and I carry it on. I am condemned condemned . . . who is right what is this twisted version of his religion that he is compelled to ignore the very basic rules of God, ignoring and hating his wife, piling on guilt and creating fear in his children, kicking cats and insulting everyone and admiring no one. A HYPOCRITE HYPOCRITE.

I am free I am free. I don't want to take the guilt he shoves into my brain, I don't have to take it.

The power struggle over control of my spirituality continued after my father's next ruse to sneak me through the Lord's back door. Persuading me that what I really needed was an extra dental check-up, I dutifully got in the car. But he didn't drive me to my usual dentist. Instead, we pulled up outside a clapboard house with a giant swastika flag hanging over the door. It was the Nazi headquarters of Virginia. I was a trifle unsettled.

We went into the house next door to the Nazis where the 'dentist' had his office. It turned out he was yet another Praise-the-Lord faith healer, who did a little orthodontia on the side. I didn't want to be a disobedient daughter, but I was getting tired of being tricked. I stood rigid and resentful as the oral surgeon lapsed into tongues, harassing my back with wordless yackety-yak.

When we got home, my father was still enraged at my religious reluctance.

'If you don't get healed, then God help you when you have that operation!'

Meaning that God help me, because Daddy won't. Meaning that if after being sliced and diced on the operating table, I was paralysed – or died – it would be my own fault for having a belief deficiency. What was he trying to do – *scare* me into a miracle? At the most frightening hurdle of my life, my father was threatening me with my own biggest fears. All in the name of God.

This was religious persecution, in reverse.

In his quest for spiritual enlightenment, my father attended a variety of Christian think-tanks. These pietist powwows hashed over all topics pursuant to 'getting with the Lord'. I peeked at a sheet Dad had brought back from one of his discussion groups. His name was written on the top, and beneath, in eight different scribbles, was a list of his attributes. I was gripped. What was my father like with other people? Did *they* think he was preachy and domineering? How did they respond to his biblical browbeating? I looked at what these strangers had written about my dad:

Caring for others
Neat

Sense of humor
Friendly

Could sell anything to anyone
Fun to be around

Enormous ability to deal with people
Courage to try many things
Interest in others

Fun to be around
Neat
Enjoys helping others

Full of beans, good humor
Good dresser, articulate

Good with people
Born salesman
Sense of humor
Positive
Interested in others

Smart
Calm
Pleasant
Good
Caring
God-fearing

Who was this man? He sort of sounded like my dad, minus the anger. I was pleased that my father was well-liked, but unfamiliar with some of these vaunted qualities. 'Born salesman'? He couldn't sell me the Catholic Church. 'Interested in others'? I never felt that interest directed my way.

He may have been God-fearing, but I was Dad-fearing.

By the time I was sixteen, any natural inclination to develop my spirituality within the confines of the Catholic Church had been bulldozed out of me by my father's militant Christianity. However, I was too afraid of his volcanic damnation to clue him into this.

I would do anything to get out of going to Mass. I'd hole up in a tree for the entire church hour. Or I took long walks in freezing sleet.

I would do anything – including hiding in my closet.

It was Sunday morning, and I could hear my father moving around in the hall outside my bedroom door. I guessed that any second, he'd check to make sure I'd gone to church. Too late now to set off on one of my inclement treks, I slipped into the closet.

I was wedged among dresses, sweaters, coats and shoes. It was suffocating, but the discomfort was preferable to the claustrophobia of the Church. As I settled against the angora buffer of my mother's pullovers, I heard my dad's voice.

'Kate?'

He came into my room. I could see him through the crack of the closet door.

After establishing that I wasn't there, I expected him to leave. He didn't. What he did do completely disarmed me.

He walked over to a framed photo that was hanging on the wall. It was a picture of me in a tutu and *pointe* shoes with my ballet friends. He stood in front of it for a long time.

Then, he sighed. A sad, caring-for-others sigh.

His fire-and-brimstone act had masked one simple fact: he was worried about my back, too.

Without knowing he did so, my father spoke to me.

'Poor kid.'

He left the room.

I never went to church again.

15

Sugar Mountain

September 4, 1977
I can't wait till tenth grade! I think I'll calm down before
people know me very well, so they won't think I'm weirder
than I am!

September 5 – School Eve
Ah yes, to once again start the great façade of school – the
worrying, the scares, the triumphs, the pleasures, the
satisfaction. Collected in this book will be most of the
above.

September 7
School is all right, but I have to settle into it again. I'll have
to do a lot of smiling and friendliness to get where I can be
comfortable. I mean, a LOT of smiling and friendliness.

At the beginning of each new school year, I felt I had to
practically launch an entire PR campaign to make sure people
liked me. I thought that in order for it to work, the campaign

obviously couldn't be based on my real personality. So instead I focused on just getting through that first barrier of general acceptance. Hence, smiling and friendliness were something I had to 'do'. Once I was accepted, then I could relax. Then I could *really* be me. Whoever that was.

With Ann, I could really be me. I met my new best friend at ballet class. At eighteen, she was fully a woman to my Little Miss Fifteeny-bopper. Ann Appleton was elegant, beautiful, voluptuous. That and her aqua-glo eyes drew people to her.

Ann had just come back from spending a year in New York City. A gifted dancer with a rare sensuousness, she had originally gone to New York on scholarship to one of the big ballet-company schools. Then she discovered disco.

The exciting underground movement was just now bubbling out of the urban hotspots. The way Ann told it, discos were a hedonist's paradise, where every man could be Superfly, every woman could be Queen of Clubs, and every song was about sex. More, More, More without Shame, Shame, Shame – Dance, Dance, Dance (Yowsah, Yowsah, Yowsah).

Sitting outside the ballet studio in the Indian summer twilight, Annie spun glittering tales of her city kitty days. I listened, rapt. She punctuated her stories with a graceful sweep of her diamanté cigarette holder – very *soigné*, I thought. I was dazzled by her, and by what was OUT THERE.

Envious of Ann's Studio 54 glories, I wanted in with Andy, Halston and Liza. The delirious hustle of the Disco Round was the lurex lure. Venus pick-up trucks blasting 'Cat Scratch Fever' were a crackerbox contrast to the Quiana sheen of the Native New Yorker. I didn't want to miss the disco boat. I hoped against all odds that it would still be fashionable by the time I was old enough to actually be allowed into a disco. I was realistic enough to guess that it wouldn't.

I compromised by turning school dances into my own private disco deliverance. Wearing scarf dresses in synthetic satin, I bruised my butt doing The Bump. I'd pretend it was Steve Rubell and Bianca Jagger serving the punch, instead of Mr Duffner and Mrs Heater.

In ballet class with Ann, the Spandex shimmer was supplied by our leotards. The Good Times were supplied by our friendship. We had a million inside jokes that would detonate at the most inappropriate moments. In the middle of a slow, sustained adagio, for instance, one or the other of us would collapse laughing so hard we'd pee in our tights. Our teacher would pointedly ignore us.

My parents met Ann's for the first time after one of our performances. As always, new acquaintances brought out the supercheek streak in my dad. Upon being introduced to Ann's father, Dad broke the ice with a sarcastically bombastic 'Hey – Big Ed!' Needless to say, Ed wasn't all that big. Knowing that Mr Appleton was a lawyer, my father then volunteered, apropos of nothing: 'Yeah, I thought about being a lawyer once, but they're all a bunch of crooks.' My father enjoyed disarming people by 'giving them the needle', as he called it. As long as you weren't the one getting jabbed, it was funny. It was kind of a character litmus test.

Struggling to rise above my father's apparent rudeness, Ed turned the conversation to me.

'Your daughter is a talented girl – very bright,' he offered.

My dad grunted non-committally. Perhaps feeling that he wasn't getting his message across, Ann's father tried again.

'We love having her over to our house. She's a real delight.'

Again my dad grunted. In desperation, Ed tried a third time.

'You must be very proud of her!' he practically demanded.

Finally my dad spoke.

'Yeah . . . she'll burn out by the time she's twenty.'

Ed gave up.

He must have thought my dad was most odd. I would have had to agree. I could never figure out why my friends' fathers seemed more impressed with my accomplishments than mine ever did.

Perhaps from this lack of feedback, I had a surging urge for impact. I didn't want to dwindle into mediocrity. I egged myself onwards and upwards, fired by the wig-kickin' women of the twentieth century: Zelda Fitzgerald, Peggy Guggenheim, Edith Piaf, Josephine Baker, Anaïs Nin. I read everything I could about these artists and muses, dreamboats and dingbats. They were my patron saints. These dames had moxie.

October
Why are we here on Earth? I'LL BE DAMNED if I do something unnoticeable with my life. The thing that scares me the most is the idea of attending a secretary college, then sitting down to something like that until I'm married, and then settling down and having kids. God, I am afraid! I want to LIVE! Why can't I live? I want a life, something to bury myself in when other disappointments hit me. It's not like I can bury myself in accounting.

My burning for distinction began to singe my sweet amour with Chris Azalea.

February 1978
I want to make Chris happy, and yet I can't. Something of me gets in the way. How I anger myself when I see his confused expression after I say something hurtful. Why do

I feel unhappy when I'm around him? Are these my 'teen years' or something? How peculiar.

Now I'm beginning to get my relationship with Chris in the proper perspective. Before I was thinking: Can I stand putting up with moral uprightness the rest of my life?

But now I say, 'Who the hell cares?'

Chris was downright upright. In the beginning, I liked that. Because I was three years younger than he was, it was a relief feeling that I didn't have any sexual catching-up to do. But a year on from our magical prom night, the original list of things I loved about him were now giving me a wedgie. There was only so much goody-goodyness a future moxie-filled dame like me could take. I didn't 'feel free to talk dirty' or to let rip my 'stored-up kinkiness', as I complained to my journal. Chris was forever reprimanding me for being too wild, too unladylike, too . . . interesting, as far as I could make out.

Chris was a Victorian patriarch trapped in a teenager's body. He was easily shocked and tried to censor my exuberance. He practically fainted one day when I announced, in front of his ten-year-old sister, 'High-heeled shoes tip your ovaries.' I'd read this in an article and was keen to share the news. He was keen for me to shut the heck up.

I raged in my notebook:

I'm in a pent-up, angry mood, about to cry or punch someone out. Chris told me today that the way I was acting pissed him off. The way I was 'acting', he said. ACTING – CAN'T HE GET IT THROUGH HIS HEAD THAT I WASN'T ACTING – I was me.

When I get with people I like, I lose all my mental blocks, and any fronts I might have – I become open and me. *So now he tells me that I am not acting myself, and why did I get all hyper? ?%!*@!, CHRIS! I'll bloody well decide where and when and how much I'm acting like my self. There is no 'self' to ACT. A self isn't one thing, it's made up of many quirks and personalities. It doesn't all come out one bland, peanut-buttery mess of GOO! Anyway, I'm getting off the track.*

The matter at hand is – what the hell does he want me to do about it??! Am I to REALLY PUT ON AN ACT and sit, quietly, no fidgeting, nice, bland, gentle – but quietly sparkling with hidden intelligence lurking DEEP below the surface?

I wasn't *that* good an actress.

March
A thump comes in my gut when Chris tells me about his 'great' days, as if he were bragging about them. I have nothing to contribute – his life is just one success after another. Someday he'll find a nice girl and they'll get married and she'll be so content to hear about his great days and hang on to his every word and will know about music but not be too smart so he can correct her and teach her about always going to a party with him, not alone and first, and heavens not alone. What do I want? No, it's not just something that I want, it's something I desperately need.

What I desperately needed was something Chris had – an outlet for his talent. He was beginning to make a career out of his jazz piano genius, and I was feeling sorry for myself because I was still stuck in high school with no chance to be fabulous.

The competitiveness I felt with Chris tipped me off to my own ambitions. I didn't want to be a docile accessory. I was ready to go to the party – alone.

Mutual disenchantment set in, eroding our coupledom. Without too many complaints on either side, we began the long drift apart. Summer was heating up, and I was frustrated by my erstwhile boyfriend's continued virtue. While Chris was worrying about his God, I was worrying about my bod. I had read enough Anaïs Nin to know that my Delta of Venus was getting short shrift. I was nubility on a hair-trigger. Even just lying in bed with no clothes was an auto-erotic experience.

July 3
I slept naked between the sheets last night, and the slow stopped trip to sleep was rushed and made new by the cacophony of feelings: I felt daring and sexual, as if I were having a party in my room and no one else was invited. Sheets slid silkily, but not suffocating. It reminded me of swimming naked. How delightfully barbaric.

Even though the summer was boiling, every day I cycled into the sticky air, escaping from home and into my sixteenth year. One of my regular stops was a bookstore in the mini-mall about a mile from my house. Backlick Books was where I met Hush.

Before Hush Popple, the song 'Sugar Mountain' didn't mean anything special to me. Neil Young and his challenging facial hair were more my older brothers' department. But Hush was twenty, and since he lived in a Sugar Hill Villas condo, took it as a personal thumbs-up from Neil when the man sang in his wavery quaver, 'You can be twenty on Sugar Mountain.' Neil may have given Hush permission to be twenty on Sugar Hill, but I'm not so sure he knew anything about Hush's dogged attempts to deflower me.

July 8
'What do you want me to do?' Hush asks me. 'Romance you?'

Hush Popple was a college drop-out with powerful body odour. In the shop, his animal smell mingled with the dry scent of new books, spines yet uncracked. My drugstore *Muguet de Bois* mixed its musky-sweet lily of the valley into the unlikely bouquet. The whole pot-pourri was heat on heat.

Hush was forever trying to get me to have sex with him. I was thrilled by his desire for me.

July 17
Hush has such wondering eyes when he looks at me – like he is about to devour me but can't quite because I am so striking and queen-like. But perhaps he simply reflects that which is flying out of my eyes.

I was reluctant to take the plunge because I'd only known him for a few weeks. Besides, ballet came first. At this point, it was the only one coming.

July 19
My attitude about sex is that there is no attitude. There are only vague feelings that HP will have something over on me if I submit to his persuasive suggestions of high times. Someday, of course, I will consider this idea totally weird and will see sex as THE ULTIMATE GESTURE OF SHARING, or more importantly: a cheap way to have fun.

July 20
*Sexual tension is just great – fear of the unknown. I keep
on thinking of watching his kittens, then being made gently
aware of Hush's hands on my neck and thigh. A scary
thrill.*

*I felt like I was looking over the edge of a cliff, daring
myself to jump. But now that I think of it, it was probably
more like squinting my eyes up at the apex from the lowest
possible starting point.*

July 23
*HAH. I was about to be romanced by Hush but now he has
weird ideas of how I would want only romance and not the
physical stuff. God, he's in the dark! The only way I will
make love with him is if I am properly in love with him or
there are signs of a good friendship. The old boy – the old
boy . . . is enchanted by my body and cannot keep his
delightfully honest and curious hands off me, but I refuse
refuse REFUSE on grounds that I DON'T KNOW A
THING about him. And I'm so worried that the bastard
could care less what I feel like and more about what prick
gymnastics are going on. We'll see we'll see.*

Hush, stymied by my stubbornness on the sex front, tried
arguing his way into my pants. I was hung up on the fact that he
was four years older, he said, and on my virginity.

The only thing that impressed me about being sixteen to his
twenty was that in the state of Virginia, it was illegal for us to
have intercourse. His friends at the bookshop hated the whole
idea of him messing around with me and hissed 'statutory rape'
at us every time they passed.

As for my virginity, I wasn't hung up on it at all – I was

wielding it like a weapon. Or hiding it like a rare truffle waiting to be unearthed by the best sniffer.

That July day, I pedalled fast through the muggy haze to Hush. I had come straight from ballet class, and I was still wearing my practice clothes. My hair was in braids. I parked my bike in Sugar Drive and ran up the steps to Hush's condo, where he was waiting for me at the door. He led me into the air-conditioned cool, down to his bedroom.

Without speaking, Hush took off all of his clothes. Then, gently, he peeled away my baby-pink ballet leotard and tights. He marvelled silently at my obscenely virginal perfection. There was less marvelling going on when I grabbed a quick nervous look at the messy display between his legs.

'It's ugly, isn't it?' he said softly.

All I could think of was the jar of pig knuckles floating in solution next to the cash register at High's Dairy Store.

Hush pulled me down to his bed. Slowly, reverently, he caressed me. I inhaled our naked skin, deeply, my brain trying to learn what my body already knew. His animal smell overwhelmed mine, trapping my lily in its valley. Then Hush moved his face down between my legs.

Now *that's* what I called speaking in tongues. I was amazed. Was it allowed? I had never heard of such a thing before. How did he think of it? The idea that I had inspired him to perform such an intimate tribute was overwhelming. I felt so . . . worshipped. It was so *personal*. I was too alert, too curious, too *awestruck* to enjoy the sensuality, but I loved the gift of his southern kisses. I was also glad that he didn't force me to interact with his pig knuckles.

Hush left me *virgo intacta* – but my head was truly fucked.

After we finished, we dressed. I put on the clothes I had in my dance bag: stretchy red short-shorts and an infantile t-shirt featuring marching turtles. With my pigtails, I looked about eleven.

Hush walked me out to the sultry afternoon. I straddled my bike. Before we said goodbye, he looked hard at the turtle shirt. He seemed disturbed. Switching his gaze to my eyes, he said with measured emphasis:

'Never . . . wear . . . that . . . shirt . . . again.'

In the meantime, Hush had met an 'older woman'. He told me he was confused.

August 3

Hush was trying to figure out how much each one of us meant to him. Michelle is twenty-four and seduced him the first time she met him. Apparently, she has a fetish for 'younger men'. When he told me she had been making an effort to understand him, my mind locked and I turned him over to her.

I asked him, 'Is it better to be understood or to understand?'

He replied, 'It's best to have both, which is why I need a twenty-year-old girl.'

Then he left me and went home to Michelle. It's an excuse to stop seeing him because I was beginning to hate him anyway.

Six months later, I heard that Hush had started wearing women's clothes.

16

White Punks On Dope

1978 was the year I turned punk. Even the news turned punk:

- *Jonestown mass suicide – cyanide in Kool-Aid kills 900.
  'Guyana punch' regularly served at punk parties.*
- *Toxic Shock Syndrome turns every girl's period into
  Russian roulette. 'Toxic tampons' worn as punk jewelry.*
- *Nancy Spungen dies. Seditionaries sell Sid Vicious
  t-shirts with 'She's dead. I'm alive. I'm yours.' scribbled
  under his picture.*

And a few calendar pages into 1979:

- *Sid Vicious dies. Punks clamour to stay in the Chelsea
  Hotel room where he killed Nancy.*

What had happened to that 'We're No. 1!' spirit of the seventies? It was on its hands and knees, that's what – crawling slowly towards the big Eight-O. And disco's 'Me first!' was getting shouted down by punk's 'You suck!'

164

Bored with Studio 54, the US media began to pick up on the kooky new phenomenon. They were quick to point out that British punk had a point and that American punk didn't. The reports were always so smug about this. I wondered why the newspapers weren't more positive about their home-grown punks. It couldn't hurt to occasionally read:

> *OK, so it's not like there's 'no future' for you corn-fed American teens, but we're sure you've got enough angst in your pants to justify a few extra safety pins.*

But we never did. Why couldn't they muster a little patriotic loyalty for our own suburban brand of nihilism? We were constantly informed that British youth was very angry. The implication was that American youth wasn't. After all, this being America, what was there to be angry about?

It was explained further in one article:

> *In the US, the hard-driving, frequently monochromatic music – with cocky lyrics about such topics as sniffing glue or hitting 'a brat' with a baseball bat – offers intensity in place of subtlety and is humorous more often than not. In England, however, punk rock is deadly serious stuff. It expresses the discontent and ultimate frustration of a teenage generation that sees no future. Fans dye their hair red, yellow and green and wear black eye make-up and purple lipstick. Some wear torn t-shirts, splotched by red-paint 'bloodstains' and burned with cigarettes, plastic slacks and pointy shoes with stiletto heels. For decoration, they favor large safety pins, worn piercing their ear lobes, nostrils and cheeks.*

Humph – if it was so all-fired 'deadly serious', then why the big focus on fashion? American punks got no respect.

And in Washington DC, it was hard to get any respect – unless you were the President, and even that wasn't a sure bet. DC's strange brew was a little like the average television evangelist: square but dangerous. The nation's capital was also the murder capital. In DC, the bloodstains were less likely to be red paint.

If the guns didn't get you, the politics would. DC's main industry is the government, which effectively kills off non-conformists and artistic pranksters. Only in a bureaucratic town like Washington would punk be reduced to consideration of whether it could work in an office. One paper commented on 'the punk look':

Punk is a very anti-establishment look. And in places where you have to relate either to clients or management, such outrageous styles as orange or purple hair make a bad impression.

In the cultural void of the greater metropolitan area, I strained to hear those far-off tom-toms of war. I found a weak-signalled college radio station that played 'progressive rock music'. The 'progressive' bag was a big, lumpy one, jumbling together Patti Smith, King Crimson, Blondie, Peter Gabriel, The Ramones, The Clash, the works. I hopped aboard the Trans Europe Express and tried to pretend that southern boogie had never existed.

Before there was any kind of forum for 'progressive rock music' in DC, there was *The Rocky Horror Picture Show*. After we got gussied up in her bedroom – away from parental eyes – Ann Appleton and I would drive the fifteen miles to DC in her turquoise Datsun to take our place in the Friday night *Rocky*

parade. While my folks thought I was snuggling in at a sleep-
over, we were bugging out to the big city.

The weekly midnight movie at the Key Theatre was the hub
for troubled youth celebrating their inner mutant. The idea was
to pick your favourite freak from the film, dress up as him, her
or it, then act out their part right there in front of the screen
with the rest of the theatre. With *Rocky Horror*, baby maybe-
no-futurists could be secure in the knowledge that in addition
to their parents not understanding it, it would also piss them off
as a bonus.

'Don't dream it – be-ee it,' sang Frank N. Furter, the
transsexual Transylvanian who was *Rocky*'s hero. I don't know if
we were being it, but Ann and I were sure dressing it. She
made a fine Frank, and I threw my lot in with the tap-dancing,
red-haired Columbia. I figured I could wow the crowd with
Columbia's big number, but the crowd was always too busy
wowing itself. Every Friday night, things got ugly in the aisles as
twelve or thirteen equally determined Columbias savagely
tapped on top of each other in their flimsy quest for recogni-
tion.

The line for the movie was like a club, or at least the original
protoplasm for one. It splashed over Wisconsin Avenue like an
exploded burlesque queen: lipstick, glitter, fishnets and feathers
everywhere. And that was just the guys. All the prima donna
boys dressed up as Frank N. Furter.

Danny and Nathan were two of the biggest prima donnas.
We met them in the line. They were both sixteen and tall, with
silky brown hair tumbling over their shoulders. Nathan's was
halfway down his back. They were too young to really be
hippies, but before the big bang of punk rock, long hair was the
default statement of rebellion for young men.

In their transvestite-for-a-night clothes, the boys looked like a couple of twisted sisters let loose in Liberace's wardrobe. Their ankle-dusting capes were black, but there the similarity to Sir Furter's rich satin cloak ended. Nathan insisted his wasn't a shower curtain. The ring holes gave him away.

Danny's fishnetted pins weren't bad, but Nathan had bow legs and instead of stilettos, he wore yellow clogs. Before the proliferation of specialist shops for every fetish interest, primordial punks had to scramble for accessories. Nathan was doing his best.

When talk got slow, the boys shouted out, 'Gabba gabba hey!' and, 'God save the Queen! She ain't no human being!' heralding our impending punkness.

The pre-film floor show was a ritual in itself. As a thin, twitchy guy called Glen took centre stage, the lights flickered down and The Tubes' 'White Punks on Dope' stomped out of the speakers. With every yelp of the campy anthem, Glen spasmed a shock therapy samba. As the song crescendoed, his voltage increased. At the climax, a strobe light froze Glen in snapshots of his own dementia. Then he'd wipe out in a wet pile of skinny limbs. Next to Glen, the actual movie was a talk-down from the cliff.

After punching the *Rocky Horror* time clock, Ann and I would straggle back to Venus. That late at night, there was only one place open on Main Street. It was a ginormous twenty-four-hour diner called Aphrodite, and this creature of the night became our headquarters.

Aphrodite's decor was Greco-wacko – a blend of caveman rock walls, fake Tiffany lamps and individual jukeboxes in each naugahyde-padded booth. The menu read like a catalogue of global comfort food: blueberry pancakes, deluxe cheeseburgers, escargots *bourguignonne*, turkey club sandwiches, Chinese roast pork on garlic buns, moussaka, six kinds of cheesecake and a dizzying array of pastries, pies and soda fountain mountains.

We'd sit there at two in the morning, Ann in her cover-ghoul make-up, me with red food colouring sweating in bloody rivulets out of my hair and down my face. The food colouring was my lamentable attempt at Columbia's candy apple coif, but in pre-MTV America there was no drugstore technology for day-glo glamour. Winging it, I raided the kitchen cupboard for my wrong-coloured hair. Like Nathan's shower curtain and clogs, my improvisation wasn't quite on the money. All I wanted was a little passive anarchy, not a DIY prom scene from *Carrie*.

Getting a red-palmed grip on my deluxe cheeseburger, I pumped Ann for more New York poop. I never got my fill of hearing about her bulimic room-mate who could eat entire boxes of Entenmann's cookies and Sara Lee cheesecakes. For some inexplicable reason, this activity seemed alluringly decadent. As we discussed the room-mate's damaged behaviour, we'd order more and more food: Reuben sandwiches, onion rings, milkshakes, rock-hard chocolate-chip cookies the size of your face. When I summoned a stack of pancakes after polishing off my cheeseburger platter, the waiter made a face and grumped, 'Some dessert!' I ignored him and ordered a diet Pepsi, too.

While enjoyable, eating my way through Aphrodite's menu was not compatible with the pursuit of a career in ballet, which I still considered my eventual goal. I tried to check my voracity with Dexitrim–nerve-jangling appetite suppressants crammed with caffeine. They didn't work. All they did was make me eat faster.

After a summer of Aphrodite and *Rocky* consumption, we were ready to take the training wheels off our counter-cultural revolution. Danny, Nathan, Ann and I began going to the Atlantis, which had just opened as Washington's first punk club.

The hidden world of Atlantis lurked in the bowels of a building covered in eagles and gargoyles. The dark garnet edifice was right in the middle of DC's seedy F Street. It was next door to 'Dor-née Corset Shoppe', a dusty lingerie store with entertaining seasonal window displays. Hallowe'en prompted a festive array of mannequins in black crotchless panties topped off with jack-o'-lantern pasties. In spring, Dor-née reminded you to 'Remember Mom' with a less than motherly panorama of nipple-less nighties – all in pastel pinks and lavenders, natch.

The Corset Shoppe shared block space with a groovy pimp-wear boutique called '4 Dudes'. The sign's '4' was enclosed by the circle-and-arrow symbol of the male. There was no mistaking the dude factor.

After negotiating the spectacle of 4 Dudes' leather pusher coats and Dor-née's ventilated crotches, the Atlantis Club seemed positively low-key. The entrance of the club always smelled of enchiladas mixed with Lysol. I'd wear a swirly-print mini-muu-muu and the trashiest Wild Pair shoes I could buy. My high ponytail was pulled through the middle of a Question Mark & The Mysterians 45 that had belonged to my brothers when they were about my age, sixteen. I'd picked '96 Tears' because it was an alt-vault classic, an ur-wave perennial. I wanted to flaunt my proud punk lineage. To complete the street cred, I'd clamp my teeth around the metal horse bit in my mouth, which was hooked to the ponytail with a chain.

Danny and Nathan toughed up their act, too. They cut their long hair into short spikes and ditched the bad drag for more respectable punk leather jackets. Ann simply adapted her Frank face to a more gothically correct Siouxsie Sioux do.

Every weekend at the Atlantis, we'd pogo ourselves into oblivion. We invented deliberately stupid dances, trying to out-Quasi each other. Ann and I laughed so much we'd wet our pants. Between the Atlantis and ballet class, we were getting through a lot of pants.

I was electrified by the new music and new friends and new places to go. I felt improbably hard: lickety-split solid gone with my bad self, man. Luckily for my bad self, my parents were tolerant of my increasingly eccentric clothes, solid gone or otherwise. Wearing clown costumes to kindergarten had alerted them early to my overdramatic daywear tendencies. Anyway, I was still doing the school plays and getting good grades, but come the weekend, I was Sister Midnight.

Whenever we gave Danny and Nathan a lift in Ann's car, we'd deliberately blow their punk fuses by keeping the radio dial on disco. Even while riding the new wave on our punk surfboards, we'd never forsaken amyl BPMs. We'd crank up Odyssey's 'Native New Yorker' while the boys raised a stink in the back seat.

Danny, Nathan, Ann and I fused our musical differences in time to witness the birth of the DC hardcore scene. Together, we went to the first ever Bad Brains show. To begin with, we thought it was a hoax. The 'Punks' Party', as it was billed, was set for Friday the thirteenth. The directions on the invitation sounded suspicious: were 'Mane Lane' and 'Bay Way' real? They were. The rhyming roads led us to the singer's mother's house in suburban Maryland, and down into the basement with a handful of other thrash seekers.

It was astonishing to see a black punk band – and one that was local, at that. Inspired, Nathan started his own band, The Teen Idles. Ann went a stretch down the hardcore route with them, while I stuck to artier nuevo waveo. I tried not to let it bother me that she was getting more interested in hanging out with the boys.

January 1979
Danny and Nathan call Ann all the time, and woo her with punk news and escapades. Now the word is out: Danny told Ann that Nathan has a crush on her. Then he proceeded to ask her out. Where are standards? She ignored him. But how is she going to get around this precarious little situation? They both think she's 17. She told everyone in July that she was 19. Then she told folks she was 18. Then 16. Now 17. She's got an ID that says she's 18. She's really 20. Danny told Ann that he has his eye on another girl, but that she's way out of his range – she's 19. Danny wants to live with Ann in New York if she's the breadwinner. Nathan says he's saving himself for her. Danny thinks I'm the brains behind the team. Neither of them are emotionally involved with me, thank God. That's enough for now.

Ann and I honed our disaffected youth routine over Aphrodite's teeth-cracking cookies. We devised a game involving fantasy interactions with our heroes. The cast list, like the diner's menu, was indigestibly eclectic:

Debbie Harry and Blondie
Mick Jagger
Rod Stewart
Mikhail Baryshnikov
The Flintstones
Kimba the White Lion

It is hard to justify the randomness of these personalities, other than to cite them as the result of sugar-fuelled delirium. We *had* been mightily excited by Blondie's recent DC gig. Debbie Harry was supernaturally beautiful, as well as being the last word on stupid dances. On her, stupid looked smart. Debbie was the coolest woman in the world. She was our queen.

In our game, we imagined we were best friends with all of them, especially with Debbie. Because Rod and Mick had been trying the youngsters' sounds on for size with 'Do Ya Think I'm Sexy' and 'Shattered', we granted them honorary coolness. Anyway, their songs were on Aphrodite's individual booth jukes.

Mikhail was on hand to supply balletic horniness. The Russian superstar was cute and could pack out a dance belt, and besides, we were still going to be ballerinas, right?

The Flintstones and Kimba were always a little problematic in our whimsical world because, as they were cartoon characters, they were two-dimensional. If they turned sideways, no one could see them. Despite this handicap, they were enormously popular with our other pretend friends, especially with Mick, who often borrowed brontosaurus skins from Barney Rubble for stagewear.

The location for any superfriend scenario was always New York City. New York had everything: Studio 54, CBGBs and all the major ballet companies. I know my priorities jostled uneasily in this grouping, but my Mick and Barney daydreams proved I was capable of maintaining highly irregular interests.

The *real* superfriends convened not in NYC, but Aphrodite. One night, Danny and Nathan came all the way out from Washington to meet us at the diner. The boys sat sipping milkshakes with us, wearing their black leather jackets scrawled all over the back with 'Buzzcocks' and 'Sex Pistols'. The next day at Venus High, the word was out. I'd been spotted at Aphrodite with the Sex Pistols. My punk pedigree was now unassailable.

At Venus, I'd found a kindred spirit in Desirée Lafont. Half Swedish and half Puerto Rican, she looked like Cleopatra but cuter. Desirée had a black Lulu bob, cappuccino skin and dimples. With her white lipstick and Egyptian queen kohl eyes, she was walking exotica. The animated hamburger that passed for jocks called her 'Deathray', baying like maniacs. These were the same lunks who howled 'Ringling Brothers!' at me in my thrift-store garb.

Des and I escaped from hoi polloi boys into drama class, turning it into a personal salon of the arts. We'd bring in thermoses of coffee and sit in the corner alcove, creating our own café society. Together we were Left Bank Paris, we were Dada Zurich. We were two little teens hopped up on beans.

Desirée liked the same things I did, and we made each other laugh hysterically. She played me Roxy Music albums and baked me a cookie in the shape of Bryan Ferry. I told her about the Atlantis Club and took her to see The Tubes. We made collages for each other, cutting up magazines and pasting them into absurdist works of beauty and love.

Desi gave me a plastic harmonica shaped like a lobster claw that we named Babbo. She only had to say 'Babbo' to me and I would shake with soundless laughter for the next five minutes. She impersonated the worst ads on local television until I was convulsed, unable to breathe for busting a gut. The stupider something was, the more uproarious it was. Everything was a joke, but the jokes bonded our serious friendship.

And for me, our friendship had flowered just in time. I needed another collaborator, because Ann had just dyed her hair blue and moved back up to New York City. She'd gone to fulfil her new punk destiny, which had replaced the old ballet one.

Also fulfilling her punk destiny was Monster Jill. I'd met Monster Jill the same way I'd met all my DC friends: in the line for *Rocky Horror*. Jill was young, and blonde, and pretty – until she opened her mouth. She had crazy teeth that snaggled over each other like the aftermath of an oral earthquake.

Monster Jill was sweet and flaky. She would only eat food if it was colour-coordinated, like fries and mustard, or burgers and chocolate Yoo-hoo, or green Jell-O and peas. But since her favourite colour was blue, she was very skinny. There wasn't very much blue food available for matching.

Jill wanted to make 'the scene', the way we all did. But what *was* the scene? It was usually supplied by New Yorkers who breezed into DC with their punk rock combo or new wave troupe. In contrast to DC's rep as Palookaville, New York was the mecca of cool. Any musical export from the mecca, no matter how shoddy, was considered bitterly hip.

One bitter hipster was Klaus Nomi, the German performance artist who sang in an operatic falsetto. Klaus had stormed the Atlantis with his squeal appeal. Monster Jill was smitten, and when he left town, she left too. She moved to New York and limpeted herself to his Krazy Kolored entourage, acquiring insta-cool. She also acquired some of the entourage's bad habits, including an enthusiasm for heroin. A few months later, she OD'd her way right out of the scene. She was sixteen.

Ann remembered seeing Monster Jill once outside the

Mudd Club, stumbling drugged and dazed after Klaus in the dark, calling out lamely, 'Kloss . . . Kloss!' She'd died trying to be 'in' with Klaus, but she never did learn how to pronounce his name.

17

Teenage Kicks

August 1979
In ballet class, I'm better than almost all of them, but I am
one of the most unpleasant, physically. I'm doing weird
and destructive things to myself. I'm eating compulsively,
like I never have before. It's disgusting that I continue to
give myself snappy little pep talks in these notebooks that
I'll never reread until too late; and tomorrow I'll just eat
again. My entire happiness rests upon being thin. My
entire future rests upon it!

Since I was nine, I'd never stopped railing against my fabricated
fatness. When I looked back at dance photos of myself over the
years, I was blind to the slender girl in tutu and tights. This was
because ballet-induced paranoia convinced me that I was a
chub. Even a few years earlier when I was only 100 lbs, I'd
chastised myself for my perceived obesity. My notebooks were
signposted by regular citings of my perfectly healthy measure-
ments, always accompanied by, 'I disgust myself' or, 'I am filled
with self-hatred'. I concluded that since whether I starved

myself or stuffed my face I weighed the same, I might as well stuff my face. The fat prophecy fulfilled itself as I filled myself. Now, at seventeen, I was slowly but inexorably heading towards Chunkytown.

Full-fledged bingeing began in my senior year at Venus High. Every day for lunch, I would have an apple and two no-cal cans of Shasta pop. Then when I got home, I would gorge. I did my hunting and gathering from a variety of High's, Dart Drugs and 7–11s. The complicated foraging ploy was a tactic to throw the cashiers off my scent. I didn't want them fingering me as the pig I was, so I would buy a 'normal' amount of junk food from numerous locations. Laden with the weapons of my self-destruction, I'd come home, close my bedroom door and snarf it all down. Salty alternated with sweet: Chee-tos, Maple Nut Goodies, Sugar Babies, sour cream and chive potato chips, pecan praline ice cream, more Chee-tos, Junior Mints. Oh, and a diet Dr Pepper.

The main course of my never-ending feast was always dough-nuts. And not just any old fried dough – no way, mister. I'm talking Krispy Kreme Doughnuts. These babies are the Jewel of the South, the pride of North Carolina. All hail Krispy Kreme.

The yeast-raised loops of love are a Dixie tradition that goes back to 1937. The Krispy Kreme shop near Venus was jazzily glassed and rakishly angled, complete with the monumental red and green 'marching Ks' roadside neon sign. The Ks both wore crowns and held aloft ring doughnuts at the end of their outstretched K arms. Krispy Kremes had been Elvis Presley's favourite doughnuts. Elvis may have been the king, but Krispy Kremes were the power behind the throne.

A hunka hunka burnin' dough is the devil in disguise. The siren call of Krispy Kreme is the 'Hot Doughnuts Now' sign in the front window of the shop. Its fanatically awaited glow signals the arrival of newborn doughnuts. When I'd see the sign shining divine in the neon wasteland of Route 1, I'd step on the gas just to park faster. I'd be forcibly foreplayed by the dough-gasmic aroma, which perfumes the air, the hair and the heart. Slurping back anticipatory saliva, I'd take a deep breath and enter the theatre of my downfall.

Every Krispy Kreme shop is a theatre. A long glass window separates the audience from the performance – always the same, but never boring: the birth of a doughnut.

In the production room, foetal doughnuts are first witnessed rising in tall warming cases. Then, after floating across a shallow pool of hot oil like a battalion of dough boats, they beach themselves against the dripping rack. The rack in turn shimmies the naked 'nuts under a Niagara Falls of hot sugar glaze. They emerge on rollers, gleaming, golden, gorgeous. The hot Original Glazed is edible paradise – like biting into an angel. I could eat six at once, no problem. Eight or ten was typical. Twelve was going to town.

Along with the Original Glazed, there were Chocolate Iced, Chocolate Iced with Sprinkles, Chocolate Iced Kreme Filled, Chocolate Iced Custard Filled, Maple Iced, Lemon Filled, Raspberry Filled, Cinnamon Apple Filled, Powdered Blueberry Filled, Glazed Creme Filled, Traditional Cake, Powdered Cake, Chocolate Iced Cake, Glazed Cruller, Chocolate Iced Cruller, Glazed Devil's Food, Glazed Blueberry, Glazed Sour Cream and Cinnamon Bun.

I hung myself on those dough nooses.

November
Well, needless to say (it seems), I tip dangerously over 120 lbs. I am too depressed lately. I've lost all desire for ballet and doubt my future success in anything.

My ballet teacher thinks my upper back is getting more curved. This has been a source of much more anguish for me. It does hurt. I have an appointment at the hospital next Friday. Well, we'll see.

I began drowning my sorrows in the bottle. Not Johnny Walker, but Miss Clairol. I finally dyed my mousy hair red after a year of messing around with food colouring. The shade was 'Flame'. And demonstrating my commitment to punk, I gave myself a mohawk. Or at least what I felt was a subtle compromise between balletic tresses and punky spikes. Instead, all I managed to do was inadvertently invent the mullet. With bangs. My 'mohawk' was a bristly patch of turf on top with the remaining long hair dripping down the sides and back. My mother screamed when she saw it.

December
Mom wants to know why I purposely make myself look ugly. One day she doggedly tried to get me into a pair of disgusting polyester slacks at Woodie's bargain basement. Blechh.

She was probably just trying to finish the job I'd started.

After making the Honour Roll one last time at the beginning of twelfth grade, apathy set in. Spare vim was scant, especially for my schoolwork. Soon I was skipping classes regularly with the aid of forged excuse notes. One exhilarating run of non-attendance lasted almost three weeks.

I managed to shrug off a little ennui for a special presentation in English class that captured my interest.

March 1980
The guidance director gave us a four-day course on communication. It was very revealing. She spoke of a way

to analyse verbal communication:

Level 1: pleasantries, small talk – merely an acknowledgement of the other person.

Level 2: orders, directions – something is accomplished.

Level 3: meaningful exchange of ideas – most people preferably communicate on this level.

Level 4: feelings, emotions – this level strips one naked – one is taking a chance when revealing this deeply.

Last night I realized with a sad start that my father and I rarely get above Level 2. I never talk to him. Sometimes I try, but traditionally I've felt intimidated by him, acutely aware that anything I might say would sound preposterous to him . . . that he would 'correct' any 'wrong' thoughts, or not even listen to me to begin with. I don't think he hears me when I speak to him.

My mother and I deal in 3 often. She doesn't get enough appreciation for her art, her wit, herself.

When she hits a Level 4 nerve (like suggesting that I should give up ballet and have the operation) I am rendered positively incoherent. I get all choked up and garbled; fractured sentences haltingly make their appearance: 'Don't say . . . anything like that. Never . . .' She'll switch to a Level 1 groove to avoid confrontation: 'Oh look, there's Sooky, look at his silly stomach flapping as he's running.'

One of the all-American rites at Venus High was the 'Senior Superlatives' section of the yearbook. In this handsome leather-bound volume, the section was the first thing you flipped to before laughing at the alphabetical mugshots. The Superlatives were those students deemed 'Most Popular' or 'Best Athlete' or whatever, as decided by their peers. I was voted 'Most Unique', which aside from being grammatically redundant, seemed like a pretty good thing to be – on the surface. But if you knew the Venus kids the way I did, 'Most Unique' was a backhanded compliment. Heavy on the backhand.

' "Unique". What's that? Is that like, "weird"? Who's that freakin' weird chick? Puckrik? She can win it – she's freakin' *weird*, man.'

And so I was Most Unique. With that superlative, twelve years of school dried up.

July
Oh these teen years. It's a slump I've been in for a few years now. But I'm still around, and it's hard to believe how many times I wished I could skip the time right by, skip my unhappiness and depression. But as a result my life was lived inattentively, precious time frittered away as I wallowed in self-hatred. It is noted here only every few months as I could not bring myself to really examine myself and be disgusted. What was the use, I thought, of recording my misery for then and all time? Such lack of self-confidence, all because of 25 extra pounds. Well, this is to be changed, I am changing. I'm out of school, 18, and must look forward to my life.

I looked forward to my nightlife.

August
The 9:30 Club is fun – a sparkling clean version of the gritty old Atlantis.

The mythical Atlantis had sunk – to reappear a year later as the 9:30 Club. The 9:30 was *the* DC showcase for everything that was happening at the left turn into the Orwellian age: punk, new wave, ska, rockabilly, reggae, art noise, go-go, hardcore. Desirée and I danced under the high ceiling or perched on the tiny stage, watching videos on the monitors. Videos were new. MTV hadn't started yet, and it would be years before it dominated the taste of the nation. The club was just about the only place where young music lovers could see the latest videos. We throbbed to everything from The Stray Cats to Bow Wow Wow.

The 9:30 was more than just a club. It was a living room, the place you left home to come home. I went just about every night, slamming out of the door to my dad's 'You going to that drinking and wiggling place AGAIN?' Shrugging off his disapproval was getting easier. The 'drinking and wiggling' remark was reminiscent of his old 'going down to that HOLE' comment, the criticism twinned with wicked potential. Except that now, the question left me tickled instead of stung.

And as for my wicked potential, there wasn't much drinking, but there was plenty of wiggling. The futurist synthy sounds of the early eighties demanded it. You could get away with a little happy-go-lucky fringe-shaking to Soft Cell and The B-52's, but Spandau Ballet and Gary Numan required heavy-duty posing.

Desi and I were in attendance for all the minstrels of the moment. If they played Washington, they played 9:30: The Cramps, The Damned, The Birthday Party; Simple Minds, Suicide, Psychedelic Furs. Even William Burroughs.

One night, Bauhaus passed close by us on their way to the stage. I caught a waft of their odour – the scent of fresh vegetables – and decided they smelled British. My general impression was that Brits didn't seem to wash as much as

Americans, but I found this disregard for hygiene dangerous and sexy. I loved how they looked, too – British beauty at its best reminded me of an attractive weasel. All those sharp, clever faces, all those pointy yellow teeth. British men were smaller than the average jock, but perhaps like cherry tomatoes, they were grown for more flavour than bigger, blander American guys.

When I finally took my eyes, ears and nose off the bands, I noticed a dance floor full of my kind.

May 1981
We've watched each other at 9:30 for a year – we finally introduce ourselves. Suddenly, we are the fluffies! Fluffy hair, balloon-y clothes, poppy records! We do everything together.

The club was a roomful of instant friends. Janet Tall Hair had ice-blue eyes and a helpless laugh that took you down with her. Her scared-stiff quiff regularly caused Chevy-fuls of Georgetown jocks to screech to an outraged stop. Little Germ worked behind the bar and served me my first ever Cape Cod. Chicago Chris always had strange luck. When he wasn't finding stolen Rodin sculptures in his garden or stumbling on pin-stabbed voodoo dolls, he was being hauled in for murder line-ups. Kim Dubby and Wannabe Dub were a boyfriend/girlfriend DJ duo. They had a baby girl called Mowgli Gillogly. Orange Pop and Yellow Greg were charmers with citrus-coloured hair. All the girls adored them – and Tommy Vacant, the physics major. In his Nutty Professor lab coat scribbled with formulas, Tommy danced like a spider monkey.

Florida Larry had a Sahara-dry Southern drawl. His 'punk name' was Pepsi Gadaffi. Larry shared a 16th Street apartment with Steve Miller, twenty-two with kind brown eyes and a child's smile: pleased and shy, all at the same time.

Like me, Steve had boogie-oogie-oogied through the disco years and had surfaced at 9:30 to see what the eighties had to offer. I wrote in my notebook that I wanted to 'align myself with this boy who expressed himself with such clarity and who listened with great intent'.

The flowing of thoughts between Steve and myself is a beautiful feeling. Very calm, very fluid. Are we like water together?

I had a crush on him.

June 16
Steve and I have yet to touch one another, and this withholding heightens our awareness of each other. I purposely do not participate in the casual social kissing and this makes us intensely conscious of the slightest meeting of hands; the closeness of our thighs when sitting. This is a calculation on my part, shyness on his, I think. It is not a heartless calculation, rather, I am savouring these tiny encounters. This had better not all blow up in my face.

Uh-oh.

July 6
Steve is gay.
Why me? . . . that's all I have to ask. I was making small talk with Larry and I casually asked him why Steve bothered to ingratiate himself with Bob if it caused him so much pain. Larry looked at me a moment, then said, 'I

shouldn't betray a confidence, but . . . there is a reason for all this tension. Bob and Steve used to be lovers.'

'Oh . . .' That certainly was a novelty tidbit – Steve was bisexual? I was unperturbed. For some reason, as my eyes flickered over him dancing away on the floor, this facet made him more attractive to me. It heightened his sensual-ness.

After studying my face for a reaction to that news, Larry leaned in again.

'Desirée told me that you have a certain interest in Steve.'

I nodded affirmation.

'Well, I should tell you that he is gay.' He knew that I may have construed the Steve/Bob thing as a one-time fling.

'Really?' I said. 'Isn't he bisexual, though?' I thought the physical overtures to me were certainly of a hetero nature.

Larry conceded reluctantly, 'Well, he may be bi, but I know that all the relationships he has had in the past few months have been with guys.'

So where does this all leave me? My heart whispers to my brain, 'What??! Maybe it'll work out after all?!!'

Then my brain retorts sharply, 'Wake up, you fool! Wait, shmait – extricate yourself!'

Steve and I are of like mind on the subject of non-sexual touching – it is an important thing and people don't do it enough. It's healthy. But I don't know how healthy my enjoyment of it is. I may be responding to his hands and lips in a sexual manner. I am starved for touching. Yet, it is established that he is gay. So what does he feel? What compels him to brush his lips against mine?

I don't know I don't know I don't know . . .

Ann is coming up from Williamsburg today. Thank God.
She will have insight and soul-salves.

Ann had shucked her punk husk and was now in law school at
my mother's old college.

Oh – but I think of Steve entirely too much. It is lovely to
feel, *however. I am positively dripping with melodrama*
and pure love.

I was dripping with melodrama and pure love. Starved for
touching, I stuffed my face. My full belly couldn't quell my
hungry heart. But my new friends staved the pangs.

Steve, Larry, Des and I hooked up and hung out with the
Fat-X-Sam sisters. Fat-X-Sam was Francie and Nancy's phone
number, and it was an easy handle for the two, who were never
seen without the other.

Although they were sisters, with only a year between them,
they couldn't have looked more different. Bossy Nancy was
skinny with excited hair and bony fingers that jabbed emphasis
to her wise-guy remarks. Ample Francie was the opposite:
queen-sized with a soft voice and a slow saunter. Who was the
casting director for this family, anyway? Though she was the
elder at twenty-two, Francie's girlish giggle sometimes made
her seem younger, less assured than smarty-pants Nance. Francie's humour was more sweetly whimsical than her little sister's.
They had the same eyes, though: spooky bright blue jewels.

Francie and Nancy lived in an office building on 14th Street,
DC's major whore esplanade. When we weren't at 9:30, we
flopped at their small apartment. The place was filled with
knick-knacks from a lifetime of rummage sales – anything that
could remotely be considered cool from every era of cool. It

was a compendium of pop culture: fifties lamps, sixties clocks, seventies TVs, eighties records, big plastic quart bottles of Coca-Cola – Francie was addicted. And lots of cockroaches.

Along with each and every new record, Francie and Nancy bought all the music 'zines imported from England. We blackened our fingers on *NME* and *Melody Maker*. We scrutinized the fine print like Columbus with a map of the New World. It was really important to know everything about the latest anything. The fluffy looks and sounds we enjoyed had now been christened 'new romantic'. The first issues of *i-D* and *The Face* were essential Blitz Kid reading.

Early club kids had to sniff out sedition for themselves, do all the legwork. It made the scene seem much more personalized and special. We thrift-shopped and wore our new old clothes like a badge of honour, which they were, in a buttoned-down town like Washington. We were five-and-dime dandies, spruced and loosed on DC. It was easy to shock people – just wearing all black was enough to make people scream, 'Hey! It's not Hallowe'en!' at us as their cars squealed off.

Ten bucks at the Salvation Army got me fully dolled. For general daywear, a rockabilly approach was useful. Tapered trousers. A purple shirt. A man's checked jacket. A boy's black wingtips. Desi called them 'Boy Scout shoes'. Any vaguely androgynous effect would then be destroyed by my purse – usually a long, thin sixties handbag covered in fun fur or patent leather.

Come eventide, the new romantically inclined piled on the chandelier gear: ruffled tuxedo shirts with rhinestone brooches at the throat; jillions of jingling bracelets; Japanese tabi socks; Middle Eastern scarves; fingerless lace gloves; ropes of pearls; pixie boots; jodhpurs; kilts. The busier the better, although occasional restraint was employed for the sleek pencil-skirted,

French-twisted image of the Human League girls.

The look was pretty much unisex, to the horror of conservative Washingtonians. People were so entertainingly outraged by our wayward wear. Once a woman in Georgetown peevishly exclaimed, 'Why, that's not even new wave!' and we burst into laughter. Difficulty in pinning down non-prep dress always filled Normals with consternation.

Fluffies roamed in packs of plaid slacks and daring hair. Everybody started cutting theirs raggedy-jaggedy. Hair covered all the bases in one weird style: long-short-tall-fat-slicky-frizzy. Bow Wow Wow rat-tails plaited up any loose ends.

I made the mistake of buying my new wave do from a Venus establishment called The Hair Corral. The salon was a mock-up of the inside of a barn, complete with horse stalls where each unlucky buckaroo sat for a shear. The stylist's hair looked like a burned Brillo pad. My heart sinking, I asked for a 'punk cut'. She turned me into Mrs Brady. I tried to disguise the suburban effect by tying a rolled scarf around my head. I ended up looking Brady Bunch-ier than ever.

My fellow fluffies were forgiving – we were all new to cool. Every now and again, we'd take a break from Francie and Nancy's kitsch-cramped flat and our study of tunes and trends. Piling into Francie's '62 Malibu, we'd take a tri-state cruise to unpillaged thrift stores and funny old diners. Setting sail from DC, her big aqua boat would glide through Maryland and Virginia to Little Taverns and Krispy Kremes. The time Francie threw her half-eaten Chocolate Iced Kreme Filled doughnut at the driver who took her parking space passed permanently into fluffy lore.

Little Tavern looked like a toytown cottage: a tiny white hut with a peaked green roof. It specialized in miniature hamburgers complete with teensy buns. Little Tavern's slogan was 'Buy

'Em by the Bag!' In our tours of highway style, calories were less the objective than aesthetics and humour. It was hilarious just to say, 'Yeah, we went to Weenie Beenie today.' We took a lot of pictures.

When I'd tiptoe in at four in the morning, my father found it hard to believe that all I'd been doing was gum-flapping with my friends at the Watergate Howard Johnson's. It seemed suspiciously innocent. While he had 'drinking and wiggling' branded on his brain, I had ice-cream dribbling down my chin. HOJOs was the home of the Tasty Tester: dodeca-scooped ice-cream sundaes that melted into a sweet grey sludge of indistinguishable flavours after about three bites.

While fluffies washed down the wonders of yesterday's future with mouthfuls of melted Tasty Testers, Washington's harDCore punk scene erupted. The new romantics' frills were ruffled by 'straight edge' punks. Fluffies faced off against 'spikies'. Spikies thought fluffies were goofy and silly. Fluffies thought spikies were too serious, and angry just for effect.

The *Washington Post* reported on the summer's frightening new youth trend, slamdancing.

The spit of British punk has been replaced by more fundamentally American violence of hurling bodies. Young men's bodies slam into each other, arms and elbows out, fists flailing, like razor-edged Mexican jumping beans popping madly on the dance floor. This ritual of resistance is fuelled by dancers who are young, mostly white teenage boys given to shaved heads, more extreme than a Marine cut, sometimes in a Taxi Driver *mohawk.*

The media had finally stopped mocking American punk. Quoted extensively in the piece was twenty-year-old Henry

Rollins. Henry had just packed his last Rum Raisin cone at the Georgetown Häagen-Dazs to become the new singer of LA hardcore leaders Black Flag.

'I don't consider this dangerous. If it was I wouldn't care anyhow. I've got scars all over my face and most of them were given by my friends. So what.'

Us fluffies played it safe and stuck to wussie wave. We were rewarded for our dedicated posing by the cavalcade of British bands that came to the capital: Duran Duran, Adam And The Ants, U2, The Teardrop Explodes, Echo And The Bunnymen.

They all played for gatherings of less than two hundred. U2 played to about fifty of us. Siouxsie And The Banshees, who'd built up their loyal hordes since the early punk days, reeled in a respectable crowd at the University of Maryland. The fluffies were all fuzzed up, because Steve had secured an interview with Miss Sioux herself for the college newspaper.

After the show, we all went to the Holiday Inn to meet Her. In the lounge, the DJ honoured the Banshees' presence by playing his meagre stash of 'new wave': Pat Benatar, The Police. I felt embarrassed on America's behalf.

When Siouxsie strode into the room, she looked about nineteen feet tall. Her long legs in thigh-high boots scissored lounge atmos to ribbons. Shocked black hair framed her painted face, which was simultaneously expressionist and expressionless.

Siouxsie had hauteur and *froideur*, for sure. Regally bored, she chain-smoked while half-baked goths laughed loudly and excessively at any chance utterance of hers.

Steve nervously introduced himself and began the interview. It was soon apparent that she'd neglected to begin with him.

Siouxsie's long silences pulverized Steve's confidence. Trying to contain her disdain, drummer Budgie was buddying up with the awed kids. But before his jollification could take hold, Haiti Ho stole the show.

Haiti Ho was an exuberant girl who'd mixed fluffy with hippie and come out flippy. Haiti punked up her Afro puffs with safety pins and plastic baubles. She wore her baby-doll dresses with lots of confrontational eye-shadow that glowed gold and blue against her black skin.

She arrived late at the Holiday Inn to see Siouxsie towering over the adoring rabble. Overcome with excitement, Haiti started running towards her, screaming, 'Sushi! Sushi! Sushi!' She forgot to put on the brakes. Safety-pinned puffs and black-leather legs thrashed in the wreckage. Siouxsie's gin and tonic spilled down the inside of one thigh-high boot. The interview was over.

Our evenings weren't always so traumatic.

July 24
Last night there was a five-cent admission price at the 9:30 for two lousy bands, The Worms and The Beatnik Flies. Desirée and I, expecting musical matters to be as dire as they were, strolled in anyway, hoping to run into pals. Pals we did run into: Steve and Larry among the notables.

At the door, the doorman says, 'Here they are, the twins!' Elsewhere, in the club, 'Are you two sisters?'

I mean, brown-eyed, coffee-skinned, black-haired Des, and green-eyed, fair, red-headed me – yeah! Nobody ever asks Francie and Nancy if they're sisters, and they really are.

Mainly we loitered in the corridor outside the bathroom, making a constant stream of patter about people, bands, and the plots of old I Love Lucy shows. Then when they played 'real' music in between sets, we'd run up and dance.

At about 1.15, Larry suggested we go to a disco, The Fraternity House. I, envisioning a warehouse-sized place with funk music booming out, quickly acquiesced. I should have known: lights flashing disturbingly nightmarishly, beautiful-faced but truncated young men gliding through smogs of amyl nitrate. The music was goofy, too – this Hollywood-y sort of bombastic, non-soulful thumps and SFX. The floor (postage stamp) was jammed.

Welcome to hi-energy.

Then Steve, Larry, Des and I propelled ourselves to the Georgetown Deli where we laughed ourselves hoarse over stupid things: Desirée's pterodactyl cries; the incessant referral to coffee as 'cuppa joe'. Also – the 'fluffy' concept: fluffy as applied to anything not readily identifiable as such – Fluffy the Cockroach, Fluffy the Disembowelled Goat.

Then we left and Larry drove us back to my car, parked in front of Ford's Theatre on 10th Street. The four of us got out and admired the lovely Waffle King with its gold and red mosaic of wavy lines. We laughed at the sign in the window which said, 'There's no place like this place, so this must be the place!' We must have stood there for another good half an hour. We saw Kim Dubby and Wannabe Dub trudging home from work at the 9:30, and hailed them over.

This sort of thing goes on all the time – these evenings, the desultory, haphazarded pace, the good feelings, the good spirits, the grand friends.

As high as our fluffy jinks were, they couldn't disguise the reality of my go-nowhere world. Maybe I was Most Unique, but so what?

July 31
I haven't done a dance class since last October. That's nine months! My motivation, feeble as it had become over the last year, petered out altogether. The months of June, July and August 1980 are a smudgy blur to me now, and surely were then. I've sat in a stupor, eating (reaching 140!) and being miserable. In February I started working at a consulting firm. I've been plugging away here at work, answering phones, typing letters, alternately elated and frustrated. Naked despair takes over: why am I doing this? What a nothing time-waster! Where is my career in an art – where are all my glittering contacts? What about my brain? I want to be on a stage, stirring myself and an audience. I have many possibilities to pursue, yet here I am, kicking my heels instead of my butt.

Is this what they meant by 'teenage kicks'?

18

Love Action (I Believe In Love)

The day the world turned day-glo was the night I met B.

I'm at the 9:30 with Desirée, Steve, Larry, Francie and Nancy. It's September and I've been nineteen for two months.

On-stage is a British haircut band that we've seen in videos. The new romantic group lace their synth pop with avant-garde pretensions. The fans eat 'em up but the critics spit 'em out. A typical review in one of the British music papers describes their songs being 'as aesthetically exciting as a bursting sausage'. The theatrical singer overdoes the bombast. Generally, I like that sort of thing, but I'm not too sure about this bunch. I came to 9:30 anyway, just because I always came to 9:30.

I dig not the music, but I enjoy their futurist burlesque. So do my old *Rocky Horror* pals Danny and Nathan. I haven't seen them since they'd taken the hardcore high road. Their updated leather jackets inform me that they're now in a band called Youth Brigade. The boys are right down front alternately pogoing and laughing at the singer.

I don't care about the singer. I'm watching the bass player. He has sleepy eyes and a cartoon smile. He wears a black shirt and baggy Bowie trousers. He has a padlock and chain around his neck and an elegant mini-quiff on his head. He is B.

After the show, I see B walking around the club on his own. None of the bands ever do that – they always disappear into the dressing room, nixing the mixing. I screw up my courage to approach him.

I say: 'Hi – I liked your show.' I think: I like *your* show.

'Thanks,' B answers. He has a London accent, although I don't know it yet.

B is trendy in a way unknown for a straight man in America – and really cute. He has been twenty for four months. As we make shy but friendly chit-chat, my friends at the table next to us beam delightedly at my hands-across-the-water success. Francie whips out her camera and clicks it wildly in our direction, trying to document the moment. A week later she'll give me the photo: a close-up of B's right ear. I'll glue it in my notebook. I'll love that ear.

Before too long we're cracking jokes and laughing. B is charming and throws himself into acting out funny stories. I'm flattered that he's court-jestering me. B tells the one about the ultraswoopy megaquiff he used to have. Every day he had to hang upside down and lacquer it with an entire can of hairspray. Once, while running for an audition with Elvis Costello, B says, he passed out on a tube platform, asphyxiated on upside-down Harmony fumes. He came to with a policeman standing over him and a suspicion of glue-sniffing. Skew-whiff quiff aside, B played great at the audition and got the gig with Elvis. He tells me he turned it down. I tell him it was the right move, because then we wouldn't have met here, tonight, at the 9:30.

Dying to make some kind of physical contact, I hitch my arms under his knees and give B a piggyback ride around the now empty dance floor. My friends leave the club in twos and threes, smiling back at our silliness.

The singer from B's band comes up from the dressing room as the music stops for the night. Going back to the hotel is mentioned. There's awkwardness and general foot-shuffling between B and me. I don't want to leave, but I don't know how to stay.

B makes it all right. He says, 'Wanna come?'

I'm relieved, then anxious. The singer gives me a disapproving look which suddenly heightens my awareness of how sleazy it all seems: me hanging around, us going to the hotel.

B laughs and takes my hand. 'C'mon, short-arse.'

We set off on our walk around the block to the Harrington, a down-at-heel downtown hotel. I point out my parrot-green Toyota Celica, which is parked in front of Ford's Theatre. B's impressed. Apparently in England, it's not the usual thing for teenagers to tootle around in cars. I tease him, 'That's because your country's too small for roads – and garages.'

He teases back, imitating my accent, 'Gar-RAHHGES! Can't you colonials speak proper English?'

'I guess not, after we whupped your ass back to England – losers!' I jab.

'Nothing to do with me, chicken – I'm Irish.'

I hear my father's voice in my head saying catchphrase number seven: 'Clever, these Irishmen!'

B describes his infant hop from Cork to London. Deep in his blue eyes and getting-to-know-you talk, I barely notice the transition from street to lobby to lift to hall to room.

As he shuts the door behind us, I look around his portable world. The TV's late-night flicker strobes softly on the double bed. Nervous again, I launch into meaningless chatter about the hand-washed socks draped over the air-conditioner.

B plays along. 'Yeah – you just can't get the help any more.'

The sock topic seems exhausted. There's nothing left to do but kiss.

We kiss.

We sink to the hotel bed, and fit into the imprint left by other lovers from other times. B holds me, and I breathe him in. I smell fresh vegetables, then the sharp tang of his sweat. His odour is strong, definite. It is B.

Eternities scroll by in his arms. My time-lapse heart shoots out new roots, and buds, and sparks. It's a valentine shined by excitement. I have never moved so fast moving so slow.

'Should I take my clothes off?'

My voice in the dense silence startles me.

I can tell it startles B, too. Was that a weird thing to say? Oh, jeez. I don't know what the hell I'm doing. It's not like I've ever done this before.

'Um, OK.'

Then B smiles. I'm beginning to love that smile. It curls up at the ends like a doodle.

Now what have I gotten myself into? It was my big idea to take off my clothes, and I'm at my fattest ever – at the putrid sewer bottom of my self-worth. I hate my body. *He'll* hate my body.

He doesn't.

His hands, his lips, his cock tell me he loves it.

B's fingers restore belief in my body. I haven't been touched for so long – not since Hush. Every pore of my skin is mewing like an abandoned kitten.

Losing my virginity. How can I lose it – I know just where I'm putting it. My mind's in split-screen. I think about my maidenhead. What *is* a maidenhead? I picture my profile carved into an ivory cameo – something a great-aunt would wear at the throat of her high-necked blouse. In *Shogun*, medieval Japanese called the vagina 'the golden pavilion'. An orgasm was 'the clouds and the rain'. Anaïs Nin wrote of the 'salty honey' between her legs. Natalie Wood and Warren Beatty experienced *Splendor in the Grass*. But none of my sources revealed how much it hurts.

It hurts. Shyness has squeezed my golden pavilion into a tiny tepee. What's going to happen? Skin presses against skin, then *through* skin. So private! No one's visited me *there* before. B is a welcome guest, but it does hurt. I hold him inside me. I hold my breath until the pain stops. It stops when he does.

I did it! I did it! I did it! I did it! I did it! I did it! I did it! Did I do it right?

No, no, no, it's not like that, Katie. Look, B is kissing me, cuddling me. He draws invisible eyes, nose and lips on my face with the tip of his finger. I breathe him in again. His smell has become our smell.

We hold each other and talk soft talk until grey shafts of light leak through the window.

When I stand up, I drip blood on my rockabilly jacket crumpled next to the bed. Like a rider after her first hunt, I am blooded.

When I got back to Venus, the grey shafts of light had blonded into morning sun. I met Desi at Aphrodite to relive the rapture over coffee. Then, buzzed on wonder and joe and still in my bloodstained jacket, I went off to my office job.

Why didn't I play hookey and stay with B, who had another whole day left in Washington? Why didn't I seize the day and milk the love? This was the big time, baby – the clouds and the rain, splendor in the grass. Or was it so big? Maybe it was just tacky. Cheap. I'd gone back to a hotel with some guy in a band – how original. But wait a minute wait a minute – what about my mewing skin, my sparking heart? What about his smile, his hands, our smell? What was real: the doubts of the day, or the surrender of the night?

I was confused. Again I replayed the morning's leaving scene for clues.

In the room, I'd started to get dressed to go. B didn't want me to go – he wanted me to stay with him, to sleep.

'What are you doing later today?' I'd asked him, trying not to sound like I was fishing for an invitation. I wasn't. I think.

'Oh, there's supposed to be a photo session with the band.'

'Oh.'

There was no invitation. My awkwardness returned.

'Well, I guess I'd better go – I've got to go to work . . .' I'd said, almost as a question.

'Well, if you really have to . . .'

I didn't really *have* to, but it seemed important not to crowd B in case he'd changed his mind about liking me. What was the etiquette in these situations? Oh no, was this a *situation*? I couldn't stand that. All that love action dried up and powdered down? Desiccated groupie – just add water. Boil her. Boiler.

Fuck that! That wasn't *this*. This was *us*. Me and B.

Months later there was a picture of B and his band in *Smash Hits*, photographed in front of Washington's Capitol building. I bought the magazine and studied it again and again. It was eerie: the photo had been taken the morning I'd left him at the hotel. In the picture, B looked sexy and sleepy. I searched his face. Was I in his eye?

I sent him a letter, trying hard to strike the right tone, ie not desperate. Then I sent a few more. They were jaunty, clever, easy-breezy.

After the fourth letter in three months, I gave up. It seemed completely pathetic. So I'd lost my virginity to him. Big whoop.

B was probably relieving girls of their virginity all over the world, and all I'd done was shuffle myself into the same deck of dodos. In trying to prove to myself that I wasn't just another one-night stand, I was only proving that I was.

His first letter arrived a month after I'd stopped believing in him. I was stunned when I opened the spindly mailbox at the end of our driveway and saw the pale blue envelope. It was snowing, and I ran back inside, out of the cold and up the stairs. Sooky galloped along beside me into my room, and we hit the bed at the same time.

I curled up with Sooky and we stared at the envelope for ever. B had misspelled my name, but that didn't matter. It was a letter! I finally opened it and read it just under one million times.

January 11, 1982
Oh dear – how do I begin . . . ?
. . . my first thought was to tell you that it took me all this time to wade through my mountains of fan mail, and I've only got round to you . . . no? Fair enough . . . truth is, mon cheri, *since we met, I've been here, there, everywhere, returned to London to do the new LP, came home for Xmas, and lo and behold – I find you've written me a veritable book!*

I noticed the absence of Xmas cards in the pile, so you've probably forgotten all about me by now. If so, stop reading now, and take up origami (I hate waste).

How are you, anyway, dearest, still as small and cuddly? Good! . . . y'know, no bullshit, in all my travels this year (he said) I've met none so charming and witty as thee – will you marry me? . . . problem is, this small matter of 3,000-odd miles doesn't really help, does it?

Now, the GOOD news, (depending on your point of view), is that I should be returning to your fair shores in late spring, which is better than nothing, I suppose ... then I can give you the 12" platform boots I bought you for Xmas – you'll love 'em!

Now LISTEN short-arse, if I don't hear from you again, I'm gonna play my bass in the bath and frazz myself. So ...

... all my love, B

He was affectionate! He was funny! He was worried that I'd stopped writing to him! He made a joke about marrying me! He made another joke about killing himself if I didn't write back!

My mind was beyond blown. My head was a-whirlin' and a-twirlin', my heart was shake'n'baked. I had dog-with-his-head-out-a-fast-car's-window euphoria. I checked the bottom of the letter again, just to make sure I'd grasped the concept. It was still there: 'all my love, B'. Love! I'd been really careful not to use the 'L' word in my letters, and here he was, strutting in with the big guns, reckless as all get-out.

Well, if he had guns, I had cannons, cruise missiles, H-bombs of ardour. His slim blue letter was the red button that triggered full-scale romantic warfare. I immediately launched a postal campaign to lasso his heart to mine.

I poured out the entire essence of my being in my letters to B. In drawings, collages and thousands and thousands of words, I determined to portray an irresistible me that he would be foolish not to adore. I wanted to make him laugh and to make him think. I wanted him to want me.

In creating the sunny, funny visuals, I was a one-woman craft corner – a playschool laureate with paper and glue. I had Desi take elaborately staged polaroids of me to be used in hokey photo-love stories. The premise of one such project cast me as the gal he'd left behind, with 'Baby Clamma', the child he didn't know we'd had. Clamma was played by a giant baby doll who shared my chubby cheeks and long red hair.

Shot after shot revealed my maternal incompetence as I poured a mountain of talc on Clamma's bottom, forced her to eat doughnuts, and read to her from *Fear of Flying*. The last picture was a family portrait, featuring 'mother and child' standing next to a photo of B taped to the wall with 'Dad' scrawled underneath. The spoof was presented in a saccharine 'Your First Baby' album.

B responded less prolifically, yet always passionately. I lived for his mushiness – the trait so abhorred when I was eight. As his band travelled the world, I began receiving postcards from India, Finland and Japan. In retaliation, I whipped out my trusty scissors and old magazines and fashioned a jokey 'Greetings from Venus' postcard depicting Mayor Elvis Presley promoting the neighbourhood space programme.

I wrote on the back:

You're not the only one making the world your playpen. 'America's Tenderloin' – that's what native Venusians called this blessed patch of God's green earth. Cows, diners, pick-up trucks and toothless rednecks . . . imagine strolling down the main drag, past countless gas stations and fast-food chains, hearing the soft repartee of lovers: 'Gimme some sugar, honey,' and 'Get into this truck now, woman!'

In describing my life, I wanted to place myself in his. I sketched for him endless little caricatures of me with my family; at the office; in the 9:30. It was my version of Pioneer 10's friendship plaque – the licence plate on that car to the stars. The plaque had drawings of a naked man and woman along with a diagram of our galaxy. It was a calling card for aliens. Well, B was my alien, and I wanted him to know that he was welcome in my world.

I was wild with the impossible romance of it all. I could not talk about anything else. Ann, Steve and Desirée were at first amused, then bored, then worried. To them and anyone else with common sense, I was flip city. After all, I was obsessed with a man I had only met once, and just for a few hours.

My friends' reservations didn't even give me pause for thought. I was oblivious to reason.

I was shiveringly, seraphically in love.

B wrote to confirm that he would be returning to America in the late spring. It was at this point that my scoliosis awoke from its catnap to resume corkscrewing me. Possessed by contempt, my crooked spine accelerated its twist. The bottom half of the 'S' snarled forty-three degrees, while the top half buckled all the way to sixty-seven. My back was folding in on itself and taking my heart and lungs with it.

My shiny valentine was getting the squeeze, too. I wrote to B:

My heart's a fiery incinerator – it wants you for fuel and is burning me instead.

19

Party Fears Two

I couldn't believe the timing.

My surgery for spinal fusion was booked for the beginning of May – just when B had said he was coming back to America. I didn't want a Bette Davis scene for B and me, all *Dark Victory* and bandages. I wanted Disney – joyous and technicolored, but with some sex thrown in, obviously.

I tried to bargain with the doctors to postpone the operation again, but they refused. When B wrote that the band would not be touring America after all, I welcomed the surgery the way a martyr welcomes the Catherine wheel. As there was now nothing left for me in this world, I figured I might as well hurtle violently into the next.

If I was perfectly honest with myself, I had to admit that I was revelling in the tragic romance of it all. My circuits were wired the same as any other earthling's. When it looked like something was about to be taken away from me, I wanted it more than I ever wanted it before. This applied to B, and to dancing. On a secret altar at the back of my brain, I burned a never-dying candle to both.

In the Limb and Brace Shop at Walter Reed Army Medical Center, prosthetic legs and arms hung high on the walls like grotesque decorations. The man-made hands had a built-in grip like GI Joe, the fake feet were pre-shod with grey socks and shiny army shoes. I'd been coming here for the last five years to have my baby humps stroked, poked and X-rayed. Usually I left the hospital after these sessions running out the front door to freedom, escaping the plastic limbs, the medicine air and a life sentence with a permanently broken back. Usually, I left.

But now, they'd caught me. Since my increasingly curly-wurly back had made surgery unavoidable, I tried to adopt a more positive outlook about life after fusion. My main concern was how well I'd be able to dance after the procedure, if at all. I'd begun to accept that a ballet career was now out of the question, particularly as I'd spent the last few years chowing down on Krispy Kremes. But maybe, even with a rod in my back, I'd be able to do *some* kind of dancing.

In the thoracic and lumbar spine, there are seventeen vertebrae. My surgeon intended to destroy ten. I quizzed my doctors on the details in order to calculate my dance chances. How flexible would I be after I'd recovered? One of them said, airily 'Oh, you'll be able to touch your toes', as if even that would be more than enough for the average bear. But I wasn't the average bear. I was a dancing machine built to razzle-dazzle, not to fizzle and clunk to a stop. Toe-touching wouldn't really cut it.

The truth was, the doctors didn't know what I'd be able do with ten frozen vertebrae. Spinal fusion was a relatively recent surgical technique. And my back was worse than most.

The surgeon explained that any operation on the spine could potentially disrupt the delicate spinal cord. A slip of the scalpel, he warned, and I'd be paralysed from the neck down. While I was reeling from this information, he pushed a form across the desk for me to sign relieving doctors of all blame in this unfortunate event.

As I wrote my signature in a slow daze, the doctor described how he'd open my back from between my shoulder-blades right down to the base of my spine. After hitching back the buttock muscles, he'd cull bone from my pelvis for extra fusion material. The surgeon would then shatter my ten offending vertebrae with hammer and chisel, twisting off any protruding bones like drumsticks off a roast chicken. After jacking up my spine in a new improved line, he'd reset the whole mess with some fancy medical superglue mixed in with the hip-bone chippings. The straightened spine would then be stabilized by a metal Harrington rod hooked into the bone. After unzipping and ripping me, the doctor said he would ask me through the fog of anaesthesia to move my feet. This would determine whether or not I was paralysed.

In preparation for the next day's surgery, I was taken back to the ward and strapped into a traction on my bed. The idea was to loosen up my back so that it wouldn't provide too much resistance to chicken-bone-twisting. I had canvas harnesses around my head and my pelvis, attached to both ends of the bed. My feet were in stirrups. Through a complex pulley system, every time I pushed down with my feet, my head and hips were winched apart in opposite directions. By the time I disentangled myself from the self-induced torture rack, I was fully rubberized.

The next morning I awoke swallowing back excitement and dread. I thought of St Catherine being led to her flaming wheel. The cause was just, but boy was it unfair. An intern popped me with knock-out juice. Giggles deepened to wooze, then to blankness.

The surgery took four hours. It was very bloody – ten pints of red stuff was replaced by the blood I'd donated in advance.

I awoke in intensive care, nauseated from the anaesthetics. As I dipped in and out of haze I was aware of low lights, the hum of equipment. A kidney-shaped plastic bowl cradled my face so I could feebly vomit into it at my convenience.

In the fuzz of drugs and physical trauma, I had one thought. Feet. Must move feet.

They moved. I wasn't paralysed.

A nurse summoned me loudly round to consciousness.

'Kathy! Kathy! Your parents are here! Kathy!'

Yeah, sure, fillet me but don't bother to learn my name.

My mother was at my side. My dad strode into the room with a vigour he didn't feel.

'Hey Kate, you look great!' he bellowed with false heartiness. I had tubes in my mouth, my nose, my arms. Even in my mashed potato state, his attempt at normality sounded ridiculous and heartbreaking. I felt bad worrying my parents. I threw up and drifted away again.

By the next day, the anaesthesia had fully worn off. I was now aware of my spine. Or rather, the tree trunk in my back. Pain with the circumference of a thousand-year-old California redwood radiated fatly through my body.

I was lying on a very narrow bed called a Stryker frame that looked and felt like an ironing board. Someone had slipped little-old-lady support stockings on my legs to ward off blood clots. I was turned every few hours so that I wouldn't get bedsores. In order to pivot me, the orderlies had to strap another ironing board on top. Thus Katie-burgered on bed buns, they'd flip me over. The only thing missing was the flame grill.

When belly-down on the Stryker frame, my face pressed

through a window cut through one end. A mirror had been placed on the floor so I could see who was standing next to me. If I wanted a drink, it was placed on a stool underneath my 'face window' with a long straw to reach up to my lips. One tube moved fluid into my mouth, another passed it out the other end.

This, along with all the other attendant discomforts of major orthopaedic surgery, was intolerable. Until the drugs kicked in.

All the spinning I'd done as a kid couldn't compare to this. Thanks to regular injections of morphine I was tripping, conjuring B fantasies at will. My hallucinations looked like the party scene from *Masque of the Red Death*, with H. R. Pufnstuf and Kimba the White Lion thrown into the mix. Tom and Jerry chased each other non-stop on my ceiling. Other times I drifted high over the earth, still strapped to my Stryker frame. It was a narcotic variation on my youthful angel dreams.

I'd come through the surgery without a hitch, except for one thing. After they took the catheter out, I couldn't pee. The retained urine distended my abdomen. A day went by. Another day went by. My belly was now a piss-filled balloon. The orderlies tried everything to make me let 'er rip: they turned on taps, flushed toilets, poured liquids into glasses in front of me. Nothing worked. Their attempts to be helpful were the most sadistic thing I'd ever endured. I was in a cold sweat: my teeth were grinding, my eyes were rolling back in my head. I was suffering the vicious urgency of having to pee without actually being able to go. My bladder stubbornly refused to give up the goods.

There was nothing for it but to put the catheter back in. Since Walter Reed Army Medical Center was a teaching hospital, an incompetent private was entrusted with the reconnection. He couldn't seem to make head nor tail of my tush, and made a hash out of it. While the twerp butter-fingered the job, I languished in hellfire. Finally, a female nurse was summoned, who re-installed the tube in a jiff.

Thank you little baby Jesus, the yellow waters ran. And ran. And ran. Christ how they ran.

The nurse, the orderly and other staff and trainees stood around the end of my bed, watching a plastic pouch fill up with my piss.

'Willya look at that! Mmm-HM!'

'It's still goin'!'

'That girl be *backed* up!'

The human body is uncanny, but uncouth. Its rude reality meant that in the hospital, humour was earthy, mordant. Things that couldn't be discussed at the dinner table were the bread and butter of hospital entertainment.

Bedpan time was no exception. There was a funny black orderly who'd just stick one arm through my curtained-off corner to spray half a can of air freshener before he came in to remove my bedpan. I'd giggle as he shouted from behind the curtain, 'PeeeeYOU! Lawd, someone CRACK a window on this girl! That is the smell of BEELZEBUB!'

Hospital life stripped dignity, privacy, modesty. The army orderlies were all guys, and all around my age, nineteen. It was weird being so vulnerably helpless before the opposite sex, but the drugs melted my shame. It didn't matter to me – when I was spacing on Demerol and just wanted my ass wiped, I didn't care who did it. My mother said, 'Don't tell your father that the orderlies are boys.'

My dad wasn't going to find out if my bottom-wipers were men, women or giraffes, because after that first day in intensive care, he stayed away. He was too squeamish. My mother and sister continued to visit, though, as did my fluffy friends. Skinny

Fat-X-Sam sis Nancy let me borrow her Walkman, which was the first time I'd experienced this new technology. After sleeping all day, I'd lie awake in the night plugged into Stravinsky and The Associates.

Each day the fat radiating pain in my back got slimmer. It went from a redwood to an oak to a birch to a sapling. I was weaned from morphine to Demerol to codeine, right down to aspirin. But my butt still hurt like a bitch. That was where the surgeon had manually pulled a muscle to access the pelvic bone. I visualized my gluteus maximus sluggishly boinging back into place like a slow-motion rubber band.

The glute-wrenching aside, I was sort of in love with my doctor. He'd taken me apart and put me back together again, baby. It was extraordinarily humbling to feel so indebted to someone else for my health. In fact, I had a soft spot for pretty much anyone who was my carer.

Dave was my carer. The young orderly was a lonely private from Tennessee. He had sandy hair and a soft Appalachian twang. Dave didn't fit in with the other army grunts, who were mostly macho and stupid. He wanted to read new books, hear new music, learn new things. When he wasn't working on my ward, he'd come in just to talk. We started to warm to each other. As the drugs wore off and my delicacy returned, I wanted only Dave to take care of my bedpan duties. He executed them with great gentleness, dabbing me tenderly with the toilet paper. With Dave, I didn't feel embarrassed.

After being rotisseried on the Stryker frame for four days, it was time to get up and walk. For this, I needed a body cast. I was trundled down to the cast room to get tricked out in plaster.

Completely naked except for panties, I had to lie on a two-inch-wide canvas strip suspended between either end of a metal frame. I was required to hook my hands and legs through overhead stirrups to support myself. Three technicians worked fast. First they wrapped me, mummy-style, in cotton gauze. Then they dipped more gauze in hot wet plaster and wound it quickly around my torso. After I was cocooned from armpit to thigh, one last strip of spackled gauze was tied around my middle and cinched in to make a waist. I looked how I felt: like a remedial crafts project.

While I dangled from the overhead stirrups, the technicians snipped the canvas strip and whisked it out the back of the cast. Carrying me like a museum artefact, they carefully moved me to a table while my tortoise shell dried. With a midget power tool, a square window was sawn out over my stomach so that my diaphragm could expand. At the top of the cast, a 'V' was cut out so I wouldn't keep banging my chin on it. *Et voilà* – it was a cavegirl corset with a sweetheart neckline and a TV tummy. I was going to have to wear it for nine months.

The doctors kept chuckling, 'Don't gain any weight – or get pregnant.'

Huh? I'd never considered the restraint imposed by a body cast. I ignored the pregnancy bit, but I was intrigued by the idea of the cast acting as a diet aid – a sort of chastity belt for gluttons. Things were looking up. The surgery had left me taller and thinner. And if fifteen pounds of plaster wasn't a doughnut deterrent, I didn't know what was. So what if it made me look like the Michelin Man?

The top of the cast was covered in moleskin to keep it from chafing my underarms raw. Whenever I sat, the cast hiked up my body, forcing my arms out and my shoulders near my ears. I resembled a Venus High wrestling champ in repose.

But at least with the cast I could now stand. By craning my neck in the mirror, I glimpsed the bright blue nylon cord that stitched my back shut. It was knotted at the top of what would become a seventeen-inch scar.

I spent the next seven days getting used to walking again. The cast *was* heavy. Between the extra weight and my atrophied muscles, I was Humpty Dumpty perpetually on the verge of a great fall.

Eleven days after I'd checked in, I walked out of the hospital. After living through that, I reckoned I could survive anything.

After lying around on the couch at home for a couple of days, I was bored. I was sick of lying around. I decided to go visit Dave. I could wipe my own bottom now, but I still missed him.

I was afraid to drive while I was still clumsy with my new bulk, so I walked in the searing summer heat for half an hour to get to the bus stop. The bus took two hours to get from Virginia to north-east DC, where the army barracks were. Dave was surprised but glad to see me. We spent the day the way we always did, talking. He drove me back to Venus that night. We kissed for the first time in my driveway, his hands cradling my head. It was a bit of me not encased in plaster.

'We can't do this. I've got a boyfriend,' I said, feeling the B-blaze battling Dave-warmth.

'I know, but it feels so good.'

I knew what he meant. It did.

It was the end of an odd plaster-of-Paris near-amour. I felt wistful. Dave's hospital tenderness had been my favourite medicine.

Two and a half weeks after the surgery, I was out dancing in my cast with my friends. Confident now to drive my car, I met the fluffies back down at my old 'drinking and wiggling' headquarters, the 9:30. I did plenty of James Brown-style fancy footwork to compensate for not being able to move my torso.

The big question was, how to hit the youth boîtes without

looking like a funky bathtub? The righteousness of denim saved me: huge-o big man jeans and an oversized flannel checked shirt disguised my orthopaedic predicament with a certain yokel verve. Also, my baggy thrift-shop uniform of men's shirts, slacks and jackets did double duty in rendering me more than just walking pottery. I had my shoulder-length hair braided into cornrows to minimize maintenance. The funny thing was, I didn't look half bad.

Until I turned sideways, that is. Then I was the human cube. One night while walking through Georgetown, a pack of black boys yelled out at me, 'Hey! She got titties on her *back*!'

Even though I was meant to have only one cast for the whole nine months, I managed to sweat through three. It was a typical Washington summer, humid and edging up to a hundred degrees – and I wasn't about to make any concessions for my stitched-up back. Blast the plaster: I was busy movin' and groovin', boppin' and shoppin'. It wasn't long before my cast started to smell like a hamster cage. I'd lie on the floor and slide my hand down the top, up the bottom, in the window, reaching all the skin I could with rubbing alcohol to cool it down. A plastic ruler with raised increments provided the perfect back-scratching tool.

A few months into my portable confinement, my stitches were removed. The pain was shocking. Nobody had warned me. The doctor cut the blue nylon cord in a few places, then yanked it out. Unfortunately, the stitches had grown into my skin. I panted in agony.

B's letters had dwindled down to the occasional postcard from Zagreb or Luxembourg. I was holding on for someone who wasn't there. By this stage, my love was entirely an act of faith. My father put his faith in an invisible god. I put mine in an absent B. It was my Courtney Slusher crush all over again: all give, no get.

I wrote to B:

Longings of the basest kind – that's what my letters reveal. Longings for the bass player, to be more precise. And the desire to keep my head, in case I am spurned. But why do I remain so cautious in that regard? Every word you send me is infused with consideration and affection. I guess I wish there were just more of them.

These really aren't love letters I'm sending to you. In reality they comprise a manuscript, portion by portion, for a novel about a pint-sized whirling dervish in a polka-dot dress. Lots of color. Lots of action. Lots of idealistic notions that pay off. So it's up to you to get it published – as soon as I devise the ending. I think I need to flesh out your character a bit.

Yours yours yours, as ever, FOREVER!!
Love, Katie

My brain was stagnating, as well as my heart. A month after my operation, I was already feeling like an enlisted nun cloistered against her will. I began spending a lot of time in my bedroom with my cat.

June 16, 1982
My bed is beginning to be my favorite place. I'm perfectly healthy but I like to sleep a lot. I daydream and then I fall to sleep and dream some more. I'm not really living in the present. I'm living in the future. The future is when I get a call from B that says, 'Hello, I'm in America'.
Then I'll wake up.

Sept 13
Well I awoke, slowly and reluctantly, not eagerly and joyfully blinking in the strong light of B's love as I had so anticipated. After a spate of postcards in June/July, correspondence from his end stopped abruptly, leading me to acknowledge that I have been phased out of his heart. I don't think about this in any terms of finality, though — even though it's been more than a year since that one glorious night, and love affairs conducted by missives are tenuous at best. I remain confident that, given the opportunity to meet again, the forgetful lad will be re-intoxicated by me. (If the complications, ie excess girlfriends/ boyfriends, continued countries-wide estrangement, etc aren't too manifold and unwieldy.)

Meanwhile, I have distracted myself with summer romances. I feel like I have more masculine attentions thrust upon me now, more than ever, since my operation. I mean, I'm wearing a 15 lb cast, for God's sake! Maybe there's something to be said for the irresistibility of bulk.

That's right, Bionic Woman was picking and choosing her beaux. I wasn't giving up on B, but I wasn't giving up on me, either. Despite my formidable plaster blockade and its gamy hamster niff, I had more boy interest than ever before in my life.

It wasn't easy fooling around in a cast, but that was part of the fun. Working out how to get around it was like solving a Rubik's cube. Despite my diversionary tactics with the locals, though, I missed B. B, I knew, was my kismet.

I wrote to him:

I was so instantly taken with you, then consumed by you — my starving schoolgirl heart ran away with you never intending to come back – and there were times when I wasn't getting feedback from you at all. I have a strong instinct for self-preservation – the preservation of my soul, of my mental health, and I realized I was losing both in my frantic, seemingly futile devotion to you. What emptiness! Another letter in the post, then yet more countless days of the empty mailbox . . . and can't you see that I started to despise myself for letting a ghost of a lover suck all the energy and drive right out of me?? And I'm supposed to be so strong . . .

After months of silence, B's letters started up again. I was ecstatic. He had excuses, he'd been touring, plotting to visit me, he was very sorry – whatever, I didn't care. Just as long as the next chapter of our never-ending story was being written.

Then, just before Christmas, I got a letter that was different from the others. It looked manic – written entirely in capital letters and carelessly singed by a cigarette.

MY DARLING . . .

I AM IN A TERRIBLE STATE – A REAL MESS. MY RECENT MENTAL AWAKENING HAS HAD ME ALMOST THINKING MYSELF OUT OF EXISTENCE – I CANNOT RELAX, I CANNOT SLEEP WITHOUT STUNTING MYSELF WITH HALF A BOTTLE O' SCOTCH OR A HANDFUL OF TRANQUILLIZERS . . . I'M REALLY DEPRESSED, BUT SO FULL OF IDEAS AND POSITIVE ENERGY – IF ONLY I COULD RELAX . . . I'M SCARED . . . SCARED OF DOING SOMETHING REALLY STUPID.

I WANT TO SEE YOU SO MUCH. I'M POSITIVE

THAT YOU'RE THE ONLY PERSON I CAN WORK
THIS OUT WITH.
* I LOVE YOU, LOVE YOU, LOVE YOU, LOVE YOU,*
LOVE YOU, LOVE YOU, LOVE YOU, LOVE YOU –
SAVE ME MY LOVE.
* B*

Perplexed, I showed it to my sister. She said, 'I'd be careful, if I were you.'

She'd recognized that B was in trouble, but the only thing I saw was how much he needed me.

He'd scrawled on the envelope, 'Eternal love and devotion'.

My stucco straitjacket was buzz-sawn off for the last time in January 1983. When the technicians left the cubicle, I sat alone in my hospital gown on a little wooden chair, hugging my newly tiny shape with crossed arms. I hadn't been able to cross my arms for almost a year. To feel myself against myself was wondrous.

Every mundane movement became profoundly sense-laden: lying down and curling into a ball, sitting and feeling my back curve with the chair, standing with my arms hanging flat against my sides. Fresh out of the chrysalis, is this what baby butterflies felt?

Opening my gown, I stood naked in front of the mirror and saw: TITS – whee! A WAIST! HIPS! I had my body back.

I looked at my cast, emptied of me, a shell on the floor. I walked over to pick it up and couldn't believe how heavy it was. I thought about keeping it as a grisly trophy – sort of like an elephant foot umbrella stand. Then I realized I never wanted to see it again.

When I got home, I put Chaka Kahn on the record player

and gonzo-danced around my bedroom. Then I tried on all the clothes in my closet. Then I took them all off and stared at my body some more in the mirror.

B's next letter after the 'SAVE ME' missive came a few weeks after I shed my plaster skin. It was a return to his characteristic mix of amusing anecdotes and ponderings on his burnin' yearnin' for me.

It ended:

Fact: I love thee.
Fact: I need thee.
Fact: We will be together.
Fact: People don't think about sending Xmas presents when they are bed-ridden, puking up their guts due to alcohol poisoning.
Fact: I promise to make it up – in spades . . .
Totally yours for eternity . . .
B

I was so naive. I didn't have the slightest idea what alcohol poisoning was, or how you got it. I thought it might be something like food poisoning – maybe B had drunk something that was 'off'.

Whatever it was, it seemed chronically romantic.

Just like us.

20

True

It is two years since I was nineteen. It is two years since I trusted B with me in a downtown DC hotel. I phoned him last night to quadruple-check that he knew when to meet me today here at Gatwick. We were both excited, laughing, serious, scared.

'I love you, chicken,' B said, 'See you tomorrow.'

He's not here.

The eight-hour flight has wrung me out. My tongue feels like flannel. The adrenalin that has powered my all-night alertness is starting to turn on me. Shimmer spins into jitter.

He's not here.

My guts knot. A fear-stink rises over my skin.

He's not here – what do I do? I'm completely alone. I don't know anyone in England. I can't even work the phones at the airport. They look like slot machines. And the British coins come in about fifteen different sizes. Once you figure out the right one to use, you can't just push it in the slot machine and make your call. No, first you have to dial the number and wait for 'the pips', it says on the instructions. Number one, why is a public phone so complicated that it needs instructions; and number two, what the fuck are 'the pips' when they're not dancing behind Gladys Knight?

In a smog of panic and pips, I finally speak to B's mother. It's sort of hard to understand her – she has an Irish accent. She says he's on his way. I begin to breathe again.

B is an hour late.

It's B! Is that B? He's wearing jeans, not Bowie trousers. His hair is longer. It's Krazy Kolored fuchsia, and so are his hands. It *is* B. It's my rose-tinted B.

It's too real. I'm used to unreal. For two years, it hasn't been real.

No words. We fall together and kiss. Our kiss is deceptive: bigger on the inside than it looks on the outside. It has to be – it holds the DNA for us-ness. It holds two years of hope, loneliness, enchantment, despair, passion, obsession and wanting wanting wanting.

It holds our hearts.

We kiss in the middle of Gatwick Airport for forty-five minutes.

We finish at the same time.

B puts my hand in his mouth and drags me like a happy dog towards the London train. He buys the tickets and tells me why he was late.

'Sorry baby – I was so nervous about seeing you that I couldn't sleep last night, so I dyed my hair to give me something to do. And when I *did* fall asleep, I missed the alarm.'

I hold his pink hand and stroke his pink hair.

We arrive at a flat that belongs to the singer in his band. We go into the bedroom and lock the door.

Eventually, we have to come out. I only have five weeks in London, so clearly we can't spend the *whole* time in bed.

We make the most efficient use of our slender time by combining sex with sightseeing.

We're having sex everywhere: daytime in the maze at Hampton Court; night-time on the playground swings next to Lambeth Bridge; any time in the compartments and toilets of British Rail trains. We do the town.

And when we're not shtupping, we want to. An old man at a pub sees us smouldering at each other over the pint glasses. He walks by, laughing.

'Just watching you two is bad for my heart!'

The iconology of London is revealed on wheels: black taxis, red double-deckers. The kingdom-y skyline, crenellated by Big Ben and his friends, is picture-postcard perfect.

At Camden Palace, I spot my first pop star: Billy Mackenzie from The Associates. He'd crooned in my Walkmanned ear through long hospital nights. He looks small and smiley, like Gene Kelly in *An American in Paris*.

B takes me to a new club called the Batcave. It's off Carnaby Street, where I'd walked with my family eleven years earlier. The orange and yellow pavement is gone, but the Batcave dwellers don't mind. The purple-lipped goths look good 'n' undead, like Siouxsie squared to the nth. They're serious about this grim reaper routine.

In the days, the English summer air is light and polite, not like the wet doggy heat I'm used to back home. B and I dance out into the daisies and down to Brighton. He told me there'd be pebbles on the beach, but he didn't specifically say there wouldn't be any sand at all. That's why I'm surprised to see only rocks. Even though it's July, the water is freezing. Soft pale families with sun-blistered backs determinedly wade into the frosty waves. Phrases like 'stiff upper lip' and 'spirit of Dunkirk' enter my mind. I discard them for the phrase that fits: 'desperate'.

Continuing the national theme of pain as entertainment, B buys me a stick of 'Brighton Rock'. I gnaw on it a little, but it hurts my teeth. They sure love their rocks at the seaside here. The sweet's like a Christmas candy cane, but with more colours and less flavour. The word 'Brighton' spirals down the centre of the stick. I'm impressed with British candy technology.

There's more unexplained phenomena along the row of seafront shops: 'spastic' statues. Why? They're always of a little girl with a neat page-boy and a discreet brace on one leg, or of a small blond boy with an Air Force Academy haircut and a crutch. The effigies are about three feet high and include a puppy or a kitten. I can't believe the bad taste – 'Spastic' is what American kids hurl as abuse when they're not screaming 'Retard!' To add to my confusion, the statue never depicts anyone with cerebral palsy, or even acting remotely spazzy. Under the circumstances, the word 'SPASTICS' splashed in red across the front of the donation box seems a tad harsh.

I can't believe I'm the only one on the street standing in front of these figurines, laughing, pointing, taking pictures. And I don't understand why, by the time I turn around to B, he's halfway down the boardwalk.

Back in London, I'm struck by establishments that advertise the availability of air-conditioning and ice. Hey guys – WW2 is over! And roaming the cutely named 'Boots' drug store, I find underarm deodorants that come in 'fragrances' such as 'pink', 'blue' and 'soft green'. How Salvador Dali can you get? I take a moment to try and imagine a blue smell. Theirs doesn't match mine.

I'm intrigued by what appears to be the national leisure pursuit – public vomiting. I've never seen such a prolific dappling of urp splats on pavements. They are numerous and consistent enough to be considered traditional folk art. This organic expression of the inner Brit can usually be found congealing outside pubs, with optional up-the-wall splash detailing. And if one is unlucky enough to have missed the exhibit on opening night, the work conveniently metamorphoses into something longer-lasting. The resulting phantom barf puddles are reminiscent of the 'nuclear shadows' left behind by victims of the H-bomb.

I hang out at Air Studios while B's band finishes off the album that will subsequently finish them off. I'm amazed to see Heaven 17 and Haircut 100 playing pool in the bar. It is unimaginably glamorous to see so many pop stars up close. After they leave, I sneak into Haircut 100's studio to go beat crazy on Nick Heyward's bongos.

B discovers that I can sing. I already know this about myself. One morning in the bath, I'm R&B-ing 'B-A-B-Y', enjoying the acoustics. B is overwhelmed: 'Hey, you can *really* sing.' In the space of my five weeks, he writes two songs for me and gets the record company to pay for studio time. As we're finishing up the second song, Batcave regulars Sex Gang Children straggle in to do their recording. We exchange pleasantries. I feel so rock 'n' roll.

It doesn't register as extreme that B nearly always carries a four-pack of beer with him. He's a Tennent's Special enthusiast. The purple cans pile up under our bed.

I had resolved two years back that B and I were going to be perfect no matter what.

The hand covering my eyes is my own.

21

The Night They Drove Old Dixie Down

I could dance again.

In the eight months since being released from my cast, I'd been finding out what my new spine could and couldn't do. Miraculously, what it could do was enough to call myself a dancer. For this, I lived every day in eternal gratitude to Jesus H. Christ and his all-girl backing band Mother Nature and the Fates. Even the doctors were impressed with how I'd reclaimed my chops. I'd taken their feeble toe-touching forecast and upped the ante to all-out dervish delirium. OK, so I wasn't as bendy as I used to be, but I could still leap and twirl to beat a barrel of ballerinas.

I could dance again! This glory was oddly underscored by the mournful wail of the Dixieline train. Its lonesome moan just about broke my heart every time I heard it. I had moved to Richmond, Virginia, the feisty two-hundred-and-fifty-year-old ex-belle of the state which in prettier days had been the capital of the old South. It was the first time I'd ever lived away from my parents. The timing was right: after my woman-of-the-world turn in London, my little pink bedroom back home was just too little, pink and back home.

It was September, but nobody had bothered to tell the head-peckin', redneckin' summer sun, which blazed long into the fall. Barely back from my epic reunion with B, I had half-heartedly begun a three-year Bachelor of Fine Arts programme at Virginia Commonwealth University.

I'd signed up for VCU before I'd gone to England, just in case the B deal was a disaster. After the summer's cataclysm of love, however, college was recast as an afterthought. Twenty-one and luminous with new belief in B, I felt justified wallowing in romantic anguish now that we were again apart. This was where the dolorous twilight cry of the train came in handy.

The BFA degree meant that I got to take a lot of dance classes. At VCU, I reinvented myself as a modern dancer schooled in Graham and Cunningham. Unlike ballet, these contemporary techniques allowed for individual quirks and jerks. And the twentieth-century moves were a better match for my athletic build and attack.

Every day I cycled to class past the Mosque Theatre, a Hollywoodified pile of minarets. When Elvis Presley played there in '56, he'd stopped the town's clocks for ever. Post-Elvis, Richmond was a fly in time's spider web. The place was a retro wet dream. Pearl's Coffee Shop had dark wooden booths and individual jukeboxes playing country music. The bar in the pool hall was lit by giant glass pool balls hanging from the ceiling. And there was a big ol' fifties Krispy Kreme a-ways down the highway, shining its Original Glazed glow on my soul. A TV movie about the Kennedy assassination was being filmed in downtown Richmond. 1983 Broad Street looked more like 1963 Dallas than Dallas ever would again.

I lived in Oregon Hill at the end of South Laurel Street, the end furthest from the James River. The closer you got to the river, the closer Oregon Hill got to you, till it was breathing right down your neck.

The neighbourhood was cracker-poor, its streets lined by ramshackle rows of clapboard houses. Every single family sat out the swampy heat on their tumbledown porches, lollygagging the day away in slow rocking chairs. To my city-slicked eyes, the denizens of Oregon Hill looked like a cross between *Deliverance* and *Dawn of the Dead*.

At all times, the Hill had an atmosphere of barely suppressed violence. A sinister silence smothered me whenever I walked down South Laurel towards the James. As I passed the last dull-coloured hull of a home, I could feel a streetful of eyes boring into my back. With one look they could paste a stranger like a BB shot picks off a possum. I could relax when the stock-car races were shown on local TV, because then the zombies turned their porch rocking chairs to face inwards towards their living-room televisions.

At the river end of the road was a honky-tonk called Mudbugs. The bar was a low cement block painted brown, crowded by a steady stream of leather-bellied rowdies. I was too chicken even to take a peek inside.

The river itself was a wide sluggish whirl studded by rocks and an aborted bridge that had changed its mind halfway across the water. Little kids dangled off the bridge's rusting lip, midstream, flaunting their limited gene pool along with their derring-do.

I'd rented, for peanuts, a two-storey maroon brick house with peppermint-green trim. The house was next door to a converted storefront that used to be a café and cake shop. Still overlooking my veranda was a weathered sign reading: MEALS – Eat In or Take Out. PASTRIES. Rolls. Bread. Ice Cream – Ice Burgs. Banana Splits – Sweets.

The family who lived in the ex-cake shop were anything but sweet. Abundant in number and Southern of moniker, they had names like Jeb, Lurleen and Arla Fern. The mother was a swollen muu-muu of a woman, a bloated behemoth who fiercely defended her brood from any neighbourhood trouble.

One time, muu-muu Lulu banged the tarnation out of my door to scream at me about some invented slight against one of her litter.

'Did you tell my Valda Lou she looked like a pig?'

I hadn't, but I couldn't have put it better than that. Valda Lou and a couple of her siblings hid behind their monolithic mom, poking their snouts through her folds of fabric and flesh. I shook my head and shut the door.

The savage matriarch/myriad young 'uns dynamic was mirrored in the family's mongrel hound dog Chevy, who bared her teeth at me whenever I was within twenty yards of her pups.

Apart from the mother, one person in particular stood out from the cake-shop clan. This was Dirtwoman. He was the oldest son.

Dirtwoman was a simple-minded transvestite who earned his keep sweeping out the nearby porn cinema. A chubby man in his late thirties, Dirtwoman had a desire for frills but no eye for style. I'd see him trudging lumpily home from the Gaiety XXX in his overalls, and then an hour later trudging lumpily back out in what looked suspiciously like one of his mother's muu-muus.

I had to hand it to Mama – she was just as casual as casual can be about her colourful first-born. When grits were on the table, she'd step out to the porch and bawl, 'Jeb! Arla Fern! Virgil! Dirtwoman! Lurleen! Dreama! Valda Lou! Soup's on!' like her half-witted cross-dressing kid was just as normal as the others. But then again, context is everything.

It surprised me to discover that Richmond had a flourishing

drag queen scene. Tranny prostitutes pranced nightly in front of the Richmond Ballet School just around the corner from my house. But what really seemed queer was the tolerant coexistence of good ol' boys and good ol' lady-boys.

Oregon Hill was the Hell's Angels' beat. The bikers all lived in a condemned house across the street from mine. Applying time-honoured American ingenuity, they'd replaced the front steps of their home sweet home with a ramp. This allowed them to roar their motorcycles straight into the front parlour – no fussin'.

When they weren't turning their house into the Rolling Thunder Run, the Hell's Angels lolled around on their porch drinking beer, just like everybody else. Just like everybody else, that is, except me. I was different, and Oregon Hill knew it.

In between belching and growing beards, the Hell's Angels gave me the fish-eye. With my sissy front steps and my raspberry hair, I was clearly an outsider. Even though I'd hardly spoken a word to them or anyone else on the street, the Hill decided it hated me.

One day I was in my bedroom, writing a letter to B, when suddenly I heard THUNK! against my front door. Then another THUNK! Then a volley of THUNKS! slammed against the house. Alarmed, I crept to an upstairs window and slid a glimpse down to the street. Fifteen or twenty young teenagers were milling in the road. Looking closer, I saw that they were all holding rocks and half-bricks. One boy wound up a pitch, and THUNK! another brick smashed against my door.

A mob was stoning my house! I was flabbergasted. I held my breath, trying to hear what they were saying. Through the rabid gabble of voices I made out, 'PUNK ROCK . . . RED HAIR . . . SHE'S A PUNKER . . .'

After that, the stoning of the House of Punk Rock became a regular Oregon Hill event.

Even the neighbourhood dogs ganged up on me. One night I awoke to strange noises coming from the veranda: yips and yelps and guttural snufflings. *Now what?* I thought, tiptoeing to look through the shutters.

A strange canine posse sprawled over my porch. Bathed in quiet late moonlight were dogs big and small, tawny and scrawny, scruffy and stocky. They were all just . . . hanging out. Every now and again one of the mutts let off a howl.

This place had it all: delinquent dogs, teenybop mobs, zombie porch rockers, Mudbug brawlers, riverbed inbreds, biker deadheads, cake-shop mongrels, muu-muu mamas . . . and Dirtwoman. And despite the formidable competition, *I* had emerged as the weirdo of Oregon Hill.

B's letters flew to my maroon and peppermint pad almost daily, and my output was just as abundant. The plan was for me to return to London pronto so that the magic could continue. Love would be subsidized by our looming pop music career. B's letters were pages of passion whipped with football coach-style gameplans for our musical future. He outlined strategies for fleecing the record industry by utilizing our combined talents. Inspired by the potential marketability of a little redheaded gal from ol' Virginny with a voice as big as the Blue Ridge Mountains, he wrote and recorded songs, sending demo tapes over for me to write the lyrics. He exhorted me to come up with band names, angles, video ideas. B was cynical about the music business and not particularly interested in artistic fulfilment. He wanted to hit the ground running with commercial demos that would snag us an immediate deal. B figured that after the hit singles and the funny money, *then* we could afford to indulge our inner artsy-fartsy. He wrote to me: 'I don't want to spend six months trying to get a deal.'

On paper and over the phone, we marvelled at the haphazard circumstances that had brought us together. The distance and improbability that were the hallmarks of our affair intensified the already torrid charge of our lava love.

Every aspect of our saga was transcendent: the way we'd met, the years apart, our decision to make music, our belief that we'd rewritten the book of love. The language of our letters was florid and emotional.

I'd start out playful: 'Lambchop – how do I dig thee? Let me groove the ways: you make the kitty litter fresher, the coffee a little stronger.' By the end I'd have spun into exultations:

You have brought out in me that which has never existed before. I am laid open for you – just gather all of me up to you and love me for all eternity. I am yours – I am begun in you – we go on forever.

I treasured B's equally fevered sentiments:

I am a man who is pretty much in control of his destiny – I am never stumped for direction or decision in my life. But I ask myself this: WHAT WOULD I DO IF I LOST YOU? I really don't know.

THINK, angel – if we are smart about our dual futures, we could travel the world together, sit together on planes, laugh at funny foreigners, check into the same hotel room every night, be guests of honour at the only disco in Cairo, be late for everything, have food-fights in the world's best restaurants and complain loudly – we could really PLAY – we would have FUN FUN FUN . . .

Baby, we ARE going to have fun! We will have so much fun for a while, and you may get sick of me one day and leave me. But I promise you this – whatever time we have together will be the best years of our lives.

Then, obviously thinking the last bit sounded downbeat and too much like real life, B hastily included an overriding clause written tiny and upside-down in the corner of the page:

. . . But, you will fall in love with me forever and marry me and have lots of funny kids that we will eventually hate, but you'll still want me and I you, forever.

Once when B tried to reach me during a weekend visit at my parents' up in Venus, he experienced my father's anti-boyfriend technique first hand. He wrote:

I called you yesterday at home, but you were out. Pop answered, administering his characteristically bubbling line in conversation.
  'Er, hello, is Katie there?'
  'Nope!'
  'Oh, er, well – could you tell her that I called?'
  'OK!'
  'Goodbye, then . . .' CLICK!
  He doesn't exactly waffle, your dad. No wonder he was a colonel – if he were ever captured and interrogated, all they'd get is, 'Nope. OK. Nope. OK.'

My father had relayed the message to me in his usual manner: 'Some Limey called for you. He sounds like a frooty-tooty.'
  'Thanks, but he's not a Limey – he's Irish,' I'd answered.

'Even worse.'

Case closed.

My father and mother had been trying to ignore away the high-wattage adoration I'd been beaming out to B for the last two years. Maybe they thought it would just splutter out. With regard to boys, their policy was 'Don't ask, don't tell'. But I longed for them to ask, I was desperate to tell. The only other serious boyfriend in my life had been Chris Azalea – and that was back when I was a little kid. Now when I sugar-plum-fairy'd into the living room waving the latest B letter in the air, I hoped my mother would say, 'Tell me all about it.' Instead, she said nothing.

'I'm in love!' I'd sung out once, rhapsodic at B's first letter. My mother had tsked dismissively and said with a little laugh, 'Oh, you're not in *love*.' Then she changed the subject. I guessed correctly that my father's attention span for the subject would be even more limited. From that time on, I understood that vagueness in these matters was appreciated by my folks. Bearing this in mind, I hadn't gone into great detail about my trip to London.

However, I had let slip enough for my parents to know that I was planning to return to B's land of Dali deodorants and spastic statues. My mother was disappointed that I didn't want to continue with the university. My father, surprisingly, was easy going.

'Do whatever makes you happy, Kate,' he told me. 'If you find out what that is, you're lucky. I was never that lucky, myself.'

Meanwhile, I was still attending most of my classes at VCU. What with my Oregon Hill capers and general B-o-rama, I was not the most focused of students. One dance improvisation class in particular annoyed me. I hated it every time the teacher, a Martha Graham-esque octogenarian, said, 'Relaaaax ... your a-a-a-anussssss.' That comment always pursed my a-a-a-anussssss into a tight little asterisk. One day she set an exercise in which we were encouraged to relate to the window, the walls, the floor. I related to the door and never came back.

My anus and I were just going though the motions, because I knew I was promised to England. The breathing space away from B proved to me that the only space I wanted to breathe was his. The semester was three months long, so I bided my time, doing dance classes and driving back to Venus on the weekends.

While up north, I made fluffy refuelling stops in DC. I relived UK tales with big Fat-X-Sam sister Francie, who had come to London with Steve during my summer reunion with B. It had felt so cosmopolitan to meet my playmates in another city, another country. As the four of us convened in strange new places, I'd felt absurdly fortunate to be able to share my B joy with my cherished friends.

Steve liked England so much that he hadn't come back. When he wrote to me that he'd decided to live there, I was thrilled. Having the fluffy supreme installed in my next new country would make my London dream complete.

I regularly made hour-and-a-half transatlantic phone calls to B, sometimes twice a day. One jumbo yak session lasted two and a half hours. It never really occurred to me that at some point I'd actually have to pay for them. When the bill turned up, I turned white. In one month I'd racked up over eight hundred dollars' worth of calls.

As the bills mounted, I entered a near-constant state of anxiety and panic. I resorted to my old bad habit of self-induced sugar comas to blot out my woes. I jacked up my doughnut jones with frequent runs to the local Krispy Kreme. Once there, the sweet smack of a dirty dozen mellowed the pre-B purgatory of boredom and depression.

I sent a postcard to Steve in England:

November 1983
Dear Steve,

Hark – what is this? After a brief period when I thought tension was over came this: one slashed tyre; another huge phone bill (bigger than a dinosaur and uglier too); a dance performance filled with tension because of phone bill worries; a return to my parked car after second performance feeling elated, only to find spare tyre now flat; panic because I need the car to get a job (where?) to pay for aforementioned phone bill; money not forthcoming from parents who of course know nothing of phone faux pas; and finally and most impressively – a horrible car accident with Francie while coming back from NYC. THANK GOD we were not seriously hurt – her car is TOTALLED. More later.

Love, Katie

The big aqua boat was splattsville, daddy-o. Sweet round Francie had been cruisin' in the '62 Malibu with me riding shotgun. Back from a Gotham frolic, we were a few miles outside DC when it happened. I'd been sleeping in the back seat when my doughnut ESP was activated. I sat up groggily to scan the landscape, and sure enough, the jaunty marching Ks of the Krispy Kreme sign beckoned on the horizon. Pointing towards the windscreen, I shouted, 'DOUGHNUTS!' Francie screamed and slammed on the brakes. Even though I lived for Krispy Kreme, I thought her reaction was somewhat excessive.

In the next instant, we ploughed into the back of the car in front of us. I was relieved to learn that a three-car pile-up, not my doughnut squawk, had been to blame for the crash.

I'd only been in Richmond for two months, and it'd been the most stressful fun I'd ever had. My short time there was further curtailed by my ginormous phone bills. Two weeks before the term was over, I had to quit school in order to get a typing job to pay for them.

In December, I drove down to Richmond one last time to pick up the final load of my belongings from South Laurel Street. Francie and Steve, who was back from England for Christmas, came along to witness my Oregon Hill exodus. Also in the witness box were my Hell's Angels buddies, glowering as usual from their be-ramped veranda across the street from my house. Balefully, they watched us wrestle my mattress across the peppermint porch, down to the curb and up on the roof of my dad's station wagon. This innocuous task riled the bikers more than seemed strictly necessary. Growling angrily, the whole stoopful of beards and broads merged into one belching ball of hostility. You'd think they would have been happy to see me leaving.

As Steve, Francie and I were tying the mattress to the roof of the car, we heard CLANK! Steve turned his head, and a beer can whistled past his nose. CLANK! number two. It hit the car, then rolled over to the first can in the gutter. A trickle of beer dribbled out of one end.

'ERRRRRRAAUUGGHHHHH!'

The biker's belch sounded like a bullfrog with a bullhorn. His eructation rumbled its battle cry all over Oregon Hill. As the gaseous call to arms faded into the distance, my friends and I finished tying the rope with jittery fingers.

There was movement on the Angels' ramp. Fifteen or so big

hairy shapes lurched slowly forward from the house, uncertain off their hogs. Gruff utterances erupted from mountains of denim, leather and lard.

'BA-NA-NA!'

I beg your pardon?

'BA-NA-NA! BA-NA-NA!'

Steve, Francie and I exchanged puzzled glances. Then looking down, I saw the colour of my coat and understood. I was wearing a swingy vintage A-line in bright yellow.

'BA-NA-NA!'

The Hell's cretins' primitive brains had made a connection between yellow and bananas.

SPLAT!

An egg glooped down the windscreen of the station wagon.

They'd also made a connection between yellow and yolks.

Abruptly, a salvo of eggs and empties hailed down on us. We shoved my bicycle into the back of the car as the bikers advanced.

'BA-NA-NA! BA-NA-NA!'

Now throwing their half-drunk beer cans, the hubbub of blubber lumbered closer and closer.

Slamming the back hatch shut, the three of us jumped in the car and locked the doors. I fired up the wagon and floored it, executing a hasty hairpin right in front of the ugly clump of Hell's Angels. As we peeled out of South Laurel, Steve rolled down his window to shout a farewell to our friends.

'BYE, MOUNTAIN PEOPLE!'

I watched Oregon Hill dwindle to dust in my rear-view mirror.

22

Blue Monday

I was all of a doodah about my latest far-fetched crusade. The strategy for my next British invasion was set. I'd do office work for a couple of months, pile up the clams, then move to London at the end of February.

On the day after Christmas, I had already phoned B twice to rejoice over my early New Year's resolution.

On the day after Christmas, I was unaware that my mother was lying in the room next to mine, on her way to dying.

I'd last seen her up late Christmas Eve, feverishly finishing off the cloth dolls she'd been sewing for presents. She finally went to bed around 3 a.m., feeling fluey. Then she missed Christmas.

December 27, 1983 – 5:00 a.m.
Dearest B,

The unthinkable has almost happened. Even at this point I'm not really sure what is going on. When I called you (for the third time) last night, it was a different kind of shock than the happy one of my coming to London.

My mother is terribly, horribly sick. And the horrible part is that we almost let her slip by without even doing anything.

For all of Christmas Day she was holed up in her room, curled up in bed.

'When is Grandma coming down?' my niece kept asking.

'Leave her alone, she doesn't feel well,' we admonished. And I'm sorry to say that I 'respected' her illness and didn't really check up on her. Then yesterday morning I poked my head in her door and asked if she wanted anything.

She was having a lot of trouble breathing with her sinuses and nose all stuffed up (her face had been aching from the pressure, she'd told me) and she said, 'A lovely . . . cool . . . milkshake.'

She hadn't eaten anything the day before and this was the only thing she'd had yesterday. But that was the last thing she said to me, and as the day wore on, all she could do was moan a little when I asked her, 'What's wrong? What's wrong?'

All I knew was that she was in extreme distress, possibly because of a recurring attack of sinus polyps, and she had a cold to make it worse and couldn't breathe.

But last night it really dawned on me that something needed to be done, urgently. Streams of blood were coming out of her nose, she was mute, her face was swollen, and she was burning to the touch. My father wasn't home and I was panicking.

When he arrived, I told him my observations and he said he'd been trying to get her to go to the hospital, but she'd always said no. But he resolved then to take her, and I got her stuff together.

She was very weak after not eating or drinking for two days, and we weren't going to be able to move her safely by ourselves, so my father called an ambulance. I was rubbing her arm and she grasped my hand and looked at me so hard, so fearfully – like she was trying to memorize my face – she wouldn't let my hand go.

That's when I called you.

An ambulance and rescue squad came; five men tromped up the stairs and into her room. They placed an oxygen mask on her face and practically barked in her ear to get a verbal response.

I remember thinking, 'This is humiliating for her – she's perfectly cognizant, but she just can't speak.'

I also thought their noisy presence was making her feel worse. I held her in a sitting position as they took her blood pressure, and she tried, feebly, to push them away and lie down.

Their walkie-talkies were crackling noisily and they talked into them: 'We have a sixty-year-old female – she's combative . . .'

So impersonal – that's my MOTHER, you idiots, she just hurts, she's hardly 'combative' – you can't say that in front of my mother . . .

I rode in the ambulance to the hospital . . . strange sense of power as cars moved over for us, and tears whenever the siren came on.

That siren's for us . . . Mommy . . . my poor sick Mommy . . .

Doctors examined her and told us she has pneumonia in both lungs and it's already entered the bloodstream. This has triggered another condition resulting in her 'altered mental state'. She also has meningitis. She was seriously dehydrated with a temperature of 104.6.

She's in intensive care now on IV feeding and antibiotics. Of course, my father's damning himself for not bringing her yesterday even though she insisted, 'No'.

Last night at 9 p.m. the doctors said she was in a 'life-threatening situation', and the turning point would be in the next six or eight hours.

It is now 5:30 in the morning, and he hasn't called, so I pray that this means she has stabilized.

If my mother weren't here – it completely transcends the realm of comprehension. I am breaking down in tears every other second, which is silly because she's in good hands now – but you can't help but think 'What if?'

More later. I love you.

Katie

Pneumonia and meningitis were merely the vicious entourage travelling with the VIP: cancer.

January 12, 1984
Dearest B,

My family and I went to the hospital yesterday for a conference with my mother and her doctor. The doctor said my mother definitely has a tumor, a rare cancer that only about two hundred people in the US have. It is situated mostly in the right sinus, with some in the sinus above the eye. Their fear is that it has already invaded the brain, but they won't be able to determine this until they actually operate.

The situation is grave, the operation is dangerous. It will take about fifteen hours. She could lose her right eye if the tumor is interfering with those nerves. After the surgery they will begin radiotherapy to arrest further growth of cancer too microscopic to remove surgically.

Lately she is feeling new effects – extreme fatigue – she wants to sleep all the time – and the doctor says this is possibly from the tumor pressing on the brain. She has ordered my mother to walk more and eat more. My mom is too weak even to lift the pop-top on her can of diet supplement.

She never knows when someone's going to come by and sweep her off to an appointment, and the appointments exhaust her. They left her in an X-ray waiting room for four hours the other day – until she was crying and begging to be taken back to her ward – they just forgot her. She's in a new ward now – maybe things will be better.

She will have the surgery in about a week, followed by two to three months of radiotherapy.

Our house is strange and empty. The living room is dark – where she always sat in the corner of the couch, sewing, knitting, needlepointing, making dolls, any one of a hundred things. Her absence is eerie.

When we saw each other yesterday (the first time in a week and a half) we were drinking each other in with our eyes – it seemed so long since we'd seen each other. At home, we're together constantly. She introduced me to the nurse as 'My sweet Katie' . . .

I have to stop now. If I think too much I cry . . . and cry . . .

Love, Katie

Three teams of surgeons working over a day and into the night saved my mother's life. Miraculously, the cancer had not spread to her brain. But as it was clawed from her skull, the disease wreaked its revenge. The cancer took with it most of the cartilage from the right side of her face, as well as the sight in one eye. The neurosurgeons had removed the tumour out through an escape hatch cut in the roof of her mouth. Finding this new peephole convenient for examinations, the doctors decided not to close it back up with plastic surgery. My mother suffered for this convenience: her face ached with constant cold from the perpetual wind tunnel in her head. But however much the surgery had ridden roughshod over her face, it *had* saved her life.

The tumour was a terrorist, infiltrating, moving in stealth, exacting a ravaging toll. And no known group was admitting responsibility – my mother's rare cancer was untraceable. Trying to fight the enemy within by stabs in the dark, the doctors asked her a series of bizarrely specific questions, including: 'Have you ever worked in a furniture factory?' They didn't ask, 'Have you ever lived in a US embassy bombarded by Russian microwaves?' Maybe it wasn't on their list.

The day before I left America for England, I visited my mother in the hospital. She'd visited me in the same hospital two years before. Despite the severity of her condition, my mother had stabilized and would soon be going back home. Filled with love and fear and shame, I walked softly into her darkened room. My mom was propped up on her hospital bed. One eye was unmoored and roamed alarmingly. There were depressions on either side of her head at both temples, lacunas left as reminders of a face that had been surgically opened like a book.

Leaving her so frail was a sickening wrench and I felt guilty. She knew this and was being very brave for me, despite her own sadness and crippling pain.

'Mom, I feel terrible leaving you now.'

'Honey, you go. Daddy's taking good care of me.'

'Oh Mom, I'll miss you . . .'

'I'll miss you too, kitty-cat.'

I hugged her carefully, trying not to hurt her more than she already was.

'I love you, Mom.'

'Oh Katie – I love *you*!'

When it was time, she released me from our clasp.

This generosity was my mother's biggest gift to me.

23

This Charming Man

This time B wasn't late when he met me at the airport. He was on time and adorable, hiding mock timidly behind a potted plant when I came out from customs. I dissolved into his arms and felt like the Waffle King sign: 'There's no place like this place, so this must be the place!'

To begin with, the place was Wimbledon, with B's family. His Irish parents, very gentle, very loving, made me feel welcome in their cosy rowhouse. The kitchen was the nerve centre, the terminus for all comings and goings. The radio next to the sink was never turned off. I listened to Radio One, trying to define my time by pop groups that wouldn't make sense anywhere else in the world: Bucks Fizz, Cliff Richard, The Wombles. Sade's 'Your Love is King' and The Smiths' 'This Charming Man' soundtracked my return to London.

Kitchen smells of buttered toast, stewed tea and the fancifully named Fairy Liquid combined into London eau de home. I couldn't get over that the Fairy stuff, which turned out to be dishwashing detergent, was called 'washing-up liquid'. It was such a whatchamacallit term, as if the elves at Fairy headquarters had been fumbling around for the right name but couldn't quite think of it: 'Ummmm, OK – we've got some green soapy junk – uh, liquid – that you use when you need to ... you know, thingy – oh what *is* it called – wash dirty dishes ... *you* know ... up. Sort of like 'liquid-for-washing-dishes-up' – oh, forget it! Let's meet back at the woodland clearing tomorrow and discuss it further. Notify the squirrels and the bunnies – maybe *they* can come up with something.'

Still on a first-date basis with my new country, I scouted the kitchen for clues as to what Britain was like when she wasn't trying to impress anyone. Through food, I built up a picture of a people.

The English edibles I encountered possessed generic brand names of the broadest possible classification: Salad Cream (which I remembered from my seventies Wimpy experience), Luncheon Meat, Sandwich Spread, Cheese Spread, and that heartburn in a bottle, Brown Sauce. They all sounded like toy food for a doll's house.

Other food was defined by the sound it made when you bit into it. Peas were mushy, potato chips were crisps. Equally onomatopoeic were the candy bars: I expected to see 'Squelchy' or 'Goosh' lurking alongside Crunchie and Wispa.

The British habit of storing their Crunchies, Squelchys and other chocolate in the refrigerator was unfathomable to me. What about the sensuality of eating it due to the fact that chocolate melts in the mouth at body temperature? Freezing it down to brittle bone cold removed it from the sexy snack category, as well as from the realm of any flavour. Then I remembered the stick of rock I'd tried to eat in Brighton the summer before. These Anglo-Saxons and Celts were plainly rugged tribes who didn't like their pleasures too easy.

Before long, I discovered that there was a great US/UK

divide on cookies. Americans liked theirs moist, chewy, gooey. Here, they were dry and crisp. And to distance themselves further from the cookies I knew, they were called 'biscuits'. 'Digestives' were one such biscuit. The name raised vexing questions – *who* was doing the digesting around here, if not me? It conjured up vivid scenes of a mother bird regurgitating predigested worms into her baby birds' gaping beaks. Still, they tasted all right, so I tried to block out any predigestion speculation.

As always, I endeavoured to keep an open mind about new experiences, but even I was stumped by such Dark Ages fare as Scotch eggs, tripe and black pudding – gore-filled guts, anyone? And I'd never endured so many sultanas and hazelnuts in all my born days. Sultanas and hazelnuts were in everything, and ruined everything.

All the toy food, tenth-century treats and cold, noisy chocolate could be knocked back with an array of unusual beverages. Tizer, Irn Bru, and Dandelion and Burdock were highly evolved soda pops that didn't feel the need to reflect anything actually found in nature. Less highly evolved was squash, the brightly coloured syrup in a bottle that needed added water to make it potable. Was wartime rationing still in effect, or what?

B's family kitchen was my cultural classroom. Lessons continued when his friends came over to visit. I offered my hand to shake upon initial introductions and they all looked at me, nonplussed. And when they did take my hand, they did so jokily, as if shaking hands was a peculiar formality. I gathered this was one practice not customary in Blighty.

It was my turn to be nonplussed when they'd greet, 'All right?' I'd politely respond, 'Fine, thank you,' until their continued laughter taught me that this British *Ça va?* was a salutation, not a question.

As the kitchen filled up with B's mates, tea, sweeties and ciggies would be offered all around. Gracious gestures left over from the war, perhaps? For Pete's sake, I couldn't get this whole Festival of Britain notion out of my head. I must have seen too many old movies about blackouts and land girls. Anyway, plucky spirit of the Blitz or not, these casual courtesies contrasted agreeably with the 'looking out for Number One' stance back home. In the States, they'd rather loan you the money to buy your own pack than give you a stick of their gum.

As the boys hunkered down over their mugs of milky PG Tips, one or two would produce the agriculture necessary for rolling their own cigarettes. When I first saw them getting out the skins, I was surprised when they didn't build a spliff. I mean, they did those too, but as an American, non-pot manual smokes were new to me. I watched them sprinkle loose tobacco out of a tiny tinfoil-wrapped brick on to the rolling paper, then coax the components into a skinny cigarette with their finger-tips. All that trouble just to manoeuvre a pinch of nicotine to their lips – roll-ups were like the chopsticks version of ciga-rettes.

As B and his friends assembled and smoked their roll-ups, romantic wartime deprivation again reared its mythic head in mine. Accordingly, the Odeon of my brain flickered up footage of heroic Limeys staving off Jerry in French trenches.

'Loose lips sink ships,' I sighed, unintentionally out loud.

'Wha'ssat Kye-ee?' Their south London glottal stop had lost my 't' somewhere along the way.

'Oh, nothing,' I chirped, snapping out of Air Raid Theatre.

Though 'the lads' were friendly enough, I always felt a little excluded once the 'all rights' were exchanged. I sensed a certain benign chauvinism, that after the bloke-folk had dispensed with pleasantries, it was back to laddish talk about laddish concerns, with no girls allowed. I wondered how much this was ingrained in British society. Since I'd been in London, I'd seen male comedians on telly cracking 'Women's Lib' gags like it was still 1969.

I'd left Venus in sub-zero conditions, slayed by snow and glazed by ice. The British butt-end of winter had a different kind of discomfort. Even while temperatures hovered around a temperate fifty degrees Fahrenheit, it still managed to be soul-chillingly cold. The frequent spitting rain left its evil mark on the natives, who moved through the dark days in walking hibernation. When the occasional meagre sunshine thawed smiles and spirits into play, I knew they had a softer side that needed protection from their own country's miserable weather.

Unlike Americans, the British didn't take sunshine for granted. Its random appearances sparked universal gratitude and renewed confidence. Citizens would actually chat in the post office queue, or meet each other's eyes on the street with a smile. But when the sun went back behind a cloud, so did they.

Maybe it was the weather, maybe it was the economy, maybe it was that old war I insisted on sentimentalizing, but I found the British generally more cynical than my happy sappy countrymen. People around my age, twenty-one, were less naive and more caustic than those back home. Cynicism's quixotic by-product, however, was the famed national sense of humour, in all its whimsy, irony, eccentricity.

Gradually, I was getting a bead on the United Queendom.

Five days after I arrived in London, I accompanied B and his band on a short tour of Spain.

February 25, 1984 – Valencia
Sunny Spain – coffee and kisses, mountains and coasts,

boyfriend who takes care of me. RELAX don't do it, when
you want to COME.

Last night's gig: B is a charismatic performer, with a
dolled-up Katie on his arm. Photographers couldn't stop
taking pictures of us – we RADIATE. I was in the audience
– DEJA VU out to WAZOO!!!! My dream has come true
EXACTLY as I conceived it.

February 26 – Alicante
A happy day of travelling and talking and talking – B and
I in hyperspace totally immersed in one another, making
each other laugh, coming up for air now and again to see
the others studying us in wonderment at the completeness
of our involvement.

By the end of the week we were back in south London, and the
pixie dust was wearing off. I was dismayed to witness a couple
of violent fist fights between B and his younger brother. And I
became aware that B was still drinking heavily. He tried to hide
his secret beers. I'd hear the furtive pops of ring-pulls from the
downstairs loo behind the kitchen.

I felt too uncertain of my own way in this new life to figure
out how serious the drinking was. After all, the old 'take charge'
B was still functioning, still coming up with songs for us, still
talking about our world domination schemes.

Soon B, the band and I were off again, this time for two
weeks in Poland. The group's third album had stiffed at home,
but there was mileage to be had abroad. In Eastern Europe,
they were indebted to British bands just for showing up.

When our plane landed in Warsaw, the airport balcony was a
frenzied crush of hundreds and hundreds of pop-famished
teenagers. Nobody had expected this kind of turnout, and the

band started whooping. The plane filled with the other passengers' excited murmurs, 'Who are they waiting for – who's on this plane?' A Polish man turned to B.

'Who are you?'

'We're The Beatles!' B laughed.

It was thrilling. There were throngs of fans calling out B's and other band members' names. Girls were crying, squealing, ripping B's clothes off. One girl jumped on his back and moaned in his ear, 'Oh B, I've been waiting for you so *long*.' I knew how she felt.

There were flowers everywhere. We were showered in flowers. A teenage boy approached me with a bouquet and announced formally, 'Can I shake hand only. Is great pleasure to see girl like you. Everybody says so.'

He turned respectfully to B and said, 'Can I shake hand only.'

We drove to Poznan, which was ugly and industrial, but which still felt like the most beautiful place in the world because I was with B. At the gig, the band played to six thousand rock 'n' roll-starved Poles who knew the words to all the songs. Afterwards, we dined at the hotel in a lavish banquet hall, elegantly supping on steak before an audience of tearful faces mashed into monster masks against the outside windows. Their unsightly adoration provoked uncomfortable feelings of rubbing our high-on-the-hog lifestyle in their hard-times faces.

The menus were enormous, but the only item that would ever be available was chateaubriand. Apparently, meat was scarce for ordinary citizens, since all flora and fauna of any significance were shipped over to the Soviet Union. Or saved for visiting dignitaries such as new romantic troubadours.

Later at the hotel nightclub, appropriately called 'Hades', rich Slavs frugged in snow boots and tube tops to German heavy metal. The live entertainment featured two tame strippers lethargically shedding their clothes and a boring magician, followed by a couple of folk dancers mazurka-ing around the tables. We soon recognized these disparate elements as the standard features of Polish hotspots. The big laugh of the night came when a drunken businessman mistook the band's guitar player, with his backcombed blond hair, for a Polish prostitute.

The next morning, I discovered that as a band girlfriend, even I was a temporary superstar. I could demand – and get – elaborate cakes and pastries whenever I wanted. On a whim, I tried it at breakfast, and it worked. Thereafter, the promoter always made sure the dessert menu was made available to me at all hours of the day or night. My tour debaucheries were those of a spoiled five-year-old.

B's debaucheries, on the other hand, were fully those of a twenty-two-year-old.

While Polish beef was shipped out to the hated Russkis, Polish vodka stayed right where it was distilled. It was a bargain – a pound a bottle. By day three, the reality of B's drinking crashed in. The cheap booze ruined a dream.

March 16 – Gdansk
I abhor weakness. B drinks vodka, spins crazily around the room, falls off the bed stupidly. He stinks and paws me clumsily. I want to throw up. When he is drunk I go dead inside. First, I feel extreme contempt . . . then pity for him in his humiliated state . . . then nothing. Absolutely nothing. Not love, not hate, just emptiness. WASTE. When this drunken thing touches me, my skin crawls.

March 17 – Warsaw; March 18 – Lodz
B partially pulls himself together – I naively hope there'll

*be no more alcohol scenes. Both NBC and ABC TV crews
film the Warsaw show and interview the band. NBC
cameras film me as well: portrait of a 'zany fan'.*

*Then, a nightmare – B drunk again – this time I'm not
neutral – my spirit is close to breaking. A casual spree for
him destroys me. Passed out, he urinates on me as I lie next
to him – I hurl glasses at the wall in helpless rage. Looking
at him turns my stomach for the lost possibilities.*

*On Sunday, in Lodz, we gingerly regroup. I stay at the
hotel and sleep during the show, which turns out to be the
best of the tour – nine thousand there! A lovely evening
with B.*

B celebrated his twenty-third birthday a few days later in a
Katowice strip club. I'd missed out on naked-lady fun because I
was too exhausted by the drama and had stayed back at the
hotel.

At three in the morning, the entire band came back smashed.
Later, the hotel's concierge told me that B had been 'beautiful'.
The man was particularly impressed with the way that B, even
in his shambolic state, kept thumping down his Irish passport
and vehemently declaring his nationality.

I awoke in the hotel bed to a commotion at my door. When I
opened it there were three hotel porters trying to hold up the
drunken birthday boy. The fact that it was his birthday gave me
the night off from freaking about his drinking.

B started to tell me some garbled story about a man he'd just
seen standing on the ledge of an apartment building, about to
jump. I put B in the bed, then, too wired to go back to sleep, I
prowled out into the corridor.

From one of the rooms, I could hear a Polish man singing
opera. I was still puzzling over that when, at the other end of

the long hallway, I saw a naked man. Each as shocked by the other, we both jumped behind pillars. Like some kind of cornball slapstick, we peeped out at each other at the same time, then snapped back again.

I found a back stairway and wandered down to the other floors, then back up the elevator to my floor. The doors slid open to the spectacle of the naked man barrelling towards me with fifty feet of fire hose stretching out behind him. He slowed to a tiptoe and put his finger to his lips, invoking me to silence. Then he said in English, conspiratorially, 'And you? And you?' – an invitation to mischief. He set the nozzle of the hose down at the door of the lift and pitter-patted pinkly back to the water supply. Too weirded by the night to see who'd get drenched, I returned to my room.

The final shows were in Wrocław at a huge hall built for a speech Hitler never made. B's combo had the Polish number one, a success they'd never achieved in Britain. They left Poland triumphant. I left defeated.

> *March 25*
> *There are two Bs – one that loves me, and one that couldn't care less about me as he pops another beer, making clear how little I REALLY touch him. DEPRESSION AND EMPTINESS: B makes promises he can't keep – and doesn't intend to.*
> *Decisions will have to be made.*

The only decision that had to be made upon our return from Poland was that we needed to move out of B's parents' house. I went to go see the first bedsit I'd circled in the *Evening Standard* classifieds. It was one room, cheap and in the centre of town. I phoned B to check that it was the kind of thing we wanted.

'It's right off Baker Street,' I said. 'Is that OK?'

'OK?' B thought I was kidding. At that moment, Gerry Rafferty's 'Baker Street' was playing in his mum's kitchen on Radio Two. Besides, who actually lived in the middle of London, apart from characters from swingin' sixties films?

'Are you sure it's that cheap and it's near Baker Street?' B was incredulous.

'Yep – W1. Right behind your old record company on Manchester Square.'

'GET IT!'

And so we moved into Robert Adam Street. In the interest of world peace, I didn't tell my parents that I was cohabiting with a man without the benefit of wedlock. It was less wear and tear on everyone this way. But in the unlikely event of a surprise visit, I'd have a hard time explaining away B's two guitars, two basses, a keyboard, a saxophone and a double bass.

It was a bedsit – one room with a hotplate, water and electricity meters, shared bathroom and toilet and no phone. For a First World country, Britain was sure doing a pretty good Second World act.

B rigged the electricity meter with his trusty screwdriver so we never had to pay for heat and light again. He also made a lamp out of a plastic 'Mr T' bust. We got a goldfish, because we felt that a pet made a house a home. We named him Colin.

B was popular with all of the other bedsit urchins in our building – he was friendly and funny and handy with the screwdriver. Before too long, everyone was benefiting from his electrical know-how, from the nouveau Buddhists upstairs to the Spanish girl next door to the fashion designer in the basement.

Robert Adam Street was a sitcom. The comedy crank was Mr Patel, an elderly Indian man who called the police on everybody, all the time, about anything. He lived at the top of the building next door to a young chef that we dubbed Margarine Man after a pivotal plot twist.

It all started when Mr Patel, snooping as usual, discovered some fancy margarine sculptures on ice in the attic. They belonged to the chef, who'd put them there for an event he was catering later that evening. We heard the shouting two flights down.

'You're running a business from here!' the old man was screaming. Mr Patel's big obsession was that people were running businesses from Robert Adam Street. The tirade continued.

'You're running a business with these . . . big yellow ducks!'

We heard the chef's voice, strangled with fury.

'It's MARGARINE, you idiot! They're SWANS sculpted in MARGARINE!'

Mr Patel's other bugaboo was that the residents were entertaining friends in their bedsits. 'That's what hotels are for!' he'd yell. 'Go to the Churchill if you want to see your friends – that's what I do!'

The subcontinental crackpot also claimed to have nude polaroids of the basement fashion designer.

Mr Patel once pitched a hissy because B was playing a tape of Joni Mitchell's *Blue*, quietly, after midnight. B lost his temper and chased him up the stairs, whereupon Patel predictably called the police. They arrived and told B cheerily, 'He's completely insane – just try not to hit him.'

While he cajoled our imminent music career out of his head and on to the demo tapes, B had signed on for unemployment benefit. In the interim before we were pop stars, I needed to get a job.

I joined a small temp agency in Victoria. The two women who ran it decided to start me right then and there answering telephones. Unfortunately, I was hopeless at being a receptionist. Over the phone, I couldn't understand the accents. The women clearly thought I was a moron, and didn't send me on any jobs. I left and joined a bigger agency, where I billed myself as a word-processing operator. This time, it was just between me and the keyboard, with no frooty-tooty accents to throw me. I got steady work immediately.

I enjoyed temp life – the pay was good and I could choose how much or little I wanted to work. However, I felt left out in British offices when the other women talked fervently about ironing. Along with public vomiting, ironing appeared to be another British pastime. They even ironed bedsheets.

'Don't you guys have perma-press here yet?' I kept asking. I'd never done any ironing in my life.

Along with my pic 'n' mix hours, I liked the fact that the firms I worked for were relaxed about my happening clothes. My togs *du jour* included polka-dot circle skirts, Bardot cinched waists, footless lacy tights, pointy-toed stilettos, tight pullovers, push-up bras, low-slung studded belts and big hoop earrings. The *maquillage* was high eighties: densely defined superbrows over kohl-rimmed eyes and pearly pale lips. My hair, now pillar-box red with the help of advanced Anglo science, was pulled up in a ponytail tied with a big tulle bow. I was decked like a techno sweater girl.

My office jobs were relatively fun. It was when I got home that the work started.

B's drinking was increasing. Sometimes I came in from my day to find him passed out on the floor. I'd root out purple cans of Tennent's Special stashed all over the bedsit: in his guitar cases, down the back of the sofa, even in the toilet tank.

One evening as B lay comatose on the bed, I huddled on the couch looking at him and crying. He and I were in the same room and I'd never felt lonelier, even when I was thousands of miles across the Atlantic waiting for his letters. I glanced down and saw a purple can poking out of its hiding place in one of his shoes. It was another pint closer to killing us. Without thinking, I picked it up and threw it as hard as I could at his head.

It cracked against his temple. Confused, B moved in a slow muddle, rubbing his head. He squinted over at me.

'Ow! That hurt!' he said softly.

I left the room, the house, the street, walking anywhere as long as it was away. I needed to talk to someone but there was no one. By the time I noticed what I was doing, I was walking down the stairs to Marble Arch tube. I looked at my hand on the banister and was flashed by déjà vu from my first trip to London in 1972: my mother saying, 'Don't touch the railings, hon, they're dirty', at this very station. For the second time, I ignored the advice, my grown-up hand tracing my little-girl fingerprints all the way down the stairs.

Low in the grey a.m. glare of the station, I called my sister in Virginia from a pay phone. Helpless, all she could do was listen as I wept. Helpless, weeping was all I could do. My money ran out before my tears.

Some nights when B and I were out at a club or a gig, he'd get more and more irrationally angry as he tanked up. Finally, he'd storm out down the road with me trailing after him, sobbing. We once marched this sick parade from the Camden Palace all the way back home to Marylebone.

During all of this, B made constant promises that he would

stop drinking. But something stronger than he was turned every promise into a lie.

EMI was around the corner from where we lived. Limos containing Duran Duran often glided down Robert Adam Street, followed by a stampede of weenyteens screaming 'SIMON! JOHN!' at the shadows behind the smoked glass.

As dozens of youthful thighs thundered by, I'd think about B's and my big pop plans. But the distance from our front door to Simon Le Bon's limo was a gulf wider than the Grand Canyon.

After four months in London, I went back to America to spend four weeks in Venus. I returned to visit my mother, who was now at home recovering from her run-in with cancer. But I also returned to escape. I was running away from tears and B. Never had I been so overjoyed to fall into the arms of my parents. I was desperate to get away from the whole mess, the drinking. I was so comforted by being home with my mom and dad that I seriously considered not going back to England. Every night I cried about B. Every day I received gush-packed letters from him. My head was so confused. I had invested emotionally in B for years, and now it was all rotten.

When I got back to London, nothing had changed. The stress stopped my periods for the next seven months.

After six months in Robert Adam Street, we moved a few blocks up Baker Street to Dorset Street. The two-room flat was in a listed Georgian building with a genteel view of moneyed London out the front window and an urban post-war view from the back. We filled the high-ceilinged space with our recording equipment, toys, fuzzy yellow and purple fun-fur pillows, musical instruments, psychedelic swirls of turquoise, tartan and zebra stripes and Colin, our goldfish.

B got roped into touring Spain with Angie Bowie. At the time it seemed like an amazing opportunity. B was the original Bowie boy – at twelve he'd had the bright orange Ziggy cut and had even slapped Immac on his eyebrows to achieve the Space Oddity look *à la* Dave. He'd awakened the next morning minus eyebrows, as well as most of the skin beneath them. The suppurating strips of rawness over his eyes eventually scabbed over in a most un-glam fashion.

With his history of Bowie commitment, even to get the chance to work with the barking ex-Mrs Bowie seemed magical. It turned out to be tragical. She was the queenpin of dissipation. Even B couldn't keep up with her.

The last time I ever saw B drunk was when he stumbled out of the cab, back from Angie's tour. Then, for no particular reason, he stopped drinking completely.

When he was sober for a month it seemed, under these circumstances, like forever.

Under these circumstances, we got married.

24

Loving The Alien

I Married A New Romantic!

It sounded like a lurid come-on from one of those *True Confessions* mags I used to read. The reality was less lurid. B and I knew that in order to stay together in London, we'd have to get married. In love forever but unnerved by the idea of forever, our plan was to wed, forget about it, then pretend we were still boyfriend and girlfriend.

'What is your Christian name?'

It was five days before the wedding. The lady at the registry office looked up at me, holding her pen over the blank on the form. I'd lived here over a year, and I still wasn't sure how to answer that question. What if you weren't a Christian? I took a shot at it.

'What – you mean like St Theresa?'

The lady didn't laugh. I guess I wasn't taking this wedding thing seriously enough.

Just as I'd kept the fact that I'd been living with B a secret from my parents, I decided to hide our marriage as well. I knew this was taking the 'don't ask, don't tell' policy a little too far, but

I didn't feel like getting into the ring with my father again. I knew he wouldn't like it, and I didn't want to hear why. Anyway, I could guess. He'd consider that I was living in sin because it was a registry office number and not a church wing-ding. I didn't want to risk losing any more fatherly affections than I already had. He'd amply demonstrated his ability to cut off others in our family for various crimes against Catholicism, and I didn't want it to happen to me. I felt that our relationship was shaky enough as it was.

And if I were to tell the truth to myself, my relationship with my father wasn't the only shaky one. B and I had lived through one bitch of a dipso year, and although he'd apparently recovered, I wasn't sure that I had. Maybe there was more to keeping this Mrs business quiet than fear of my father.

But when I took a look at the two of us, things were better than they'd ever been. Since B had sobered up, the daily focus was blessedly off booze and a tentative happiness had begun wafting in. My heart was again in fluorescence, a perfumed hothouse of roses, posies and pinks. I was excited by the possibilities opening up for me in London. I was dancing with a variety of small contemporary companies and I'd started doing session work – backing vocals for a handful of pantywaisted pop artistes. And B and I were working on our own demos. I devoted a lot of time to thinking up a catchy stage name. I'd decided on Kimba Sputnik, until my friend Steve pointed out that my real name was equally preposterous, if that was what I was after.

On my second trip back to Virginia since I'd moved to Britain, seven months after the first, I noted how different it felt to be leaving B. This time I was going reluctantly, not wretchedly.

My mother and father were delighted to have me home. My

dad, unveiling a new burgundy Honda in what he hoped was an enticing manner, said, 'This can be yours if you decide to stay.' I thought he meant 'eventually', and that I could buy it from him, but my sister clued me he meant it as sort of a bribe. He'd told her that I'd get tired of my 'bohemian lifestyle' at some point and would want to move back to Venus.

I was touched that they missed me enough to dangle automobiles in my direction, but the offer had come a year too late. In London, I was happier than I'd ever been. If someone had told me a few years earlier that I'd be living kerplunk in the middle of London with a loving and hilarious musician boy, working as a dancer and a session singer, I would have dismissed it as mere mouthings of my most impossible dreams. Pitted against my impossible dreams, the shiny burgundy Honda didn't stand a chance.

I loved my Limey life. God bless America and all, but London was my carnival and I was going on all the rides: sitting top and front on a double-decker bus, upsetting the Elvis-crested ducks in St James's Park, trawling Brick Lane Market for old copies of *Manhood* and *Wicked*. I still had an eye for the naked ladies.

And for the ladies in general. To my mall-dulled eye, Britain's greatest cultural contribution were hip chicks of the dolly-bird persuasion. These were women who'd thrown down the gauntlet to cookie-cutter cuteness to celebrate their own foxaliciousness. In High Street Kensington, Covent Garden and the King's Road, I was inspired by mam'zelles flaunting their unique selling points. Their very diversity was reassuring. In Venus, I'd been a freak. In London, I was a babe among babes.

Dazzled by female it-ness, I'd follow that day's most-fascinating-girl-I-have-ever-seen fifteen minutes past whatever bus or appointment I was trying to make. Besotted, I'd trail a tight black plastic mini-skirt, leggings, high heels and a ripped-up white t-shirt all the way down Oxford Street.

The girls I admired were all about my age, but aesthetically they'd left me way behind in their glamorous dust. I was clobbered by their beauty, their sexiness, their outrageousness. I even had a sort-of crush on a girl who worked in Top Shop. She was beautiful, with spiky white-blonde hair, fishnet stockings and the artless way of the deeply hep. I'd go into the shop just to stare at her. She'd always ruin my peeping Tom time by noticing me and staring back, which unsettled me. I didn't know why she was checking me out. Compared to her, I felt like a frump.

Other scenes seized my cultural interest. The Safeway on Edgware Road was enveloped by fragrant clouds of yashmak-clad Arab women. I enjoyed the defiance of their intricately embroidered and bejewelled haute couture stilettos poking out from their dour black chadors. I was fascinated by the more zealous types who wore what looked like a metal Darth Vader mask. I saw one Darth Vader lady with her fully westernized husband in a shop called Rich Bitch, fingering airy fairytale dresses. The contradictions befuddled me – when did the metal-faced wife get to wear such frilly-dillies?

I was about to become someone's wife. Hopefully without the Darth Vader mask. Certainly without the frilly-dillies.

For the big day, I wore a wide-shouldered stripy yellow suit that looked like pyjamas. On my feet were black patent-leather Doc Marten boots. I tied a flyaway yellow tulle bow around my acrylic corkscrew ponytail. B wore an expensive blue silk suit and an extra-tall quiff.

That June, I was twenty-two, B was twenty-four. We were married at Marylebone Registry Office, just a mosey up from our Dorset Street flat. Steve was my witness, the singer from

B's band was his. The registrar looked a bit like Margaret Thatcher with her whorled helmet hair, but her businesslike manner softened at our nerves and excitement.

As she pronounced us man and wife, B and I couldn't stop grinning.

She said, smiling, 'You are one of the most beautiful couples I have ever married.'

We believed her, because that's how it felt.

Afterwards, the four of us returned to Dorset Street for champagne and wedding cake. The cake was shaped like a giant hamburger complete with marzipan cheese, lettuce and tomato. The marzipan bun had real sesame seeds.

We all clanked coffee mugs of champagne and toasted our eternity.

I felt really depressed the next day.

A few months after we pretended we didn't get married, I went with B's band back to Poland for the last-gasp tour of their career. This time, I'd graduated from girlfriend to backing singer.

We arrived at Warsaw Airport to the now familiar Beatlemania. This time around, the crowds at the shows were even bigger: ten thousand, fifteen thousand. After every gig, we were treated to textbook rock 'n' roll frenzy. Mobs of pop-o-pathic lunachicks obliged my mini-diva trip by hurling themselves at our Mercedes. The car would roll slowly away from the venue entirely covered in crying girls. As the Merc picked up speed, they'd fall off one by one with muffled plops.

When our car approached the hotel, there'd be more berserkoid younglings waiting, eager to spreadeagle their heroes' windscreens. It was wild. Since the huge crush of people prevented us from opening our car doors, we had to be driven straight into the hotel reception area – just the coolest. It turned out those Hell's Angels in Oregon Hill had been on to something good with that motorcycle ramp.

In the evenings, as had happened the year before, we dined before hundreds of girlish nostrils pressed against the glass separating them from their dreams.

The morning after our first show in Poznan, B and I ran into two superfans named Iwona and Kinga, who had travelled twelve hours on a train to see us. I don't know where these Slavic-bops got their zlotys, but they dragged their suitcases in and out of every one of our hotels on that tour. They became our mascots.

August 10, 1985

It became readily apparent that Iwona was drunk off her little Polish ass. Later B and I noticed identical Band-Aids covering a strategic spot on the inner wrists. Suicide pact? Angst under Communism? Madness from the lead singer's caterwauling? We weren't to know. Iwona would only point mournfully (and drunkenly) to her t-shirt, which had 'CRAZY' emblazoned across the front.

A group of us went into Poznan, admiring the centuries-old houses that lined the cobblestone square. When I stopped to buy silly little toys for my ever-burgeoning collection, Iwona and Kinga tried to stop me, saying, 'Don't buy – is bad. Very, very bad. Poland is horrible.'

Iwona was so drunk: 'I love you, B. Please, don't you want to touch me? Oh, I love you too, Katie.'

This time, Iwona, not B, was the tour drunk. The Polish promoters who remembered last year's lush life couldn't get over the difference in him. Sober as a judge ... straight as a die. But he still had a few rock 'n' roll excesses up the sleeve of his leather-fringed Johnsons jacket.

After the show in Wrocław, B threw a thrillingly ridiculous rock star tantrum that anticipated *Spinal Tap*. When informed that the hotel's restaurant had closed for the evening and that we would have to make do with a tray of cold luncheon meats, B theatrically placed a slice of the salami over each eye. Then, calling the waiter a 'wanker asshole', he frisbee'd the meat across the lobby. I must have been sliding into minor rock star mode myself, because his behaviour didn't strike me as altogether unreasonable.

Rock 'n' roll and Poland were a funny hybrid. We'd go into the perfectly preserved old town of Cracow, into the cutest, quaintest little timber-framed shop, and inside they'd be selling Limahl and Shakin' Stevens badges. Evidently, Poland was where British bands went to die. And in that pack of jokers, no wonder B's band had such credibility.

When B and I got back to London, we began receiving cartoons of ourselves drawn by our Polish devotees. We were rendered Japanese-style: big-eyed, round-headed, babyishly cute. The cartoons playfully projected us into domestic contentment. Scenarios included our wedding (with 'Ideal Marriage' written underneath); B with a baby; me urging B to do a little feather-dusting around a sloppy but snug flat.

Our fans were entranced by the idea of us as the perfect pop couple.

So were we.

25

Pop Life

March 1986
Finally there are outlets for my boundless energy, my revolting enthusiasm. I'm so grateful! I feel like a Tasmanian devil, a fleshly tornado. A happy storm that twiddles and twirls anything in her path.

I was all-fired, all-singing, all-dancing. Opportunities were siren-calling me forward, ever forward. Every corner was a lottery: was my big break lurking just around that bend? Maybe! No? Ohhhhhh . . . wal dog mah cats little lady, never you mind – 'cause there's always another corner ahead . . . and ahead . . . and ahead . . .

My controls were cranked to Perma-Perk. Optimism shooed me through the days like a fly off a pie. Even one molecule more of jut in my strut would have bounced me right through the planet's gravitational field.

My crazed exuberance was beneficial, in most respects. However, one thing I could have used was Mom asking why I made myself so ugly, the way she used to do back in high school. For without a doubt, this was my positively ugliest era.

Of course, *I* thought I looked great. My hair was now chemicalled up to a densely punchbowl red. I'd shaved my hairline at the temples to make my severe pelmet of a fringe look even more severe. It was severe all right – and the increased expanse of skin turned my face into an even bigger boiled potato than it already was. I'd been slapdash with my razor technique and had ended up inadvertently nicking my eyebrows down to half their original size. Because I only noticed this some time after I'd done it, I sincerely thought my eyebrows had fallen off by themselves. I even considered going to the doctor about it, until B gently pointed out that my wonky shaving was probably to blame.

I piled my long hair on top of my head into a tall funnel-shaped bun, tied at the base with velvet ribbon. People often stopped me to ask what was inside holding it up. I wore black-rimmed cat-eye glasses, a floor-length purple fun-fur coat and red brothel creepers. I was an Addams Family dream date for Uncle Fester.

In order not to be compared to *real* beauties and found lacking, I carved myself a not-so-comfortable niche by looking like a kook.

The kook look attracted flocks of preposterously faddish Japanese tourists who took photos of me for their style fanzines back home. These carefully trendy teens would stop me on the street and before I could say 'Sushi gives you worms', I'd be posed and snapped. Close-ups of my hair, my clothes, my creepers would be published in the Land of the Rising Sun documenting the Empire where the Sun Never Sets, modelled by a girl from Deep in the Heart of Dixie.

Regardless of my challenging appearance and ongoing inse-curities, B always made me feel like the most desirable woman who ever walked the earth. I felt adored by him.

And I adored him. B was the mad scientist – always creating some space-age gadget to improve the quality of our life. He was good with his hands. Since we could only afford a cheaper black and white TV licence, he hooked up a secret button on the back of our colour set to render it instantly monochromatic in case of a raid. He designed and built his own guitars, painting them in unorthodox ways, with felt-tipped markers and varnish. He also built an electric viola, along with sophisticated recording equipment encased in a variety of cardboard boxes. The impressive thing was that they all actually worked. He was a maestro with glue. He'd once fixed a friend's dodgy haircut with Krazy Glue. He also Krazy Glued together his Starship Enterprise kits.

B worshipped *Star Trek*. He aspired to the heroic humanity of Captain James T. Kirk. He videotaped every episode and watched them on the nights he couldn't sleep, which was every night. The dragging of the TV set from the main room to the kitchen became a bedtime ritual. After watching an episode, B would get back to beavering on whatever song he was crafting for our any-minute-now career. When I'd get up for work in the morning, he'd just be going to bed. Making coffee, I'd find the funny little notes and cartoons that he'd left for me. Among these Post-It missives, there'd often be an appreciation of my singing on whatever demo we were recording. I loved that he loved my voice.

B's encouragement made me want to wow him even more. My friend Steve provided the opportunity – a PA spot at a night he was organizing at a gay club on York Way.

September 1986
I've been busy getting my backing tape together for my big

night. Or rather, B's been busy – writing, playing, producing the songs, while I throw in the occasional backing vocal. At the studio he pulls saxophone after guitar after keyboard out of bags and boxes. In these days where 'multi-instrumentalist' means the ability to play a synthesizer with two fingers, the engineers look upon him with amazement.

We both worked so hard. Before B had organized his home recording equipment to his satisfaction, we travelled far out of London to find the cheapest studios, trundling the TEAC four-track on a mumsy shopping trolley behind us. We were boogie pilgrims.

Once he'd set up our kitchen studio, crowded by appliances and the shower that stood next to the sink, he'd cook up four-track magic all night long as I slept in the next room. Plugged into headphones, the only sounds I'd hear at 4 a.m. might be the unamplified blinggg! of his guitar strings, or maybe a sotto guide vocal.

My job was to take care of lyrics, strategies, gigs, record companies. The concept was to keep it all a ma-and-pa operation: no band, just us. For gigs, I'd sing live to backing tapes prepared earlier in our kitchen. We decided that the Puckrik family nickname, Puck, would make a good name for the act.

In my notebooks I compiled lists of Puck ingredients to help crystallize my guise:

NERDY
NUBILE
CARTOONS
TECHNICOLOR
ELVIS

ANN-MARGRET
VIVA LAS VEGAS
KRISPY KREME DOUGHNUTS
PEBBLES
TOM JONES
HANNA-BARBERA HOUSE BAND
BREASTS
SPECS
CREEPERS
SPORTY
TRIPPY

Availing myself of office Xerox machines and stationery cupboards, I designed 'Puck Packs' to send to record companies and magazines. Along with our demo tape, photos and toys, the packs contained flyers heavy on hyperbole:

> *Ann-Margret picks up Chaka Khan in her dune buggy and mows down Ethel Merman in the street . . . a monster crawls from the wreckage and screams, 'Bring me the head of Barney Rubble!' That monster is Puck.*

I'd unwittingly stumbled onto the cringe-making bombast of pop press releases.

Other flyers were written in village idiot verse:

> *Feel like confuse squeak toy?*
> *Sometimes Puck do.*
> *Look like cartoon drawn bad?*
> *You know Puck do too.*
> *Less sense than a Q-tip?*
> *That be Puck to a T.*

Thankfully, I'd introduced a little sex appeal to my recent Uncle Fester fashions. For Puck, I kept the cat-eye glasses and the creepers, but I'd also sport a stretchy little cocktail dress. I was twenty-four and had never dared to wear out and out oomph until now. I also had a couple of snappy strappy dresses made, one in glow-in-the-dark Hallowe'en fabric. My hair was a high ponytail of corkscrew curls. My slogan was 'Nerdy and Nubile'. That way, it gave me a get-out for those who didn't find me quite nubile enough.

Though the general direction was poppy-soul, the first official Puck track we recorded was a cover of Tom Jones's 'It's Not Unusual'. We had to shelve it once the great man had his post-modern revival later in the decade.

We did show business on a shoestring. We considered every element of the three-song performance. Stagecraft was all: I exhausted myself before my first gig blowing up my inflatable 'band': dalmatians, penguins, balloons and Fred Flintstone bop bags. Between the blowing and the nerves, I practically hyperventilated.

Out of some old turntables, B rigged up mechanisms that twirled one of the penguins and a giant plastic daisy. He also positioned a strobe to go off at key points in the show, along with a slide projector that splashed the Puck logo over the back wall. My dream was to get a bubble machine.

We had done the business. Now all that was left to do was the show.

October 1986
I had my debut as a proper chanteuse last night at Steve's club at Traffic, and it went down a storm! As the audience hollered and hoo-ha'd, I thought they were just being polite. But then I realized that since none of my friends

were there, it wasn't loyalty prompting the enthusiasm. B
said that he never heard a reaction like that for a singer
with only backing tapes. B's ex-manager was the first
person backstage, saying goofy stuff like 'A star is born!' in
deadly serious tones. He went over to B next, pumping his
arm up and down in a frenzied handshake, saying, 'You
must be very excited!' Then he wanted to know when my
next 'dive bar extravaganza' was. Things are hopping –
motivation is high.

I had seven inflatable dogs and a glow-in-the-dark dress – but
still no record deal. Confident as ever, I considered Madonna
the competition. OK, so she had a little head start on me, but it
wasn't anything I couldn't gain on once I'd served my pop star
apprenticeship.

I was very organized. I made endless hit lists of record
companies, magazines and venues to contact, ticking off each
one as I ploughed through the music biz. I was shamelessly
persistent. I had to be, to ride out the embarrassment of being
an unsolicited nobody.

I wrote out little scripts for myself so I wouldn't get tongue-
tied on the phone to A&R men. Having to hard-sell my soft self
to bored strangers helped me detach myself from Puck: the
Product.

Puck was nerdy and nubile. She had her own brand of appeal
that didn't stoop to conquer the spuddy Mr Potato Heads of the
world. She wasn't the obvious sex bitch goddess who was so hot
she had to wank over herself onstage. She wasn't the bland
girl-next-door, either. She was like the secretary in those old
Dean Martin swinger movies, the one whose glasses he
removes saying, 'Why Miss Puckrik, you're beautiful!' when the
rest of us could see she was the ONE all along. Puck was

inclusive, not exclusive. The audience wouldn't hate her for being too cool for school – no – she'd be the first one they'd want to invite to a pyjama party. And most of all, she could *really* sing.

I pushed the Portable Puck Propaganda factor: music from in the kitchen, video from the bedroom, publicity shots from the photo booth, playback gigs to the Walkman.

I marched into every magazine I used to read back at the Fat-X-Sam flat: *i-D*, *The Face*, *Melody Maker*. Armed with Puck Packs, I'd introduce myself to the surprised editors and launch into my spiel. They'd laugh and then put me in the next issue.

Securing gigs, I roamed in and out of Fred's, Freud's and the Fridge. I played the coffee bar at St Martin's School of Art. Wearing a corseted space-goddess metallic minidress I'd borrowed from Vivienne Westwood, I warbled and wiggled my twenty-minute set. Art-kid cries filled the air: 'Oh, I wish I'd brought my camera, Super-8, etc.' I found out that the only other band who'd ever played there was the Sex Pistols.

For A&R showcases, I'd run up a pile of kiddy-style Lucky Bags that I called, of course, 'Pucky Bags'. The bags were filled with lick-on tattoos, plastic glasses, wax lips, toys and candy.

I'd go into record company meetings with a pink attaché case filled with toys, sweeties and plastic doughnuts. At strategic moments I'd open it up and pass around the can of Uncle Joe's Mint Balls while the A&R guy played with the toys.

The biz bods were impressed by B's and my shit-together approach and came down to plenty of gigs. They liked my wailin' soul voice, they liked my wacked-out look, they liked our ideas – and then they sent us rejection letters. Every time we flogged them a tape, they flopped it right back at us.

Their comments were baffling: I was larger than life; we

were too versatile. I was pleased until I realized they were citing these as drawbacks. Why was smaller than life better? What was so great about limitations?

After a few years of this, B said, 'I'm fucking tired of impressing *myself*.' I seconded that emotion.

The whole pop-star-waiting-to-be-discovered jazz was getting me down. I didn't give up – I couldn't give up – but I decided to diversify. I threw myself back into the dance scene with renewed enthusiasm. With dance, I knew the move: if you were good, you got a job. Dance success was something that was entirely down to me – no waiting around for some dopey A&R guy to tell me I was too talented to make it.

I got a job with DV8 Physical Theatre, a group that specialized in exploring sexual politics through dancing, speaking, singing, thrashing. The project was called *My Body, Your Body*. The premise concerned women who let their stifling relationships with men stop them from reaching their full potential.

I was part of a company of eight women chosen to lend our own life stories to *My Body*. We turned weeks of discussion into movement, movement of masochistic repetition, frantic hysteria, obsessive vehemence. The violent realness of our collective experiences gave the work its jolt. The piece, though powerful, was not exactly light entertainment. It was headache-inducing mayhem, carefully organized and meticulously performed.

I laughingly accused the director, Lloyd Newson, of only wanting to use performers who had screwed-up relationships. Mine, I assured him, was not. But as I built up the project with the seven other women, I realized that it was.

After denying that B and I were anything less than perfection, I began to examine what we actually were. Any way you sliced it, we were in love, forever and ever amen. But B did everything to excess. In the years after quitting drinking, he'd

276

lent addiction-strength commitment to even the most harmless habits. His boxcar-strength beers were substituted for gallons of Tizer and Dandelion & Burdock. He chain-drank tea. Every morning I came into the kitchen to find a high-as-an-elephant heap of used teabags. He smoked a lot of hash, too. Not that I minded about that, because whatever he needed to keep him off the hateful booze was fine with me. But I noticed that he *needed* it more than he wanted it. If we went out to see a movie, B would get up three times during the film to spliff up in the gents.

Doing everything to excess, he loved me hard – and raged at me harder. His devotion didn't take the edge off his temper, which blasted to rocket-fuelled fury out of all proportion to our standard-sized rows.

I was afraid ever to get mad at him, because he was so much better at it than I was. Shortly into any squabble, he'd erupt. Overtaking me on the inside lane, he'd shout at me, insult me, whatever it took to get him off the hook and me on it. Whatever the issue, it was never his fault, always mine. Whatever the issue, my crime was the same: I was selfish, B said.

Once he told me I was selfish when I wouldn't buy him a guitar to replace one in his collection that had been stolen.

'You're so selfish!' he spat at me. 'You're so selfish that you left your mother when she had cancer and needed you most!'

Guilt bomb hit at ground zero, sir. That wasn't just close to the bone – that was the marrow. Even B was surprised at how well it had worked. I was inconsolable.

I wept, 'You're right, you're right, I'm selfish! I left my mother just when she'd almost died. I'm so bad . . . so bad . . . '

It was only as B swung into Good Cop mode and was gently drying my tears that I remembered I'd left her to be with *him*.

Our flat was only two rooms big – too small to contain two

human beings' worth of anger. I soon learned to defer mine to his. The pattern was set: he was Mr Out-of-Control, I was Mrs Peacemaker. The constant strain of having to submit, to submerge, was tangling with my head.

In between notebook pages of Puck plans and lyrics, I wrote out my desperation in faint frightened pencil.

February 1988
B doesn't give me a chance to say anything when he's mad at me. He cuts me off and tells me I'm stupid and full of shit and ignorant. I'm not ignorant or stupid. It's never the original argument that gets me upset. It's his bug-eyed mad reaction when my opinion infuriates him. He told me once that as a kid he and his two best friends would take turns ganging up on each other and saying the cruellest things they could think of. They'd practise being the mouthiest and their skill would sharpen to the point where they always had an answer – louder and meaner than the last. I had no such training. This shows, pathetically, as he shouts me down and all I can do is sit there whimpering. He bullies me, stands over me, I cooperate in this power game by shrinking back. He lords and I cower. Even as I sit there, rooted to my pathetic little spot, I begin to hate myself. Why can't I stop him dead in his tracks, make his mind search desperately and frantically for a way to stop the human steamroller – make him beg for an end to the sadistic bear-baiting? He says: 'It's very easy to make people stick around when you abuse them . . . just make them think black is white . . . you hold a little back, then they're begging for it. It's like drugs.'

I'd been begging for it for years. He bragged about twisting people around. Why should he stop at me?

It only took a few minutes for any spat to go nuclear, by which time I'd be crying hysterically. The more upset I got, the more infuriated he got. He'd grab something breakable to throw, preferably something of mine. Before he lobbed it, he'd pause to check my reaction. If I showed alarm, then he'd smash it with even greater satisfaction.

Perversely, at the height of this insanity, I'd get out the dustpan and broom to sweep up the shattered fragments. Anything to make it all better, make it all stop. Scurrying down to his feet, I'd tidy the mess, practically vomiting on my sobs as he continued the attack from above. In these psychotic scenes, I felt completely powerless. If I managed to pick up the pieces of my Tom Kitten figurine, well, then at least that was picking up the pieces of *some*thing.

I remembered what an elderly friend of his mother's had told me when I first came to England. Reminiscing about B as a youngster, she'd whinnied, 'And if he didn't get his Lucky Bag, he would stamp his feet and throw things.' It had seemed cute at the time, a look through a long lens at a faraway little boy. But now I realized that the little boy wasn't as faraway as I'd thought.

A wall-puncher and a cup-slinger, B was also a shover and a shaker.

He was good with his hands.

It was Saturday morning. B's alarm had gone off, but as usual he'd turned it off and gone back to sleep. For the past year or so he'd had a job in an electronics shop. His night-owl bent meant that he was regularly late for work. Sometimes he wouldn't even show up until after lunch. Bombarding the boss with his industrial-strength charm, he always managed to sweet-talk his way out of getting fired. But even if *he* wasn't worried about losing his job, I was. There was less strain on our relationship when we were both earning.

Again and again I tried to nudge him back awake, getting more and more annoyed. Why couldn't he ever wake up on his own? It was my day off, my day to sleep in, but now here I was wide awake, instead of him. It wasn't fair.

Rankled, I sighed loudly and flounced out of bed to the kitchen to make coffee. As I rinsed out the espresso pot, I let its metal clanking against the sink express my annoyance. I heard B stirring in the other room.

'What's the matter?'

His voice already held a challenge. He knew I was irritated.

Holding the water-filled pot, I walked to the doorway dividing our tiny flat.

'What?'

'What's the matter?'

I was so angry. He knew what the matter was. The matter was, he never took responsibility for himself. Maybe being on *Top of the Pops* as a teenager had ruined him for this ordinary world. Maybe he wasn't built for the compromises life had forced down his throat. Maybe whatever. But whatever the maybe, couldn't he just get out of bed when his alarm rang?

I was so angry. Not just because of this stupid little thing, but because I wasn't allowed to be angry, ever. The price was too high. By shouting at me, pushing me, shaking me, B made sure of that.

I was fed up with the emotional clampdown. Today, I was pissed off at him, and I was going to say so. For once, I was just going to come right out and say so.

'I'm pissed off.'

'What?'

Immediately, B was out of bed, ready for the face-off.

'I'm pissed off. You never get up when you have to, and it's up to me to make sure you're up. It's not fair . . .'

My voice trailed off into the air. B was livid. He wasn't especially big, but his anger made him big. Or my fear of it did.

'What?'

Danger.

'It's not fair . . .' Why was I moving back into the kitchen as I spoke? Oh yes, because he was advancing malevolently towards me. This intimidation tango was our usual dance.

'. . . it's my day off and I have to stay awake to make sure you get up – '

'You're so SELFISH!'

On the hiss of his 'selfish', B kicked the bottom of the coffee pot and a slosh of water slapped me in the face.

Without thinking, I chucked the remaining water back at him.

The rest happened fast. B's lunge for me brought us both down to the kitchen floor. I struggled to get out from underneath him, knocking over the chair, grabbing at the stupid shower next to the sink. Then I couldn't breathe. What? What? Why?

His hands were on my throat.

Seconds later, we were at either side of the kitchen, panting. I wasn't sure what had happened. Did I scramble out of his grip, or did he decide to stop throttling me?

Without a word, B put on his clothes and went to work. I put on mine and went to ballet class.

When he came home that night, I was waiting for him.

'I want to talk about what happened this morning.'

He didn't.

'That should never happen again,' I continued.

My idea was that he'd be extremely remorseful, that he'd want to somehow make it up to me. Not that an 'I'm sorry' could wipe out that day's horror, but at least it would be an acknowledgement that trying to strangle your loved one was wrong.

All he said was, 'You know better than to have a go at me in the morning.'

I waited for the apology.

'I'm a bloke. That's what blokes do.'

Was he going to apologize?

'I have bruises too, you know – on my legs.'

Bruises from me fighting to get away from him.

'For fuck's sake! It's not like you're a battered wife or something!'

If he said so.

Gradually, the marks of his fingers on my throat faded.

So did my love for him.

26

When Love Breaks Down

The love fades, and the madness begins. The trouble is, I can't tell the difference between the two.

And I don't know how B and I keep getting it up for that big music biz slut like we have been for six years now. We've got the looks, the sounds, the management, the reviews, the record company demo time. CBS and Chrysalis are both playing footsie.

We're closer than we've ever been to getting a record deal. And if we do, it will be a catastrophe, because we are at the end of us. All the label will get for their advance are a couple of fashionable corpses.

We have been dying a long time. B's violence six months ago strangled us, but even now we shy away from pronouncing ourselves dead. Dead is just too final. After the 70 mm epic of our life together, no one wants to see 'FIN' flash up on the screen.

So now we cadaver along, artificially animated by my boundless energy. But 'boundless' doesn't really mean 'without any bounds, ever'. Even boundlessness has bounds. My boundlessness is bottoming out.

I tiptoe around to the back of us and unplug our life-support system.

It's taken six months to get the nerve, the heart, the guts to announce to B that I'm not happy. He acts shocked, but he's not shocked. I'm too afraid to know if I want to break up, but I know I want to move out. The most I can say is that I can't guarantee to be his girlfriend. After five years, we still deny that we're married.

First he tries bluffing me out. 'I'm going to move to Finland and recreate Puck with some cheekboned chicklet.' Yeah OK, that's a good plan, go, go.

He ostentatiously lays out his best suit to prepare for a post-Valentine's 'date' with a 'nice' girl in Wimbledon. Does she even exist? Whatever, have a pleasant time.

Then he comes clean about the problems. He knows he's manipulative, he says. Control masks his fear, he says. He's spent a lifetime trying to lick this fear, you know. It's always there, the fear. That's what the drinking was for, that's what the hash is for, that's what the anti-depressants are for. Fear drives him to bully. On the first day of school, he says, he was so scared that he walked up and punched the first kid he saw, just to put fear in its place. It worked, sort of. And he's never snapped out of kill-or-be-killed, even with me. It's a habit now. Feeling no control made him controlling. He's never lost his knack for bullying.

He doesn't trust any situation to work out well, even ours. Too frightened to have faith that I would *want* to be with him, his impulse is to trick me to be with him.

The manipulation disguises his dependency on me. In tears, he says, 'I've stopped drinking but the feeling's the same – I'm addicted to you.'

Now that I've said I want to leave, he sobs every night in the kitchen, or next to me in bed. The sound of his heart breaking wakes me up. It is a terrible, racking sound. It is the sound of the last rites of last hopes.

As B cries through his agony, I go back to sleep. I am temporarily numb to trauma, like those foxes who chew off their own leg to get out of a trap.

B and I continue living like this for six more weeks.

The night I leave Dorset Street, B stays out so he doesn't have to see it. Before I go, I look through two suitcases of almost ten years of my letters to him. Crying, I read every single one of them. Blind foresight makes me take a handful of them which refer to my life before us: my spine surgery, my mother's illness. I want to preserve a part of me that doesn't belong to him.

All of my belongings are in big red and white checked plastic bags. When the minicab arrives, the driver and I heave them in. Squeezed in the back, I try to figure out which flavour Magic Tree is hanging off the guy's rear-view mirror. It looks like the tag says 'Pizza Mouth', which is an accurate description of the smell. I squint and make out 'Rose Musk'. I imagine the driver trawling the aisles of Magic Tree Mart for the stink of distinction that will set his minicab apart from all others.

My halfway house is Steve's dilapidated co-op lodgings next to a railway line up from King's Cross. The house in Gifford Street has holes in the floor and rats in the garden. My bed is a slab of foam on the floor of the upstairs spare room. Every night I walk back to my new home up York Way, past dark whore-doorway humpings, skidding on used-condom jellyfish.

B says, sadly, 'I know you really want to get away from me if you are able to stand living there.'

He's right.

It's too bad that Steve is just now going away for three and a half months. It means I'll have to face loneliness alone.

The next day, I walk across Trafalgar Square through swarms of people, preoccupied by the chaos in my head. Later, I learn from the radio that I'd ambled through the middle of the poll tax riot.

I get a dance job. The timing is a lifesaver. I need something all-consuming that isn't going to kill me, like the B thing is. *The Second Sitting* is a deranged performance-art piece choreographed by Jacob Marley. Jacob is an irresistible character. He's a tawny-skinned disco monster who's equal parts creative genius and tantrum-throwing five-year-old. I know the type.

His signature step is the pony, a sixties sock-hop move, combined with balletic lost-fairy-in-the-woods arm gestures. This is characteristic of Jacob's peculiar playfulness. In his velvety effete speaking voice, he says 'super trooper' and 'oh *dear*' a lot.

Oh *dear*, *The Second Sitting* is weird. An Irish cleaning lady immaculately conceives the second coming of Christ. Then she changes her mind. She hides the aborted foetus in her broom closet until a drag queen cook finds it, stuffs it into a blender and drinks it. Along the way there's projectile vomiting and elegantly choreographed nose-and-bottom wiping. One dance number consists entirely of the eight of us stabbing each other in slow motion with joke-shop daggers. The whole thing is disturbing and childish and hilarious.

In my current frame of mind, the whole thing seems plausible.

The dancing keeps my brain from chewing itself raw over the split. I'm grateful for the gift of exhaustion. Jacob lends me a Louise Hay healing tape to fall asleep to. I'm so addled I'll try anything. I wake up in the middle of the night, terrified at the sound of a strange woman cooing, 'I love you . . . I love you.'

Then I realize it's electronic Louise, helping me with my 'dis-EASE'. I wonder what else she's been saying to me as I've slept.

I'm unable to eat. I don't really mind because I'm now the skinniest I've been since I was thirteen. I know it's warped, but I like seeing all the bones sticking out of my chest. There's gotta be some kind of pay-off for the pain.

A week after I move out of Dorset Street, B informs me he's off to San Francisco with some American woman he's met.

'Oh, she's just a friend,' he says. 'She manages bands. And she's a psychic.'

What is this Mystic Meg shit?

'It's no big deal – she just had a spare ticket,' he tells me. 'I think she likes me, but I'm not interested. If I thought she'd bought me the ticket, I wouldn't go.'

Is that so? The morning of his flight, I phone the airline to ask if there's any such thing as a spare ticket. There isn't. It has to be especially bought in the traveller's name.

Well, obviously, this is something B would want to know. I call the TWA desk at Heathrow to track him down.

'He was here half an hour ago, madam,' the man tells me. 'Travelling with a woman? Yes, well, he didn't have a visa, so they've gone to the American embassy to get him one. There are two later flights he'll be able to catch.'

No visa? Typical. Gone to the American embassy? I'm back at Dorset Street now, and Grosvenor Square is just down the road. I'll be there in minutes.

As I run, my head throbs: let him go, let him go – why can't I let him go?

I approach the embassy warily, like a predator on a new patch. The line for visas straggles out the side entrance, semi-

287

circled around the marble proscenium like the chorus of a Greek tragedy.

Showtime is now.

I feel powerful, in control. They won't know what hit them.

I scan the crowd for B. Negative. I don't know what Mystic Meg looks like, but I know she's American and has one of those new mobile phones. Still scanning, I move towards two Arab men to glean information.

I ask them if they've noticed a couple in a rush to make a plane to San Francisco. They're not sure. While I'm in the middle of explaining that I need to catch the flight too, I hear an American voice behind me.

'Excuse me, did I hear you say you have to catch a flight to San Francisco . . . ?'

It's her. I just know it is. I turn around. I see a regular-looking woman in her thirties.

She gestures with her mobile phone, '. . . because I am, too. I'm waiting for my fiancé to finish getting his visa, and then we're getting a cab to Heathrow. Do you wanna share it with us?'

Fiancé? *Fiancé*?

'Uh, yeah, OK.'

I can't believe how psycho this is. I'm standing on the steps of the American embassy talking to B's . . . what? Placebo? Meal ticket? Fiancée? He sure works fast – I only moved out two weeks ago.

OK Mystic Meg, now let's see how telepathic you are. I make with the chit-chat. Not suspecting a thing, she volunteers that B, her boyfriend, is an English – no, Irish – musician. They're travelling together to California to visit her mother.

'Is he close to your mother?' This is so sick. This is so fun.

'Well, they've only talked on the phone until now, but they get along.'

'Awww, that's good. It's nice that your mom likes the man you're going to marry.'

'Yeah, isn't it?'

'I wouldn't know.'

At no point does she appear to have a flash from beyond tipping her off to my identity. Maybe her ESP gets a weak signal next to big buildings.

I'm enjoying this so much. I feel *incredibly* powerful. And it's too bizarre – I can't keep it to myself. I'm bursting to tell somebody.

I say to Mystic Meg, 'Hold on a sec, willya?'

I scurry over to the two Arab men. I'm breathless with excitement. They look at me expectantly.

Slowly, with great weight, I tell them, 'That . . . woman . . . over . . . there . . . is . . . running . . . away . . . with . . . my . . . husband. She doesn't know who I am. My husband is inside the embassy. He doesn't know I'm here. We're both waiting for him.'

The men's eyes light up, their mouths part in delighted smiles. Oh goody – entertainment.

I hotfoot it back over to where Mystic Meg is sitting on the steps, her back to the queue.

'Sorry 'bout that,' I say, cheerfully. Standing in front of her, I can see past to my Arab confidants, who are now spreading my plot synopsis along the line via Chinese whispers.

In moments, we have the rapt attention of all fifty-odd visa-seekers.

Unaware that we are now co-stars, Mystic Meg says, 'What about you? What are you doing?'

'I . . .'

I see B though the glass door. B sees me. With Mystic Meg. His face is an unforgettable mask of astonishment, horror, panic.

I drop the Chatty Cathy crap. Mystic Meg, the Arab guys, the queue melt away. I feel like I'm staring a mad dog stare at B, but I don't really know what I'm doing any more. I'm operating on pure instinct. And it feels GREAT.

What is this I'm doing now – I'm giving B the finger? How weird – I never do that. I've been possessed by the spirit of a New York taxi driver.

With bird in mid-flip, I push past Mystic Meg, up the stairs and across the marble dais to B, who looks very, *very* apprehensive. The expression in his eyes tells me he thinks I'm going to hit him. Makes a change.

Our public crescents around us like a new moon hugging the old. The side entrance of the American embassy is now a theatre-in-the-round, and we are centre-stage.

'Fuck you!' I growl at B, my middle finger in his face, 'Fuck you! Fuck you!'

It's not Shakespeare in the Park, but it'll do.

From off-stage, I hear Mystic Meg's voice.

'B! B! GET IN THE CAB! C'MON! B!'

B is frozen.

My fury unlashes the whipcrack of my tongue. I talk low and fast.

'Fuck you, B! You liar, you LIAR. She just told me you were her fiancé. Her FIANCÉ. And that you're all big chums with her mo—'

'How did you—'

'I called the airline, asshole! I know she BOUGHT you that plane ticket! You go with her now and you can forget about us! If you go with her we will NEVER EVER get back together, you hear me – NEVER!'

What am I saying? Let him go, let him go – why can't I let him go?

'B! C'MON! GET IN THE CAB! B!'

It's Mystic Meg again.

'If you love me, B, you will not go with her.'

B's confusion looks like it's hurting his brain. There is silence. The audience holds its breath.

'B!' Mystic Meg wails, 'COME *ON!*'

Quietly, B says to me, 'I'll see you back at the flat.'

He walks on past me and into the waiting cab. It roars away.

I stand alone on the stage. The attack of the fifty-foot woman now spent, I start shrinking back down to my real five-foot-one self. The faintest feeling of self-consciousness starts to brown me around the edges as I gradually become aware of the stunned crowd. I sense that they need some sort of finale.

'Um, he's coming back,' I announce, somewhat unconvincingly.

I turn haughtily and make my exit down the steps.

Maybe I flubbed my last line, but what a performance, huh? Yay – I won!

Uh, what did I win, exactly?

I'm still guided by a little leftover instinct. For no apparent reason, I stop at Littlewoods on the way back to Dorset Street. What is this I'm doing now – I'm buying an ugly green vinyl purse? How weird – that's not like me. I've been possessed by the spirit of a Barnet housewife.

The summer of 1990 is blistering. It's May, five weeks since the showdown at the American Embassy. B's back at Dorset Street and I'm still at Gifford Street. Beneath blue skies and meaty beaty sun, we've been lurching along in passion and suspicion. The morning I leave his bed for a British tour of *The Second Sitting*, I stop back at Gifford Street to pick up my bags. There is a letter from him on the doormat. I try to put off opening it.

I know it will be something upsetting. I'm right.

It's the old 'I've met another woman' ploy. Hah – more like 'I've drummed up another dupe to fling in your face'. It's so nuts – we've just spent the night together – he drew lovehearts in the air as I left.

While he gets his hot water bottle women in, I try to sort out my feelings. Disappointment. Contempt. Anger. What is it? He invents a string of lovers for me, decides he must claim revenge, plans a jaunt with Mystic Meg, and now nonchalantly announces that he's 'seeing someone'. He's making it easy for me to hate him.

I want for B to be strong. His own strength, not the stuff he siphons out of me or another mommy/mollycoddler. Why can't he at least try? Isn't our life together, what we've done, worth the struggle to fix it?

Apparently not. His charades fill me with sadness and disgust. They're all games designed to make *me* make the decisions again. I can't forever be the motor revving him up. And yet, I can't *not* take the bait.

The letter finishes: 'If we really want to hurt each other, we'll use people as weapons – that is the kind of manipulation that made you hate me in the first place. I love you.' ARGHHH! Even in a letter acknowledging his manipulation, he chucks in a manipulative 'I love you'. His 'love' for me . . . his fucked-up love for me.

I write to B:

I remembered it was our fifth wedding anniversary. Poignant, painful. I dragged myself into Gifford Street, hoping for some sort of 'let's try again' message from you on the answering machine. Nothing. Sadness. So I dragged myself

*back out to pick up some provisions, and in those few
minutes you arrived to slip death letter number two in
through the door.*

*B, my heart leaped with hope when I returned and saw
that envelope on the floor. 'He's been here! He's been here!'
I just picked it up without looking at it and ran like
anything all the way to King's Cross, trying to catch up
with you. Baby,* I FUCKING RAN FOR YOU, *my lungs
were in my throat, I ran that mile down to the station . . . I
couldn't miss you . . . I couldn't lose you. Then I opened
that letter and sobbed the route back to Gifford Street,
obliterating the speedy path of hope with my tears.*

'HELL IS NOW', I scrawl in my notebook. Death letter
number two contains more out-of-the-blue accusations of being
a 'slut', of catting around with a make-believe man. But, but,
but . . . he said *he* was going off with someone, and not to
interfere. The double-whammies are turning my well-chewed
grey matter into bright pink bubble gum.

And all this on our wedding anniversary – nice timing. Not
that we've ever actually told anyone we're married, but our
disintegration makes the date more loaded than it ever was.

I leave a twenty-minute screaming fit on B's answering
machine. Every time it BEEEEEEEEEEEPs, I hang up,
redial, and recommence screaming. My head is a big swollen
pumpkin of screams. When B gets home, he calls me back for a
screaming duet.

Two days later I write a letter to B:

6 June 1990
*I woke up this morning and waves of sickness and anxiety
washed over me.*

I am compromising my health and self-worth by allowing myself to be dragged along on your endless roller-coaster ride of emotions, manoeuvres and unappeasable demands.

You alone have access to a 'love-o-meter', on which you measure my every feeling and motive and find me wanting. You deny me the truth and power of my gut feeling, my emotions, time after time after time after time.

What more can I do after I say, 'I love you', and you respond 'You never loved me'? After I say, 'Your needs have sucked me dry', and your answer is, 'You never gave me enough'? What more can I do? Stand in front of you and punch myself in the stomach? Literally shit myself in the morning before I can get to the toilet because of nerves? So I do that too – big whoop.

I want to get off the rollercoaster.

I am too scared to send it to him. I'm too scared because I want the impossible. I want to break it off with him, but not still love him. I want to say goodbye, but painlessly. I want to be away from him, but not miss him. Impossible.

Sensing he's pushed the Bad Cop angle as far as it will go, B tries a different tack: he proclaims unconditional love, pressure-free neutrality, space.

He admits that all the 'girlfriends', letters, sulking, etc *were* strategies. He says, 'All that shit I put you through – I wanted to make your life a living hell. I will stop now.'

Instantly, I'm plunged into severe depression and overwhelming guilt. I'm not sure if I can trust B's pledge of non-interference. I can't stop feeling completely responsible for every spasm of his heart – he's trained me too well.

And when *The Second Sitting* tour finishes, there is no escape from the unbearable blackness of missing him. My heart is a holocaust – a continent of scorched earth. Anguish.

I feel useless, unlovable and entirely absorbed by B. In trying to get away I feel more swallowed up by him than ever. My former feelings of dread and suffocation flip on a hair-trigger to neediness and insecurity. His doing 'neutral' turns me into the weepy wimp. I see that when B is stronger, I reveal my weakness, the true nature of my need for him.

Every time he holds me I burst into tears. Crying and crying . . . so nice to be in his arms without rage and misunderstanding burning just beneath the skin.

I feel like I've aged a decade in the past few months. All at once my body breaks down: a gum infection, a shivering, sweating flu; a rash all over my arms and legs. I have no sensation in my right thigh – a trapped nerve. My body's sticking two fingers up at me.

I finally understand B's recent detachment when I find out he's been seeing someone for real.

Let him go, let him go – why can't I let him go?

I'm too scared to let him go.

I knock on our – I mean, B's – door at Dorset Street. He opens it a crack. He's shirtless and wearing a worried expression.

Even as I'm saying, 'Hi – I just thought I'd stop by', I know there's a woman in there.

He mealy-mouths some excuse for not letting me in. I pretend to accept it and leave. But I don't leave. I go upstairs to my girlfriend Georgie who lives on the top floor.

Yorkshire Georgie's an artist fresh out of St Martin's, her ballerina delicacy grounded by strong brown eyes. She's younger than I am, but wiser – especially in these manic days of mine. We've been friends ever since she moved into Dorset Street three years ago. And now that I've moved out, her friendship is more important to me than ever.

Georgie listens to my report from two flights down. As gently as she can, she tells me that she's seen B with a girl – a girl with long red hair.

That's all I need to hear to push me over the edge.

Instinct's telling me what to do again. Georgie tries to duke it out, but my instinct's gotten too used to having its own way. This time I'm possessed by the spirit of the biggest-ever masochistic martyr happy to die for her beliefs.

What is this I'm doing now – I'm tiptoeing back downstairs to listen at B's door? How weird – I thought my spying days were over.

I hear B with a friend of ours – and the girl. B mentions my name mockingly, then laughs. A mean laugh.

Stop now, Katie.

When our friend leaves, I hide on the landing above. The kitchen light from within bathes the black shadows of without.

Stop now, Katie.

I slip back down to the door in time to hear B calling the girl his pet name for me.

Stop now, Katie.

Then he picks up his acoustic guitar and sings her a song that he learned from me.

Stop now, Katie.

Then it goes quiet for a while. When I hear sound again, it's the sound of them fucking.

Too late, Katie.

My instinct sure has some shitty ideas.

B once wrote in a letter that I made his soul glow like the beginning of creation. Standing out on that landing, I catch the death of my soul.

By the next day, B-autism mushrooms into toxic obsession.

Misery bulldozes the last scrap of my self-respect. After he goes to work, I let myself into Dorset Street with the key I still have. Rummaging through the trash can, I find an empty Hula-Hoops bag. He doesn't eat those – they must be hers. I read the letters she's written to him, listen to tapes of songs she's written for him. She's a singer. A red-haired singer. I play back his answering machine to hear her mush-talk messages. My need to know is eating me alive.

I discover a framed photo of B and me hidden behind some books. I put it back in its rightful place on the bedside table to remind the three of us what's what.

I leave everything else the way I found it, even the Hula-Hoops bag. I leave myself debased, demoralized, dehumanized.

The next day I go to The Samaritans. I know no one can save me now, but I'd hate to be called a quitter. I just want the records to show that on my way down, I went on all the rides.

I'm sitting in a small, dimmed room with the counsellor, an older lady. She's got glasses and grey hair, and she looks tired. I feel sort of sheepish, like my goofy plight isn't going to measure up to the *real* problems she's used to hearing. I open my mouth and start rambling. Ramble ramble ramble, B and me this, B and me that. Step by step, blow by blow.

When she not-so-discreetly hides a yawn, I falter. She cuts in. 'What is bothering you *today*?'

What is bothering me today? I can't even articulate it. I start sobbing.

'*That's* right, you just *cry*,' the lady says, sounding pleased that she's gotten a rise out of me. She moves a box of tissues closer to me.

This isn't helping – I can cry on my *own* time, for Chrissakes. The more I sob, the happier she looks. I cry a little bit more, just to make her feel that she's done her bit, then I leave.

I go straight to Dorset Street. B opens the door. I walk in and jump his bones. I'm having sex with him, but I'm competing with the girl. I'll match her in the sack – orgasm for orgasm.

Afterwards he tells me that the girl is merely an 'entertainment', 'the equivalent of going bowling'. He probably tells her I'm the American Satan.

If I'm Satan, I'm in the right place.

July 20
Am a mess. On the phone to B, beg to see him. He is dubious about the good of it. Force him to allow me. He tells me I am making a mockery of all that has gone before. Know he is right. But emotions are so much more powerful than the intellect, eh?

21 July
AM SO ANXIOUS, shaky. B tells me on the phone not to come over. PANIC. Is she there? Is she there? He begs me to stop with the ever-changing signals. He tells me the sex part of us is over. I FREAK OUT. Am so upset that finally he says I can come over. Am wild-eyed. At Dorset Street, my words and actions bring around a mammoth crying session for both of us. He pleads for me to respect his need for space. He insists that I go home to sleep and bundles me into a cab.

22 July
Crying all day. Listening to sentimental B and Katie favourites on the cassette player. Writhing in pain. B doesn't phone, am determined not to be the albatross around his neck that he was around mine. See Ann in the evening. She's moved here from the States and is working

at a law firm. She's trying to give up smoking. Her edginess, million-miles-awayness matches mine exactly. Realize, 'My God – I'm addicted to B!' Ann inhales deeply when passing a smoker. She gains comfort from sniffing her box of fresh cigarettes. I think B B B.

23 July
Back at the office job, feel so hopeless – keep crying – what the fuck hath I wrought – can't cope with all the 'space' I so badly wanted . . . finally break down and phone him, and am so GRATEFUL that he sounds genuinely glad to hear me. 'Pop over' to Dorset Street on business, and soon enough we are desperately fucking. What of his resolve on the 21st? What of my initial iron-clad self-preservation?

24 July
Meet with B to attend Georgie's gallery opening. Are 'in love' with one another. Classic quote from B: 'There's nothing like an artificial redhead'. Hah! More love at the end of the evening, though we were earlier both mouthing intentions to go our separate ways.

25 July
Start off day feeling pulled together, calm. Book and pay for holiday to Crete with the girls. Start to feel scared about that. Start to worry about B some more. Start to feel jealous and insecure again. By the time the end of the day rolls around, am in a state. Don't know where B is. Know that somewhere in London, the real redhead is craving B and sex. I am craving B and our oneness. Give myself a stern talking-to at 6 p.m.: 'Get yourself out of this office – get a fucking LIFE', but by 10 p.m. am still roaming Baker

Street, Burger King, Europa Supermarket, video shop, Dorset Street. Try to get on the tube several times, but keep going back for one more phone call to Dorset Street. Feel like a little ghost that has been cast out, a poltergeist that has been exorcized. In the night I dream about B and her. Toss and turn and wake up in a panic, wondering when the first bus to Baker Street starts.

26 July
I can't breathe in the night – I need to be with B to breathe, when only months before he was suffocating me. Get my stuff together in the morning to go home, to reclaim my side of the bed. Then B phones me. Shaky, scared, anxious – familiar, non? He has gotten fired. He wants to be with me and of course I want to hear that. Off I dash. So ironic – the straw that broke the camel's back was the day he took off to be with her. So I take off from my work to be with him. Around and around it goes. He sleeps in the day and I lie awake, stiff and scared, night-mares of his oneness with another clawing at me. Can I smell her in my sheets? I try. By now I know too much about them to trust my motives, and he is right to be scared of me, as he said he is.

27 July
This is too weird. Don't want to know as much as I do, but the fascination is powerful. Know he goes to her in the night. Isn't this fucked? Go to meet Steve and try not to fret. The thing is, when Steve puts the question to me: 'WHAT DO YOU WANT?' I draw a blank. Know I don't want to live in a bedsit with B for another six years. But I'm so jealous.

28 July
Go to ballet class, treat myself to new shoes, lipstick, but by the end of today am frantic again, trembling, making Steve nervous. Walking up Charing Cross Road, I burst into tears. Lose my travel card. Bottles of blood-red hair dye explode in my bag. It's a banned episode of The Mary Tyler Moore Show. *Pop several Quiet Life pills. 'When do they kick in?', I ask a worried-looking Steve. And when is B home? He sounds wobbly on the phone, I affect a breeziness and bomb it to Dorset Street. Once again it's a shot of the DRUG – I'm one with B. Then, her voice on the answering machine dripping with love, 'Hello sweetheart . . .' as B slams a hand down on the volume control. Once again ask, 'Don't you want to be with her – she seems crazy about you', and he tells me the bottom line is that he wants* me. *Ask myself if I wasn't here reclaiming my place in his heart and mind, wouldn't she be just what he needed? Must act with integrity.*

29 July
He phones me to come over . . . soon it's laughing, loving, eating, television. My mind is trying not *to go into split screen, imagining the same thing with him and* her. *The answering machine is going off all the bleeding time through the evening. We both know it is her. Who knows what she thinks? Sneak a listen when B goes to collect burgers, who later discovers this from messed-up cables. Admit to it, and he is very upset, agitated. Am calm, probably only because her message was innocuous. Am morbidly fascinated with information that will only hurt me.*

I am unbalanced. No, unbalanced is a day at the beach

compared to what I am. What I am is a raving DIY psychopath. I've been possessed by all the leftover spirits too venomous to mess with anyone normal.

Despite my insanity, every day I frock out to slink-machine max. My skirts are short, my heels are high, my hair is long. Its bloody sheen matches my all-over raging red halo. I can't see it, but I can feel it. So can the old lady in black standing at a Baker Street bus stop. As I stride by, she crosses herself.

The summer of 1990 is blistering. The blue skies and meaty beaty sun play up the pain. My short-term salvation comes with the holiday to Crete. In my mania, I'd almost forgotten I'd booked it.

I'm floating in the Mediterranean waves, feeling the beginnings of a timid peace. I'm still obsessing about B, of course, but this past week in paradise is showing me that there might be an alternative to loony-tooniness.

I wave to my girlfriends on the beach. They wave back. I start to swim towards them. I'm not getting any closer. I change my stroke. No luck. I'm only about twenty feet from the beach, but an undercurrent keeps drawing me back, sucking me back. I try the crawl, the side-stroke, the doggy paddle. Nothing works. It occurs to me that I might actually die. After surviving the bleakest year of my life, to kick the bucket in paradise seems like the dumbest thing ever.

I'm treading water, running out of breath. I don't yell for help, because like my time at The Samaritans office, I'm not confident that my crisis really counts.

Just when I'm about to give up the fight, I see nearby a small buoy, a rope.

Seven weeks after almost drowning in Crete, I'm still searching for that rope. I'm sitting on the bed with B at Dorset Street. He gives me half a tablet of Ecstasy. I watch him take a whole one. I've made it all the way to twenty-eight years old without ever finding the idea of drugs appealing, but this one could be different. I'm attracted by the disco biscuit's plug: all that love for your fellow man in one little pill. I cautiously take my half, and wait.

And Houston, we have lift-off. B and I are talking – fantastically honest, soul-searching talk. No guards. No defences. Easy, fearless communication – FEARLESS. If I want to know something, I ask him. If I want him to know something, I tell him. I listen with every pore open to what he wants to tell me. There is complete acceptance on both sides.

We decide to get back together.

My bliss begins to drizzle out before his. Creeping in is the horrible realization that I've made a big mistake.

Then his portion of chemical love runs out.

All we're left with is the teeth-grinding.

27

Iceblink Luck

1990 was the year that I discovered I could scream. I turned up the volume control on pain, and that's what came out. After all those years stifled in two rooms with B, it was kind of a relief that something came out.

But now it was 1991, and I was tired of screaming. Once I knew I could do it, the novelty factor wore off.

I was dancing on a three-month world tour with the Pet Shop Boys. The production resembled a big bucks version of *The Second Sitting*. The Boys provided the bucks and Jacob Marley supplied more of his twisted whimsy.

It was the best job in the world. Aside from the adventure, friendship, travel and money, I was appearing in the coolest anti-rock rock show since Ziggy Stardust and the Spiders from Mars.

Performance was seventeen Broadway shows mashed inside-out through a mad-cow meat grinder. My assortment of costumes included Playboy Bunny, Catholic Schoolkid, Big Pig, Pumpkinhead Lady and Invisible Person. Except those were no costumes, those were my life.

I danced my life story in fifty cities across Japan, Europe, Britain and America. Now that I was away from B, I almost couldn't remember what had ever been good about us. Every time I tried, all I could recall was feeling anxious, or pissed off, or like I was compromising. I contemplated what a girlfriend had said – that the times I thought I was happy with B, I'd only been a 'souped-up Stepford Wife'.

Oh yeah – Stepford Wife was another one of the costumes.

Incredibly, I was still too yellow-bellied to break up with B, to say the words 'we are finished'. And he sure wasn't going to say them. Seven months after our Ecstasy-fuelled truce, I was hoping that this time away on the tour would shred the rest of our Swiss cheese peace.

To enliven the routine of the show, the on-stage antics became more and more ridiculously pornographic. As the tour got closer to DC, I started agonizing about my father being privy to the vaudeville filth.

My dad's thing was to 'accidentally' happen upon some writhing pop video bods on MTV, then storm out of his den to where my mother sat in the living room and demand, 'Is that what *your* daughter is doing?' In this case, it was. In addition to writhing, I was ripping off my underpants, going down on other young ladies and having an imaginary penis fellated, all in front of thousands of people.

I was gratified to find that even pop stars were creampuff enough to worry about what their folks thought. Before the LA show, Pet Shop Boy Chris Lowe begged the dancers to go easy on his oral sex bit during 'It's A Sin'. His parents were in the audience, he explained.

After much deliberation, I decided not to censor the choreo-graphy for my kinfolk. A couple of years away from thirty, it was time to start breaking Dad into the fact that I was a grown-up. I just hoped it wouldn't break me first.

The show in DC was one of the best performances of the tour. Knowing that my father, sister, brothers and their families were in the audience filled me with pumpkinhead-popping pride. I was sad that my mother, who was more or less housebound, wasn't able to be there.

Afterwards my family came backstage and I introduced them to my employers. Neil Tennant in particular was interested in meeting my father. He was intrigued by my tales of the Old Tiger – the yodelling wag so religious he made the Pope look slack. I'd told Neil about how my dad would yell 'Hovna head!' when he got impatient with himself. 'Hovna' was a good old Slovak word for 'shit'.

I was excited by the 'when worlds collide' vibe of the Pet Shop Boys vs my father. Neil exited orbit first.

'She's great,' he said about me to my dad.

'She got it from her mother.'

Good answer, Pop. At least he didn't say, 'Yeah . . . she'll burn out by the time she's thirty.'

Living up to his rep, my father started getting a little sassy. 'Yeah, pretty good show, Neil – but if you really wanna improve it you'll feature Kate a little more.'

I could tell Neil was tickled.

'Yes, well, we'll certainly take that into consideration, Mr Puckrik.'

I thought I'd return the favour.

'My dad plays the accordion and yodels, Neil.'

Dad didn't miss a beat.

'Yeah, I play the accordion, and her brother here plays the guitar – yodel-ay-DEE-whoo!'

Some things never changed. Thank God.

* * *

And thank God some things *were* changing. After I got back to London in the summer, B decided to join forces with Fat-X-Sam sisters Francie and Nancy, who were taking a road trip across America.

It was the most positive thing he'd done in years. The trip was something he'd always talked about doing. And with Francie and Nancy, he'd be in the hands of road-dog professionals.

Before the three of them explored every pock-marked pit-stop from DC to LA, they stopped off at my parents' home in Venus. The news that B was meeting my folks now that the end credits were rolling made me uneasy. I wasn't the only one. My sister told me that after the visit my father had commented, 'Well, he's all right, but I hope she doesn't marry the bum.'

Oops.

With B gone, the constant gut-twisting tension slipped off like an old suit that didn't fit any more. Instead of blistering me raw, the London sun made me sing. I was HAPPY HAPPY HAPPY.

I wasn't just surviving – I was living again. Now, what to do with my life?

My ballet/punk/lawyer friend Ann, now living in Manchester with her English husband, phoned me with the news that a television show was looking for a new presenter. She thought I'd be good for it.

'What's it called?' I asked her.

'*The Word.*'

I gathered it was one of those late-night hipster pop programmes the British did so well, but I hadn't actually seen it. I'd been too busy or out of the country touring. And until Ann had mentioned it, I'd never seriously considered working on TV. Being a TV host seemed like sort of a dumb job – what you did if you didn't have any real talent.

The next day, I read about the *Word* gig in an entertainment listings magazine. They were looking for someone who was funny and could 'think on their feet', no experience necessary. It was starting to sound a little less dumb.

My first *Word* audition was in their Docklands headquarters. On the way in, I passed a gaga-looking girl zombie-ing out of the building. The 'I Auditioned for *The Word*' sticker on her lapel explained her damaged expression.

Somebody had told me that five thousand people had applied for the job. A tenth of them were crowded into the open-plan office, all clamouring for attention. Being in one room with so many show-offs felt like the first day of kindergarten all over again.

I had a series of on-camera chats with producers. Then I delivered a one-minute speech I'd prepared about Oregon Hill and Dirtwoman. At the end of the day, they asked me back for a second audition later in the week.

At the second *Word* audition, I had to interview Labour MP Derek Hatton and a new pop group from Manchester called Take That. By the end of the day, I was one of six candidates left.

Twelve days later, the phone rang.

I got the job.

I put my hand over the receiver.

'YEEEEEEEEEEEOOOOOOOOOOOOWWWWWWWW!'

The day before I'd been unemployed, and now I was a presenter on the biggest youth TV programme in the country. I needed to celebrate, but I was too stunned by my good fortune to know exactly how. I got on a bus and ended up wandering alone through Harrods, thinking I'd treat myself to some little luxury. I roamed around for two hours and came out with a fifty pence hair elastic.

I had a week to prepare for my instant television career. A producer was assigned to give me 'presenter training'. He took me and a video camera down to Leicester Square, pointed both of us at an unsuspecting civilian and said, 'Interview him.'

The experience reminded me of a documentary I'd seen on baby puffins. Each spring, there were always a few puffin young 'uns who left the nest confidently enough, but in the wrong direction. They'd flap baby-fat wings into town instead of out to sea. The local kids would carefully scoop up the little lost fellas, gently carry them down to the ocean shore, then HURL the bastards across the water as hard as they could.

I was hurled, and I flew.

When I got *The Word*, I was living in a tiny three-room flat in a series of blocks next to Edgware Road. Arabs and groovy bohemians jammed together into the six low tenements. The blocks were only about twenty feet apart from each other, with every flat looking directly into the one opposite. It was *Rear Window* on housing benefit.

The one opposite mine resounded with hours-long humping sessions. The woman's cries reverberated all around the court-yard. I was impressed by her stamina and envious of her enjoyment. She seemed to be able to teeter on the brink of coming for hours at a time.

One sunny afternoon, Fanny Annie was bellowing out her pleasure even louder than usual. I was irresistibly drawn to my open window. Then from another open window, I heard an Arab man's voice call out softly, urgently, 'Yeah . . . fuck her!' Her roister-doistering now seemed far too interactive for comfort. The *Rear Window* scene had turned into a pervy Advent calendar.

I knew I had to move the day I came out of my front door and heard a voice from Fanny Annie's flat saying, 'Oh look – it's her off the telly'. Suddenly, I realized that the monitoring went both ways. The windows into my kitchen, living room and bedroom were merely TV screens on the twenty-four-hour Katie Puckrik Show.

So far, my only TV appearance had been on the 'Wordsearch' documentary charting the audition saga. However, that brief cathode glow was enough to consolidate my 'her off the telly' status.

My normal life of bus rides and Marks & Spencer shopping sprees were suddenly accompanied by nudges and whispers. Was this 'being famous'? Maybe this was what it felt like to be the popular girl in high school. Some people wanted to be seen with you, others resented you, but everybody had an opinion. I stood outside myself and watched people watching me. Weird. I'd been a 'real person' all my life, but TV had made me unreal. Now, I was a 'personality'.

It was time to go to work. I was in LA, staying in a hotel room bigger than my entire Edgware Road flat. I'd flown in that afternoon, and after a screening of a Demi Moore movie, I was heading for a party that B was throwing for me. I hadn't seen him for three months.

B was now sharing Francie's Hollywood apartment. I rang the buzzer at the communal gate, looking around me. Contrary to what I'd thought, Hollywood was a pretty seedy part of town. Still, the balmy night perfumed by sweet tree smells turned the low-rent condos into mini-Hearst mansions.

B came to the gate. He'd grown a little goatee. He'd put on some weight. But I was shocked by the biggest difference, which was in me.

I didn't want him any more.

We hugged and kissed. He brought me inside and began

introducing me to a profusion of new faces as 'my wife'. It was over, and NOW he was telling people we were married? The stress and the jet lag started to make the room sway.

I left before I threw up.

The next day was my first *Word* mission. I had to interview Demi Moore and Barry White, and get out alive.

Waiting for Demi Moore in a reception room at the Beverly Hills Four Seasons, I was terrified. My eyes had glazed over and whenever the PR spoke to me, all I could say was 'Hello!' She'd offer me coffee or whatever, and out would pop that chirpy parakeet 'Hello!' It was like I had perky Tourette's. The PR must have thought I was an imbecile.

Before I 'Hello-ed' my way out of a job, my puffin-chucking producer held my hand to comfort me. I was so traumatized, it was a while before I noticed what he was doing. When I did notice, I was absurdly grateful. And when his hand left mine, I gave it back to him to hold some more.

'*The Word?*'

It was the PR woman. It was my turn with Demi.

I went into the next hotel room filled with lights, cameras, big men and little Demi, who was sitting miked up in an armchair. I must have been her seventieth interview of the day.

She was picking her teeth. Her lacquered lips stretched away from her gums like a mule tasting a lemon. I admired her unselfconsciousness. After all, she didn't have to impress me, just the cameras.

The cameraman said, 'Rolling!'

Instantly, Demi became *Demi Moore*, the movie star who never had spinach in her teeth. Instantly, I blanked out.

Well, not blanked out, exactly. I did the five-minute interview, without even saying 'Hello!' once, but other than that I had no control over what was coming out of my mouth. At the four-and-a-half-minute mark, I started to resurface.

I could hear myself saying, 'So, Demi – why'dya have Bruce video the birth of your children? It's not like you could yell, "BRING ON THE STUNT BABY!" Well, I guess it beats the usual, "Here's me with a camel" home movies. Do you invite your friends over for coffee and doughnuts to watch them?'

Demi narrowed her eyes and fixed me with a look. Then she shifted her gaze to my jaw, which was trembling uncontrollably.

'Your time is up,' snapped the PR woman.

I zombied out of the room feeling like the gaga girl I'd passed at the *Word* audition.

'Well done!' my producer kept saying. 'Well *done!*'

I felt well done, all right.

The next stop was Barry White's pad. The singer lived a populuxe life in a swanky LA suburb. Man-made waterfalls tumbled down the hills behind his home. He had a separate house in his backyard with a screening room. That's where he played computer football games with his friends.

And, unlike most stars, in the flesh Barry White delivered the goods. Barry was *very* Barry: big and baaaaaad, with a deep, bottom-of-the-sea voice that had the soundman furiously twiddling his controls.

To my relief, Barry was also gracious and relaxed. It was just what I needed after the Demi freeze-out. Before long, we were cackling away together. Well, I was cackling, and he was making a sound responsible for accelerating the continental drift.

'HEH HEH HEH HEH HEH HEH HEH HEH HEH HEH!' Barry rumbled.

Even his mirth was basso profundo.

Barry kept saying, 'You sho' is funny, HEH HEH! You funny. You gonna be a star – HEH HEH HEH HEH!'

I loved Barry.

That night, I rode in a rented convertible along the sleek peaks of Hollywood. The hills spilled down either side of Mulholland into distant shimmers of neon stars. I leaned back against the white leather seat, tilting my face to the spangled city's reflection in the warm black sky. I saw thousands more stars, real ones, blinking and winking a tip-off: maybe being a TV host wasn't such a dumb job after all.

I was lucky. Baby, I was so lucky.

The answering machine message was waiting for me when I got back to London.

Whirr – Click – BEEEEEP. B's voice.

'I just want you to know that I'm going to "check out" . . . don't worry, it's nothing you've done . . . talk to my parents . . . I love you . . . goodbye.'

Suicide?

'WHAT? WHAT? WHAT?' I shrieked at the machine.

Click – BEEEEEEEEP. B's voice again.

'Don't freak, I'm still here, bye.'

Bastard.

I still fell for it, though.

It took me a few days to get though to Francie and B's Hollywood house of fun. The first few times I tried, she picked up the phone crying hysterically, then slammed it back down again. All aboard the B bandwagon, I thought. Then all I got was their answering machine.

I redialled the horror hotline until Francie sobbed hello and didn't hang up. She told me that for the past week, B had been talking about killing himself. Maybe by locking himself in her car and gassing out on exhaust fumes, he'd mused aloud. She'd hidden her car keys. She felt responsible for his existence, she said.

You got a witness to *that*, sister.

As we talked about B's latest stunts, a wild kaleidoscope of fear, rage and boredom whirled in my head. B still wasn't getting his Lucky Bag, and in Francie he'd found someone new to give a shit.

'Where is he now?' I asked her.

'He's locked himself in the bathroom,' she answered, her voice quivering. 'He's been in there for hours.'

I sighed.

'Well, go tell him I'm on the phone. I might as well talk to him before he tops himself or something.'

I heard the diminishing clomp-clomp of Francie's shoes on the bare wooden floor. Before they'd clomp-clomped too far, they stopped.

She screamed.

Her scream sirened louder and louder until it was right in my ear.

'HE'S DONE IT! HE'S DONE IT! HE'S DONE IT! HE'S DONE IT! HE'S DONE IT!"

'WHAT? WHAT? WHAT?' I screamed back.

'HE'S IN THE LIVING ROOM! THERE'S BLOOD EVERYWHERE! HE'S SLIT HIS WRISTS!'

I got off the phone so she could call the ambulance. I was distraught, but there was nothing I could do. There had never been anything I could do.

Francie called me later to tell me that he was in the hospital and his condition was stable. Oh, and that he'd slit his heels, too.

Poor B. He'd shifted responsibility for himself so much he'd forgotten where he'd left it.

And poor Francie. She had a front row seat at B's Theatre of Pain.

I hoped she'd be able to get away from him. But for me, B's scene-stealing had finally gone too far. I was bowing out of the psychodrama.

And this time, I was able to let him go.

28

Oh Father

The jig is up. My parents have found out that I'm married.

A year and a half has gone by since B's self-immolation in LA. In all that time, I've only spoken to him once. Horrified by the damage we've inflicted on ourselves over the years, I'm staying away from him. Together, we're bad ju-ju.

My mother calls me, upset.

'Katie? B has sent your father a letter.'

Uh-oh.

'He says you two are *married*?'

Her 'married' goes up the scale like she's in a comedy operetta. Except no one's laughing.

Instantly, my insides feel like they're about to spontaneously disembowel. But at the same time, a hurricane of relief begins to roar through me.

Finally, I think. No more secrets.

I drop the subterfuge. My arms ache from the years of holding it.

'Yes.'

'Why didn't you *tell* us?'

Why didn't I tell them? Because they didn't want to hear when I tried to tell them about B in the very beginning. Because I wasn't convinced it was such a hot idea myself. Because I'd seen my father withdraw his love in disapproval.

It turns out that B wants a divorce. Fine. He wants to get remarried. Great. It's about time we all moved on.

But why is he telling my *parents*? When my mother reads me B's letter over the phone, I recognize his style. From the first line, the trickery is still there:

I'm sure by now, Katie would have told you that we are married.

One thing he'd absolutely be sure of is that I *wouldn't* have told my parents. The malicious impact of his letter bomb is deliberate.

I guess he hasn't moved on after all.

But that's his business. My business is here, now.

Through my poor mother's shock, I try to explain my actions.

In one phone call, it's impossible to convey the wide-screen malignancy of B and me. I stick to the basic outline of our downward spiral, punctuating it with, 'I'm so sorry, Mom. I didn't want to hurt you – I'm so sorry.'

By now I'm crying, but the relief is getting stronger.

'Can I talk to Dad?'

She tells me that she'll talk to him first, and that I should call him tomorrow. We hang up.

The next night, I call my father.

He's angry, of course. I expected that. But at least I've had some preparation.

I go back over the scaredy-cat facts.

'I was wrong not to tell you, Dad – but I was *afraid* to. B knew that I was afraid, and he sent you that letter to hurt me.'

After a while, he begins to accept the truth of this. But something else is still bothering him.

'So what's the situation with you and that *bum*?'

From his intonation, I know he's no longer referring to the marriage secret. Now he's talking about my new boyfriend, my puffin-throwing, hand-holding TV producer.

'Situation?' I don't understand.

'Yeah. What about all the postcards you send from these vacations with him? What's the *situation*?'

I'm starting to understand. And my new honesty makes me reckless.

Boy, that hurricane of relief is sure feeling *good*.

'Are you asking if we sleep together?'

'Yes.'

Why does he have to ask this? Oh well, no more secrets.

'Well . . . yes!'

My father is *apoplectic*. I am committing a mortal sin, he thunders. The Bible forbids fornication outside of marriage. He doesn't care if the whole world does it, the Bible says it's *wrong*.

And on and on he goes. I am crying, trying to get my defences out, but the sobs are choking them in my throat.

'I'm not doing anything wrong!' I wail, 'And I'm happy, Dad! I'm *happy*!'

Wasn't he listening when I'd just explained how the B-time almost destroyed me? Wasn't he the one who said, 'Do whatever makes you happy'? Didn't he tell me if I found what made me happy, I was lucky?

Sure of his position, he is unmoved. The Good Book backs him up on this one.

'You are a *harlot*!'
I'm not a harlot. I'm a thirty-one-year-old woman.

I call my father a week later on his birthday. He is cool with me, brusque.

Signing off, I say, 'Happy birthday, Dad – I love you.'
He hangs up.
He doesn't talk to me again for two years.

29

Hollywood Swinging

Things were going well with my TV auditions. I was in LA for the '94 spring pilot season, and I'd just nabbed a callback for *Chicago Hope*. Next week I'd get my chance with another new one called *Friends*. The scripts for seven sitcoms were jumbled in a glamorous heap on the slimy shag carpet of my motel room.

The heap was significant. I took pains to slob around these precious scripts, the way a film *noir* floozie drags her mink through the mud just to ram her dough down all the other suckers' throats. After reading each two-hundred-page yuk-fest, I'd oh-so-casually fling its bulk across the room, revelling in the dense THUMP as it belly flopped on to the hillock.

Yeah, another potential hit sitcom – so what? The maid'll sure know I'm a player when she tries to manoeuvre her Hoover around that mound, baby. How dreadfully dreary, Front Desk. You mean my agent's sent *another* script?

Who was I kidding? In reality, I was rolling around on the mingy matted rug, hugging that whole hot-doggin' wad of paper like it was a lover. Mmmmmmm, what did you call me again – 'Phoebe'? I *love* that. Let me just look at my lines one more

320

time – oh, you're *so* funny. And I love how your ink smells.

According to the casting directors, I was one of two types: wisecracking/attractive or kooky/attractive. For wisecracking readings, I'd wear red lipstick and all black. For kooky, I'd put on a flowered dress and leave my new streaky-stripy blonde hair down.

Every day in network waiting rooms, I'd jostle shoulder to black or flowered shoulder with hundreds of other WAs and KAs.

Get out of my damn pigeon-hole, girls.

I was staying at the Beverly Terror Motor Hotel. That's how I'd misread the sign, but I liked my version better. The Beverly Terror must have been the only fleapit in snooty-patooty Beverly Hills.

Just by stepping out of my room, I could already taste the burned coffee that stewed all day long in the front lobby urn. My neighbour Fred had loaned me a crystal tumbler to drink the charcoaled coffee out of because, as he said, 'Styrofoam cups are made from formaldehyde'.

Mellow Fred was an author in his mid-fifties with wavy grey hair. We met when I was first heaving my suitcases up to my second-floor room. He was standing in the door to his room, with a pack-rat's paradise of books, chairs, beds and washing machines stacked against the wall behind him up to the ceiling. Fred told me he used to work for Andy Warhol and was once married to Margaux Hemingway. He pointed to a framed photo on the wall. In it, Fred was sitting next to Margaux at a big table with Andy Warhol and a bunch of Beautiful People.

By the time Fred introduced me to his twin cats Eric and Lyle Menendez, I knew I loved the Beverly Terror.

Even though Fred had been kind enough to lend me his

tumbler, I didn't like to drink the battery acid that masqueraded as java. I preferred to take my scripts for a walk over to the Coffee Bean for stuff that left my stomach lining intact.

I noticed that every time I went out for a walk in LA, people gave me weird looks from the protection of their cars. In this town, all walking had to be done in the privacy of one's own home, or at a pinch, in the mall. Besides me, the only others ambulating alfresco were homeless people.

Strolling over to Melrose, I tasted the air, breathing deep to refamiliarize myself with LA. The smell fitted the city: purified pollution.

I entered the Coffee Bean in time to overhear a woman in cowboy boots and collagen lips saying earnestly to her friend, 'I'm *trying* to be genuine.' Other starlets sucked their Lo-Cal Mocha Ice Blendeds and read their sitcom scripts. I ordered a Lo-Cal Mocha Ice Blended and took my seat among the heavenly bodies.

A pock-faced man in combat trousers broke up the women's monotonous perfection. He slouched over his Lo-Cal Vanilla Ice Blended, took a slurp and continued his ode to weaponry: '. . . you can open up at a thousand yards and just . . . *kill*. Now a *machine gun* is hard – you need lots of ammunition, you need to keep reloading . . .'

The other customer sharing his table stared out into space, bored.

I suddenly missed the protection of my car.

I'd rented a Neon to bumper-car over the earthquake wounds in the street. The recent Richter twitcher meant that every third building was a cubist version of its former self, all goofic angles and zigzag floors. The devastation was playfully arbitrary, leaving strip malls unscathed next to bungalows bisected by palm trees.

Angeleno street wisdom held that animals were the first to respond to earthquakes. Unfortunately, their pets' response consisted solely of vomiting. I couldn't see how this constituted an early warning system. After all, if your Burmese was barfing on the kelim, who knew if the cause was faultline or furball?

The K-9 police units patrolling the areas most blighted by terra-not-so-firma confirmed the city's confidence in critters. I imagined Shep and Rex sitting Alsatian-proud in the back seat, while the cop at the wheel monitored them in the rear-view mirror for any signs of doggie queasiness.

'One Adam 12, One Adam 12, K-9 personnel about to blow chow. Alert National Guard – earthquake imminent!'

God bless America.

I'd been living in England so long – ten years now – that I was missing out on what made America great. Really great. Like the use of the word 'America' – which in advertising slogans was never less than constantly. Usually preceded with 'Hey' and followed by an exclamation point.

'Hey America! Have we got some Top Whack Blackjack Snack Muffins for you!'

Or:

'Hey America! Give yourself a chocolate milk moustache *today*!'

Or:

'Hey America! Cause a seventeen-car-pile up on the freeway and then sue everyone's ass off!'

Or whatever.

God bless America, mother of the mall.

The shopping mall had evolved into a sophisticated creature since my teen years at Galaxy Galleria. The Beverly Center was a multi-levelled dark star of commerce and corn dogs, as well as Juice, Sushi, Cookies, Pizza, Chinese, Salads, Submarines and

even an A&W Root Beer Stand. The lure of so many international calories was at odds with the hundreds of stores selling
you-better-be-thin-bitch clothes.

At the Beverly Center, I'd walked into Betsey Johnson where
a girl was holding up a thin-bitch dress to show her friend. She
whined, 'Will this make me look like a slut?' I couldn't tell if
'slut' was the desired effect or not.

The Betsey Johnson salesgirl did the salesgirl thing and
complimented me on my shoes, no my dress, no my whole
'faaabulous' look. When I thanked her, she noticed my 'English'
accent and excitedly told me about her recent time in Britain.

'I was working as a model there,' she said in her scratchy-
sandy LA drawl. 'It's freezing! I learned what a duvet was, fast.
Everyone eats chocolate like they don't EVEN care. And
everyone's an alcoholic, but in a fun way, you know? Ritzy-titzy
people get smashed the most.'

She was an authority, all right.

Sealing the caffeine deal at the Bean , I gathered up my *Friends*
script and bopped my Coffee Achiever walk back out on to
Melrose.

I had the scripts, all right, but I didn't feel like the kind of
person who was entitled to scripts. I felt like a fake. I wasn't the
sleek, chic Beverly Hills babe as celebrated by Aaron Spelling. I
wasn't going to squeeze a leather Harley saddle between
aerobicized thighs and Easy Rider my Buttmastered buns to
the ocean. How could I? I was too lumpy, too real. I sashayed
my Shetland-pony ass and felt womanly next to all those
doughnut-deprived dollies. But Hollywood was no place for
Shetland-pony asses.

A plastic surgeon I'd met at a party in the Valley had
hazarded a guess that my 'perfect' nose was the handiwork of a

doctor. When I told him it was all mine, he was a little unnerved, but I was downright shaken. I couldn't decide whether it was flattering or not to have a nose so faaabulous it looked like plastic surgery.

Shucks, I'd never even had my bikini line waxed. But did I imagine for a split-hair of a second that Julia Roberts had become America's sweetheart due to the capricious charm of her free-range pubes? Had Heather Locklear knocked 'em dead on *Melrose Place* by sporting southward-migrating purr fur? I couldn't imagine Heather having storage space for much of anything between her pins, ever since I'd read her troubling comment in *Allure* magazine that despite her best attempts to build it up, she had 'no butt at all'. Whatever she was sitting on, I could bet it wasn't padded with a nether Afro.

Getting in the Hollywood swing, I decided to celebrate my flimsy pilot-season success with a bikini wax. There was no logical reason for this. *Baywatch* was not on my heap of scripts. I was not expecting a casting director to require a Teflon sheen to my tidbits. Nevertheless, the shape of my bush was easier to change than the shape of my tush, so I set about getting the facts on wax.

The weather-leathered lady at the front desk of the Beverly Terror recommended a midtown beauty school as a cheap way to depilate my way to success. 'It's called Kokomo. I go there all the time, for my underarms.'

I looked at the sun-toughened skin on her arms and pictured wax strips ripping her pits down to puppy-belly softness. It seemed like such a production. What was wrong with a razor? But this was Hollywood, where everything was a production.

I revved up the rented Neon and trundled east to Wilshire. Kokomo Beauty School sat squat and low in a parking lot next to the deserted steamship elegance of May's department store.

I parked behind the school and walked quickly towards the entrance, intimidated by all the slicked-up cosmetic academics taking their back-door break. The girls had Kools dangling out of black-lacquered lips and complicated juxtas of pompadours and flickbacks. The boys were all swivel hips and dyed eyelashes. They looked like beauty-school bullies to me.

They fell silent as I moved through them. I tried to keep my pace to a dignified mince. Those Latinas and Philippinos, they didn't buy it. Their assessment was painful. I ditched the mince and galumphed the rest of the way inside.

Inside, there were harsh fluorescent lights and an equally harsh Korean woman at reception. She was middle-aged with a wide head and tall hair. She had angry eyes and a twisted butt mouth. I guessed she was in charge, because she kept shouting orders to young girls in lab coats.

After telling her what I required, the cranky Korean demanded twenty dollars, then led me back through a maze of partition walls, trainee beauticians and customers. She marched me into a tiny cubicle and wordlessly pointed at the high bed that practically filled the whole space. I understood her to mean that this was the altar of denudification. Cranky left the cubicle and I began to consider the removal of my underpinnings.

I wasn't altogether sure what the waxing procedure entailed, and Cranky didn't seem like the most approachable practitioner. I was unsure about underwear etiquette: on or off? In any event, the question was moot, because I happened to be wearing retro-girdle-ish lacy shorts. How could the invisible bikini line be drawn in drawers? After a moment's hesitation, I whisked them off and hopped on the bed. The door opened.

Two girls in lab coats walked in. I felt awkward, but I thought the best way to compensate was to make cheerful small talk.

'You're from Belgium? How interesting. Do you speak French?'

The Belgian grunted. The other girl was slightly less miserable.

At one point, the Belgian abruptly left the room, leaving the other to continue the arduous task of ripping hair from my tender giblets. The Belgian returned. I felt increasingly uneasy. What was the problem?

Then the door burst open with the Korean woman screeching like a tortured yak.

'YOU ARE DISGUSTING! YOU ARE DISGUSTING! YOU STOP RIGHT NOW!'

Indignant, I sat up on the table, primly flipping my skirt over the topiary project.

'Don't you speak to those girls like that!' I said, all protector-of-the-downtrodden. My voice came out with a weird British finishing-school overlay.

The Belgian and her accomplice froze, keeping a neutral gaze into the middle distance.

Then I realized what was going on. Cranky was screaming at *me*. The miserable Belgian had squealed on me and my panty-free knick-knacks.

'YOU ARE DISGUSTING! YOU ARE DISGUSTING! YOU GET OUT NOW!' Cranky kept screeching. Her voice ping-ponged through every cubicle in the school.

It was ludicrously mortifying. It was more mortifying than the time Trina Spinaldi told me in the school playground that I was fat. It was so mortifying that I almost relished it.

With as much self-righteousness as I could muster, I said, 'This is an outrage! Your behaviour is completely unprofession—'

'YOU ARE DISGUSTING! YOU ARE WEARING NO UNDERPANTS!'

Ah – that would have cleared up any questions people down the street may have had on the exact nature of my disgusting-ness.

'Will you calm down! I was wearing *these*,' I hissed, pulling on my lacy shorts. 'I couldn't very well get a bikini wax in these! Why don't you provide alternatives if you're so easily *disgusted*? *You're* disgusting!'

'NO, *YOU'RE* DISGUSTING! *YOU'RE* DISGUSTING! YOU GET OUT! WE GIVE YOU MONEY BACK! YOU GET OUT!'

She stormed out of the cubicle with me trailing behind, leading me back through the maze of partition walls, trainee beauticians and customers. Everyone gawked at me like I'd just been excreted out of Jeffrey Dahmer's hindquarters.

When we got to reception, Cranky went behind the desk. Handing me a twenty-dollar bill, she yowled, 'THERE'S YOUR MONEY! NOW LEAVE!'

She wasn't going to get off that easy.

'I'd like to make a complaint. I want to speak to the manager!'

'I'M THE MANAGER!'

'Then I want to speak to your boss.'

She didn't like that. Huffily, she led me over to an office next to the front door. Leaning in, she formally announced me.

'SHE'S DISGUSTING!'

I walked into the minuscule room. Two Arab men with moustaches each sat behind a desk. They'd heard my advance publicity, and they both looked nervous.

I tried to keep the humiliation from making my voice shake.

'I demand an apology from that woman. I've never been treated like this in my life! I came in for a bikini wax . . .'

At the words 'bikini wax', the men started to shift uncomfortably.

'. . . and since I was wearing these . . .'

I hitched my skirt up to my thighs to display the lacy bottoms of my retro-girdle-ish shorts. They men looked like they were going to pass out.

'... I had to take them off! If you have some sort of underpants policy here, why don't you have a sign in reception?'

I'd lost them at 'take them off'. The men looked like they wished they'd never bought Kokomo Beauty School.

'We're sorry ... we're sorry ...' one of them mumbled from under his moustache. Neither of them could look at me.

'I want an apology from *that woman*!'

'We're very sorry – we'll give you your money back.'

'I've got my money back! What I want is an apology from *her*!'

'We're sorry ... we're sorry ...' the moustaches kept mumbling. It was clear that although they'd do almost anything to shut me up and get me out of their life, making Cranky apologize was beyond their power.

Recognizing this, I conceded defeat. And with an exceedingly misplaced dignity, I glided past Cranky and out the door.

In the parking lot, I passed the tough-looking beauty-school gang. Contemptuously, they slack-jawed their Kools in my direction.

I got back into the protection of my car. As I turned the key in the ignition, the radio spewed 'Hotel California'. The Eagles had never really made sense until I'd heard them here in LA, from behind the wheel. Here in LA, they were the *only* thing that made sense.

I needed salvation from the craziness.

I gunned the Neon and headed for the mall.

At the Beverly Center, I headed straight for the Hello Kitty toy boutique on the top floor. I needed something niminy-piminy to release me from my waxing nightmare, and Hello Kitty was as niminy-piminy as they came. With her big round head and vapid expression, the cartoon cat summed up all that was safe in her big, banal world.

I dropped my armful of Hello Kitty stickers, wallets, pens and notepads next to the cash register and handed the girl my twenty-dollar bill. She looked at it for a second, curiously. Then she held it up to the light. Then she handed it back to me.

'This bill's a fake.'

'What?'

'This bill's a fake. A forgery.'

Kokomo. Cranky.

We're livin' it up at the Hotel California – such a lovely place . . .

Back in the Neon, The Eagles were soft-rockin' me out of my gourd. As I reached to change the station, I remembered something critical about this afternoon's interrupted wax.

I now had exactly one half of a bikini line.

CLICK.

'. . . we haven't had that spirit here since 1969—'

CLICK.

'. . . sweet darlin', you've got the best of my—'

CLICK.

'. . . he's the new kid in tow-w-w-w-wn—'

CLICK.

I turned the radio off. Wasn't anybody, even The Eagles, going to give me a break?

Pulling into the Beverly Terror, I parked the Neon in my usual spot. I got out and walked across the street to the 7–11. I had a fake twenty-dollar bill, half a bikini line and no mercy.

I needed to blast out the bad taste of the day with the worst junk speciality of the house. However, new product confusion stumped me in the snack aisle. While I'd been in London, American industry had made great advances in the arena of heart-clogging foodstuffs.

I pondered Sociables, Soft Batch, Munchies, Sweet Spots, Wheatables, Zesta, Nutter Butter, Elfin Delights. A chocolate bar called Idaho Spud stopped me cold. It was high-concept candy: a chocolate 'potato' complete with 'eyes' made out of coconut. The slogan on the wrapper said: 'The Candy Bar That Makes Idaho Famous'. I tried to picture the pitch meeting: 'Look CJ, it'll be great! What's Idaho known for? Potatoes! What do people like to eat? Chocolate! Let's make a *chocolate potato*!'

There was also a chocolate, peanut and cherry experiment called 'Big Cherry'. Disappointingly, 'Pop A Big Cherry Today' was not the slogan on the wrapper.

I ended up with Sugar Babies, Chee-tos, and a sixteen-ounce bottle of diet Dr Pepper. On an impulse, I grabbed a box of Screaming Yellow Zonkers. The caramel-covered popcorn had been one of the first foods directly marketed to munchie-suffering potheads back in the early seventies. I didn't really like them, but the name matched my mood.

I palmed off my counterfeit twenty on the lethargic check-out guy and left.

The next day it was my parents' forty-sixth wedding anniversary. I felt cheesy about calling collect, but I was running out of money.

My dad answered the phone. 'Ave Maria.'

The operator spoke.

'This is a collect call from Katie – will you accept the charges?'

Silence. More silence.

He didn't answer.

The world wore down, spun down, stopped. The sun was too hot, then too cold. Then dark. I drifted in space, abandoned.

The operator spoke again.

'Will you—'

'Yes.'

I was connected. To nothing. My father had dropped the phone. I could hear his footsteps walking away from me.

For five minutes, I cried into the receiver.

'Hello?' It was my mom.

My father had accepted the charges and summoned my mother. His participation in the call was now complete.

'Mom?' It was hard to stop crying.

I was sitting in the kitchen of my father's childhood home with his eighty-one-year-old sister. It was a week after the phone call to my parents, and I was meeting her for the first time.

I'd grown up hearing about this house in El Segundo. I didn't realize that my grandfather had built it himself, for his wife and ten children. Now, my father and his older sister were the only original residents still alive.

I wanted to pour some of the love I had bottled up for my dad into his sister. I saw his eyes on her face. I stared into them, searching for him. She gazed back into mine, smiling.

'You're beautiful.'

She said 'beautiful' like 'beeyooTEEful', every syllable savoured, with extra WHEE on the TEE.

'Thank you.' I laughed.

'But you don't look like a Puckrik.'

'I don't?'

She tilted her head, assessing me.

'You must have come from your mother's side. You're too happy to be a Puckrik.'

Trying to know my father, I asked her, 'Do you and my dad make each other laugh?'

She looked perplexed at the question, then said, 'No, I shock him. I shock him with my cussing and swearing. He gives me looks and wants me to be pure. I *am* pure 'n' holy, but it's just a bad habit.'

'But *he* swears!' I protested.

She let loose a little high-pitched giggle.

I was engulfed with emotion. Meeting my aunt had made LA more than just an edgy show-biz hunting ground, a place to feel flinchy about soon-to-be ex-husbands. Meeting my aunt had made LA my *roots*.

I had a history, a connection to a family. A connection to my father.

She told me about how grateful she'd been when my dad recently redecorated the old homestead.

'The Mexicans working on it would say, "When ees your brother coming next?" He would sing and make jokes and they loved him.'

She handed me photo albums stretching back to the beginning of the century. I looked at pictures of my father as a child, as a teenager, as a young man, trying to imagine what he'd been like. He'd looked like a matinee idol in his West Point ceremonial uniform – the greatcoat with short cape around the shoulders, the fitted button-down suit, the epaulettes, the sword, the works. His sister's pride was palpable.

Then, she started showing me photographs of myself as a teenager. I couldn't believe it. There were school pictures,

pictures of me in tutus, pictures of me dancing.

'I didn't even know you existed before your father started sending me these.'

Did he know I existed now?

'Your father always tells me how proud he is of you.'

Huh?

'He does?'

'Oh, yeah. Real proud. He tells me how pretty you are, how smart you are, what a beautiful dancer you are.'

BeeyooTEEful.

'He told you that?'

'Your father talks about you all the time.'

I thought of my father cross-country skiing with me across the frozen Volga River.

I thought of him building me a sprung wooden dance floor in our basement in Venus.

I thought of him smiling and saying, 'Hey Kate, you look real cute,' as I trotted up the driveway on Petra's pony.

I thought of him taking my mother and me to two performances of every ballet company that came to DC.

I thought of him getting my old Toyota sprayed parrot-green as a surprise.

I thought of him wiring me money a few days earlier, even though he'd refused to talk to me on the phone.

I thought of him.

Did he think of me?

LA was finished with me. Sitcomless, it was time to return to London. On my way back across the planet, I stopped in Venus to visit my family. I stayed at my sister's house.

When my sister and I walked into my parents' house

together, my father gave her the big glad-to-see-ya. He gave me the big nothing. If I entered a room, he'd leave it.

My father wasn't talking to me more than ever.

The day I was leaving, I sat in the living room with my mother and sister, hoping that he would come down to say goodbye.

He didn't.

Hearing him in the upstairs hallway, I ran up to intercept him.

When he saw me at the top of the stairs, he turned on his heel and walked back towards his bedroom.

'Dad! I'm leavi—'

Without even turning around, he shut the door in my face.

I didn't have my daddy any more.

My heart was atomized.

30

Fade Into You

For reasons I've never been sure of, I have in my possession a letter one of my brothers wrote to my grandmother when he was thirteen.

I was nine months old.

Boy! You should see little Katie! She's loads of fun. As soon as she sees you coming up the stairs, she scrambles to the top of her pen to greet you with a big smile and cute giggle. She's really a barrel of laughs and fun.

Reading it makes me smile, then it makes me sad. Sometimes the best reviews of your life come early, and after that it's all downhill. At nine months, there's so much promise, so much control.

But once you're sprung from that pen, the key to surviving real life is resilience, not control.

You can't control anything.

Three weeks after my thirty-third birthday, I receive a letter from my father. Two years have been lost since he last spoke to me.

I stare at his familiar handwriting scrawled across the envelope. It's like staring at him.

Shaking, I open it. Inside is a letter and a birthday card. First, I carefully study the card's bouncy verse.

With you as a daughter . . .
I've had a messier bathroom,
noisier days,
later nights,
a busier phone,
. . . and a happier life than I ever would have had without you!

Then I read the letter.

July 31, 1995
Dear Katie,

Surpri-i-ize!

I guess my disappointment in your unfortunate choice of lifestyle shouldn't exacerbate other relations. You're obviously going to do your thing.

But the shock of losing someone so dear was too much. And forcing myself to be the heavy was worse. So – here I am – talking.

I hope you can get back to the straight and narrow, as much as your profession will allow. We certainly wish you success and happiness and God willing, in something licit.

You never were a follower, so what others do should have no bearing on your choices.

Do I dare wish God's blessings and comfort in your future?!

Love,
Dad

I am stunned.

August 5, 1995
Dear Dad,

I was profoundly moved by your letter. I have been heartbroken by your silence for the last two years. I had been trying to get used to the idea that we would never speak again, but the thought filled me with overwhelming sadness. Life is too short, Dad.

It was a great step forward for you to write me that letter. In our family there is a tragic history of people shutting each other out, cutting each other off. Emotional honesty is feared.

Dad, I know you don't approve of aspects of my life. I guess all parents have qualms about how their kids turn out. But the most important thing is that one, immutable fact: that you are my father and I am your daughter. Even though you might not think so, you have been a positive influence on my life in so many ways. And I would love so much for you to allow me to enrich yours.

The most painful aspect of your freeze-out was how seemingly easy it was for you. I now know from your letter that this was not the case, and that it was a wrench for you. Dad, your love matters to me so much, and I thought I had lost it.

Two years of silence is too high a price for open communication. After hiding my marriage for eight years, I wanted to be honest with you. I wanted to turn B's destructive manoeuvre into a chance for us to be more open with each other.

Maybe it was too much.

Nevertheless, here we now are. I am so happy that you have opened your heart to me again. I love you, Dad.
    Katie

'Anybody home?'

It's a month after my father's letter and I've just flown back to Venus.

I round the corner to my dad's study and there he is, waiting for me.

I stretch out my arms to him. This time, he takes them. We hug each other. A deep hug. When we pull back to see each other, we lock on to each other's eyes with profound rediscovery. So much love is in his eyes.

We hug again and I whisper, trying not to cry, 'I loved your letter, Dad.'

Holding me, still holding me he says, 'I loved yours, too.'

We look at each other again and the love pours back and forth between us.

The relief makes me smile, then it makes me sad.

More Non-Fiction from Headline

Junk Food Monkeys

Robert M. Sapolsky

In *Junk Food Monkeys*, Robert M. Sapolsky offers a sparkling, erudite and compulsively readable collection of essays about science, the world and our relation to both. Drawing on his career as a behavioural biologist, Sapolsky here interprets the peculiar drives and intrinsic needs of that most exotic species – *Homo sapiens*. With candour, humour and sharp observations, these essays marry cutting-edge science with a rich and compassionate humanity.

'Robert M. Sapolsky is one of the best scientist-writers of our time, able to deal with the weightiest topics both authoritatively and wittily, with so light a touch that they become accessible to all. In *Junk Food Monkeys*, he tilts against reductionism and oversimplification of every sort, and what emerges in these brilliant, wide-ranging essays is a rich picture of human individuality and how it is both constrained and liberated by biological fate.'

DR OLIVER SACKS

Author of *The Man Who Mistook his Wife for a Hat* and *An Anthropologist on Mars*

NON-FICTION / POPULAR SCIENCE 0 7472 7676 5

More Non-fiction from Headline

Adventures in Wonderland
SHERYL GARRATT

From its roots in the underground clubs of New York,
Chicago and Detroit to the worldwide phenomenon it
is today, house music has transformed the face of
youth culture over the last decade.

Adventures in Wonderland is *the* definitive guide to this
extraordinary explosion. Featuring hundreds of
exclusive interviews with everyone involved in the scene
– including originators such as Frankie Knuckles,
Marshall Jefferson and Derrick May, through to Paul
Oakenfold, Danny Rampling, Mike Pickering, Sasha
and Pete Tong – it tells the stories of those who were
there, from the dancers, drug dealers, door staff and
DJs to the gangsters, blaggers and promoters.

This isn't just a book about music; it's a book about
being up for it, out of it, mad for it. It's about the
Paradise Garage in New York, about dancing under the
stars in Ibiza or Goa, about the house we built in the
UK at Future, Shoom, Spectrum, Clink Street and the
Haçienda. About the huge raves of 1989. About
Madchester, Glastonbury and a new understanding
between rock and dance music. About the rise of the
superclubs. About a scene which now exists in
Britain's remotest corners and has spread across the
globe. It's a book, in other words, about having the
time of your life.

NON-FICTION / MUSIC / POPULAR CULTURE
0 7472 7680 3

If you enjoyed this book here is a selection of other bestselling non-fiction titles from Headline

ALL QUIET ON THE HOOLIGAN FRONT	Colin Ward	£6.99 ☐
THIS SUPPORTING LIFE	Kevin Baldwin	£6.99 ☐
SUPER SHAPE	Judith Wills	£4.99 ☐
GREAT GRUB FOR TODDLERS	Cas Clarke	£6.99 ☐
UFO ENCYCLOPEDIA	John Spencer	£7.99 ☐
I THINK I'LL MANAGE	George Sik	£6.99 ☐
KICKING IN THE WIND	Derick Allsop	£6.99 ☐
AN EVIL LOVE: THE LIFE OF FREDERICK WEST	Geoffrey Wansell	£6.99 ☐
BEATING THE BIOLOGICAL CLOCK	Pamela Armstrong	£7.99 ☐
DALGLISH	Stephen Kelly	£6.99 ☐
CAPITAL PUNISHMENT	Dougie & Eddy Brimson	£6.99 ☐

Headline books are available at your local bookshop or newsagent. Alternatively, books can be ordered direct from the publisher. Just tick the titles you want and fill in the form below. Prices and availability subject to change without notice.

Buy four books from the selection above and get free postage and packaging and delivery within 48 hours. Just send a cheque or postal order made payable to Bookpoint Ltd to the value of the total cover price of the four books. Alternatively, if you wish to buy fewer than four books the following postage and packaging applies:

UK and BFPO £4.30 for one book; £6.30 for two books; £8.30 for three books.

Overseas and Eire: £4.80 for one book; £7.10 for 2 or 3 books (surface mail)

Please enclose a cheque or postal order made payable to *Bookpoint Limited*, and send to: Headline Publishing Ltd, 39 Milton Park, Abingdon, OXON OX14 4TD, UK.
Email Address: orders@bookpoint.co.uk

If you would prefer to pay by credit card, our call team would be delighted to take your order by telephone. Our direct line 01235 400 414 (lines open 9.00 am–6.00 pm Monday to Saturday 24 hour message answering service). Alternatively you can send a fax on 01235 400 454.

Name   ....

Address   ....

....

....

If you would prefer to pay by credit card, please complete:
Please debit my Visa/Access/Diner's Card/American Express (delete as applicable) card number:

Signature .... Expiry Date ....